the natural law

the natural law

A Beginner's Thomistic Guide

STEVEN J. JENSEN

THE CATHOLIC UNIVERSITY OF AMERICA PRESS
Washington, DC

The paper used in this publication meets the minimum requirements of American National Standards for Information Science—Permanence of Paper for Printed Library Materials, ANSI Z39.48-1992.

∞

Cover and interior design by Reflective Book Design

Cataloging-in-Publication Data is available from the Library of Congress

ISBN: 978-0-8132-3876-0

eISBN: 978-0-8132-3877-7

FOR KENNY

A faithful friend is a sturdy shelter:
he that has found one has found a treasure.

—SIRACH 6:14

IN MEMORIAM

Daniel B. Hurley	*Robert E. Hurley*
1973–2023	1934–2024

For the growing good of the world is partly dependent on unhistoric acts; and that things are not so ill with you and me as they might have been, is half owing to the number who lived faithfully a hidden life.

—GEORGE ELIOT, *MIDDLEMARCH*

contents

Part II. Harm

Part III: Society

acknowledgments

I would like to thank all those who have helped with this book. Most of all, I would like to thank my dear wife Christine, who helped at all stages of the manuscript and whose moral support is indispensable. My children—Clare, Louis, and Anna—also deserve my thanks, for their patience and for their many insightful comments. I am grateful for the help of my many students, who have asked questions and suggested answers over the years. I appreciate the work of Tom Cavanaugh, who carefully read an earlier manuscript, for which he provided many invaluable corrections and suggestions. For the cover art, I am indebted to Barbara Stirling, whose keen eye is always able to find appropriate artwork, and to Daniel Gerhartz for the use of his inspiring art. The beautiful cover design I owe to Rebecca Schreiber at Reflective Book Design. Special thanks to my favorite copy editor, Clare Laylock, for her exceptional copy editing, which brought the manuscript to its final form. Finally, I would like to thank all those at The Catholic University of America Press who have brought this project to realization, especially John Martino, Trevor Lipscombe, Trevor Crowell, and Brian Roach.

abbreviations

FOUND IN PARENTHETICAL REFERENCES

Abbreviation	Author	Work
De Am	Cicero	*De amicitia*
DR	Aquinas	*De regno*
In Meta	Aquinas	*Commentary on Aristotle's* Metaphysics
In Ph	Aquinas	*Commentary on Aristotle's* Physics
In Pol	Aquinas	*Commentary on Aristotle's* Politics
NE	Aristotle	*Nicomachean Ethics*
Phys	Aristotle	*Physics*
Pol	Aristotle	*Politics*
QDM	Aquinas	*Questiones disputatae de malo*
QDV	Aquinas	*Questiones disputatae de veritate*
Rep	Plato	*Republic*
SCG	Aquinas	*Summa contra Gentiles*
ST	Aquinas	*Summa theologiae*

the natural law

chapter 1

Moral Truth

> Alice laughed. "There's no use trying," she said. "One can't believe impossible things."
>
> "I daresay you haven't had much practice," said the Queen. "When I was your age, I always did it for half-an-hour a day. Why, sometimes I've believed as many as six impossible things before breakfast."
>
> —Lewis Carroll, *Through the Looking Glass*

Our minds, they say, can adapt to just about anything, even to an upside-down world. People who wear inversion glasses (glasses that turn the image that enters their eyes upside down) initially stumble about awkwardly in the upside-down world of their vision. With time, however, they learn to maneuver easily in their new world. After a while, returning to the real world, in which they walk on floors rather than ceilings, might prove challenging.

In the modern world, our perception of the human good is much like this inverted world. We have an upside-down vision of what it means to be good. We have lived so long with this inverted vision that the truth—the right-side-up vision—appears alien and distorted. It may be hard for us to believe that we are seeing things inverted.

The natural law can help to set things right. It can place the floor beneath our feet, so that we walk solidly upon the true good. The natural law, for instance, might help us resolve the following conundrum:

> *Holding Hostages*: Pat has taken 20 people hostage, and he threatens to kill them all. He has only one demand. He asks that Traci kill Louis, who is the innocent son of Pat's worst enemy. If she complies, then he will set the hostages free.

What should Traci do? If she refuses to kill Louis, then 20 people will die. On the other hand, if she chooses to kill him—in the hope of saving the 20 hostages—then she kills an innocent human being. Neither option has an ideal outcome, but which should she choose?

As Traci considers her options, she reflects that she should help people in need; furthermore, she has an opportunity to help the hostages, who are definitely in need. On the other hand, she should not kill innocent people, and Louis is definitely innocent. Neither option seems acceptable. Either she abandons the hostages to their fate or she kills someone who does not deserve to die.

In the face of such perplexity, we might throw up our hands in despair. We might rehash in our minds certain common platitudes of our times: who is to say what is right and wrong in this difficult situation? Maybe no real answer can be found. After all, different people will reach different conclusions.

No doubt they will, but it does not follow that no correct answer is available. People have reached different conclusions concerning the shape of the earth. Some say it is round; others—even today—insist that it is flat. This dispute should not lead us to despair of a correct answer.

The shape of the earth is one thing, you might suggest, but what is right and wrong for Traci is an entirely different thing. The shape of the earth is a fact, and facts are real. Facts are sometimes disputed, but one answer is always correct and the other incorrect. In contrast, right and wrong are a matter of values, which vary from person to person. When values are disputed, no answer is correct and no answer is incorrect. As people often say, "values are a matter of opinion."

Natural law ethics, which is the focus of this book, rejects this reasoning. Values do not belong to a special realm in which there are no right or wrong answers. Rather, values are particular kinds of facts. They are real features of the world (*ST*, I, 5, 1; *ST*, I, 6, 4). We do not make them up, and they do not depend simply upon our opinions. Just as we can discover the shape of the earth, so also can we discover moral truths. Through inquiry, we can discover the correct answer to Traci's dilemma. In the chapters that follow, we will pursue this answer.

Our guide when investigating the natural law will be Thomas Aquinas, one of the greatest minds of all time. Aquinas lived only a short time—from 1225 to 1274—but in that brief span of 49 years, he examined the fundamental principles that structure our universe, producing an extensive corpus of writings unrivaled in depth, lucidity, and insight.

Aquinas's treatment of ethics has particular relevance for our times. Although he lived long ago—in what is sometimes (incorrectly) called the dark ages—his thought is especially pertinent to our own day. The time in which he lived did not pose a handicap to the investigation of ethics. On the contrary, it supplied an intellectual advantage. Free from the burden of certain modern assumptions—assumptions that are rarely acknowledged and even less often examined—Aquinas provides a fresh perspective, allowing us to perceive simple truths with remarkable clarity.

Aquinas is often considered a preeminent (perhaps *the* preeminent) natural law ethicist. This attribution is somewhat ironic, since a search through his massive writings reveals very few explicit discussions of the natural law. Indeed, he wrote only a few pages explicitly addressing the topic of natural law (*ST*, I-II, 94). Nevertheless, his brief comments on the natural law are unusually original and penetrating and have indelibly shaped subsequent considerations.

Natural law ethics dates back to ancient Stoicism, a philosophical school of thought founded by Zeno of Citium in the third century BC and flourishing—both in ancient Greece and in Rome—well into the third century AD. Stoics believed that human beings must live in accord with their nature. In our day, the term "natural law" contains only minimal elements of the Stoic system; it often refers to nothing more than an objective ethical standard. This objective standard is contrasted with moral relativism, a view (expressed above) that denies the moral objectivity of good and evil (or right and wrong).

This term ("moral relativism") has a certain ambiguity. On the one hand, it is opposed to moral realism, according to which morality refers to objective realities. On the other hand, moral relativism can refer to a particular kind of realism, in which the reality of moral truths differs from person to person depending upon particular perspectives; what is right for me might be wrong for you. Although contemporary philosophical discussions typically use the term in the second way, we will use it almost exclusively in the first way (for which contemporary discussions might use the term "anti-realism" or, better yet, "non-realism"). Moral relativism (as we will use the term) is the view that ethics does not really tell us about the world. Perhaps it expresses something about ourselves, such as our desires, or perhaps it fabricates moral fictions having nothing to do with reality. In contrast, moral realism—of which natural law is one particular kind—upholds the objectivity of ethics. In this view, good and evil are truly found in reality.

As we will see, a natural law ethics is much more than an objective ethics. It is a particular kind of objective standard. It links ethics with our human nature. The Stoics insisted that we must live according to our nature, so that we may thereby take our place in the plan of the universe. According to natural law ethics, rules of behavior (or "laws" of behavior) can be discerned in the design of our nature. Objective ethics have a firm foundation in our human nature.

This book hopes to show, through the thought of Aquinas, how nature provides guidance for our behavior, how we can recognize this guidance, and how we can apply our knowledge to the actions that we perform in our daily lives. It hopes to uncover the law written in our nature. Since the book is written for beginners rather than scholars, it does not delve into scholarly disputes (although some of its ideas and arguments may prove helpful to scholars). In order that those unfamiliar with Aquinas (and those unfamiliar with the natural law) may gain a basic understanding, the presentation is as simple and straightforward as possible. For ease of reference, the end of the book contains a glossary of common or difficult terms.

You may have already noticed some parenthetical references, which direct the reader to relevant texts of Aquinas (or Aristotle or Plato). Most of these citations are from Aquinas's best-known work, the *Summa theologiae*, and they typically consist of three or four elements. The first element (after the abbreviation *ST*) is a Roman numeral, or a combination of Roman numerals, such as I, I-II, II-II, or III. This element identifies the volume of the *Summa*, either the first part (I), the first part of the second part (I-II), the second part of the second part (II-II), or the third part (III). The second element, which consists of an Arabic numeral, refers to the question within the volume. The third element (when there is one) is another Arabic numeral, referring to the article within the question. Finally, the fourth element (when there is one) consists of the Latin word "ad" and a number—for instance, "ad 3"—which refers to Aquinas's reply to the numbered objection. For example, if you run across the citation "*ST*, I-II, 94, 2, ad 1," then you should look in the first part of the second part of the *Summa*, question 94, article 2, the reply to the first objection. Abbreviations for some other works cited are provided in a list immediately preceding this chapter.

The text also includes another kind of parenthetical reference. These references, which consist of a name followed by a year, refer you to the bibliography, where you can find a complete citation if you are interested. These references are not meant to provide scholarly citations. Rather, they provide a representative source where certain views may be found.

part I

Realism

chapter 2

Error Theory

Nothing worthy can be built on a neglect of higher meanings and on a relativistic view of concepts and culture as a whole.

—Aleksandr Solzhenitsyn, "The Relentless Cult of Novelty"

We talk of actions being right or wrong, good or bad, but we rarely pause to reflect on what these words mean. What do we mean, for instance, when we say that murder is wrong? The answer to this question is not obvious.

Some Inadequate Accounts

Some have suggested that when we say that murder is wrong, we are simply giving a command, as if to say, "Do not murder" (Hare 2013). This account, sometimes called prescriptivism (since it claims that moral terms express a prescription to behave in a certain way), seems wrongheaded. For one thing, "Do not murder"—unlike "Murder is wrong"—can be neither true nor false. Consider the following scenario: Daniela says, "Please pass the salt," and then José responds, "That's false." How odd, we might think, for José to respond in this way. Daniela was not asserting something as true; rather, she was making a request. On the other hand, consider a different scenario: Daniela says, "Yawning is morally wrong." We would not be at all perplexed when José responds, "That's false." Prescriptivism confuses these two kinds of statements, those that can be true and false and those that cannot.

We often describe actions as right or wrong even when we could not possibly be giving a command. Suppose that Jim steals a car and then Kay comments to Chuck, "Stealing that car was wrong." Kay is not giving a command to Jim, who is not present and who has already acted. Nor is she giving a command to Chuck, who—unlike Jim—has no desire to steal cars.

If we are not giving a command when we say that murder is wrong, then what are we doing? Another suggestion, called emotivism, claims that we are just expressing our own personal wants or desires (Ayer 2014). "Murder is wrong" means something similar to "I don't like murder."

This account seems misguided as well. When Daniela says that murder is wrong, she is not talking about herself and her feelings. She is talking about an action, the act of murder. Suppose that José makes the opposite claim; he says that murder is right. Daniela and José seem to be disagreeing with one another. Both of their statements cannot be true at the same time. Either Daniela is correct or José is correct. But if emotivism is right, then they are not disagreeing, since neither is talking about the act of murder: each is talking about his or her desires. Daniela is saying that she does *not* like murder, and José is saying that he *does* like murder. These two statements can both be true at the same time.

Another suggestion seems more helpful but ultimately unenlightening. According to this account, "murder is wrong" simply means that people should not murder. This latter statement, at least, can be true or false. Still, the new statement has not made great strides in explaining our difficulty. Someone who is perplexed over what it means to say that something is right or wrong is likely to be just as perplexed over what it means to say that somebody *should* or *should not* do something. A simple descriptive statement like "Kyra is eating breakfast" is clear enough. It means that the woman named Kyra is engaging in the activity of eating breakfast. The slightly modified statement "Kyra *should* eat breakfast" is more ambiguous. It less clearly concerns what is actually the case. Rather, it concerns what *should* be the case, whatever that means.

Yet another approach suggests that the statement "murder is wrong" should be understood just like the descriptive statement "snow is white." We mean that snow has the quality of being white. Similarly, the statement "murder is wrong" means that the action of murder (or of killing innocent human beings) has the quality of being wrong (Zimmerman 2001; Moore 1903).

Unfortunately, this approach, which might be called naïve realism, seems to be no help at all. While we know what it is for something to be white or red, it is far from clear what it means to say that something has a quality of being wrong. We can point to white and red objects, but we cannot point to "wrongness." This bizarre quality seems to be no quality at all.

The View of Error Theory

Perhaps this absence—the lack of any quality of wrongness—is precisely the problem. Descriptions of right or wrong are so hard to understand because no such qualities of rightness or wrongness can be found in reality. Rather, we have made up these qualities in our minds, much as we have made up accounts of unicorns or leprechauns. "Murder is wrong" is a perplexing statement, then, because it purports to identify a quality of wrongness that simply does not exist. It is as if we made up some quality "borundity" and then said, "That oak tree is borund," or "Randy is rather borund." No one would know what we mean.

This last explanation of moral terms is called error theory, since it claims that moral statements are all erroneous: moral statements purport to identify qualities in the world, but in fact they merely assert fanciful qualities (Mackie 1990). Error theory is an instance of a family of views often called moral relativism. In general, relativism (as we will use the term) claims that moral qualities are not something real in the world.

Diverse relativistic views all agree that moral qualities are not real, but they often disagree over what moral terms mean. Error theory claims that moral terms are meant to express something real in the world but that in fact they express fictional qualities. Prescriptivism, which is also a moral relativist account, does not claim that moral statements are fictional; rather, it claims that moral statements express a command. Emotivism is also a moral relativist view, but it has yet another view of what moral terms mean (Ayer 2014). According to emotivism, moral terms do not express something fanciful, nor do they express a command. Rather, they express our own subjective desires.

Naïve realism is different from all these views (Zimmerman 2001; Moore 1903). It maintains that moral qualities (like being wrong) are in fact real. Naïve realism, then, expresses an objective view of ethics. In this respect, naïve realism is like natural law ethics. As we will see, however, the two views have little else in common.

Surprisingly, naïve realism has something in common with error theory. These two views agree on the *meaning* of moral terms. Both claim that moral words like "right" or "wrong" are meant to express something real in the world. In contrast, emotivism claims that these words express a desire within the speaker, and prescriptivism claims that these words express a command from the speaker.

Error theory, you might suppose, looks like a moral realist view rather than a relativist view. After all, it claims that moral terms express something real in the world. This last statement, however, does not fairly represent error theory. The claim of error theory (mentioned above) is subtly different. According to error theory, moral terms *are meant* to express something real in the world. That is what the words *mean*. It does not follow that they do, in fact, express something real in the world. When Daniela says, "Murder is wrong," she means to convey something real about the world. In fact, says error theory, nothing real corresponds to her statement. Naïve realism and error theory, then, agree concerning the meaning of moral terms; they disagree concerning the reality of these terms.

Of the relativist views expressed so far, error theory seems to have the most in its favor. It correctly identifies how we use moral terms. We do not use moral terms simply as commands, nor do we use them to express

TABLE 2-1. Some ethical theories

Theory	Realist or relativist?	What does the word "right" express (according to the theory)	What is found corresponding in reality (according to the theory)
Prescriptivism	Relativist	A command or prescription	In right actions, nothing is truly right.
Emotivism	Relativist	A feeling of desire	In right actions, nothing is truly right.
Naïve realism	Realist	A quality of rightness	Right actions have a special quality of rightness.
Error theory	Relativist	A quality of rightness	In right actions, nothing is truly right.

our emotions. When we use moral terms, we are talking about things in reality, most often about human actions. Error theory recognizes this aspect of our moral statements. It remains a form of relativism, however, because it insists that moral statements do not actually express something real. They are meant to do so, but in fact they are talking about something fictional.

Some Problems with Error Theory

Error theory may not have the same problems as prescriptivism and emotivism, but it has problems of its own. When we make things up, for instance, we often form definite ideas concerning them. Most of us have a reasonably clear idea of what unicorns or leprechauns are like, and we can describe them to other people. These creatures are imaginary, but their features are not a complete mystery. Why, then, when we fabricate the quality of "wrongness" (as error theory claims) do we leave it empty and meaningless, as empty as "borundity"?

Furthermore, error theory has some distasteful implications. Do we really want to say, for instance, that the statement "rape is wrong" is a fanciful statement identifying nothing real about the world? Do we want to say that the statement "helping the needy is right" has nothing to do with reality? Do we want to say that the statement "discrimination is wrong" is just fabricated, much the way people have imagined unicorns? Do we really want to live in a world in which morality is a fiction, in which people can behave however they wish?

Error theorists think they can manage this concern. They claim that all moral statements are false but that some of them can be useful. The statement "murder is wrong" does not express anything real about the world, but it might be useful for restraining people's behavior. In other words, it might be a good idea to lie to people (perhaps even to oneself), encouraging them to believe false things about the world—that is, to believe in moral qualities—in order to get them to behave as we want.

Such utility, however, is a dangerous tool. It can be used by tyrants to demonize their opponents and to control the populace. When error theorists claim that some moral ideas are useful, we should ask, "Useful for whom?" or "Useful for what end?" False claims and lies can be useful for evil people and evil goals.

Error theorists have no way to avoid this last problem because they cannot even acknowledge that some people and some goals are evil. According to error theory, the statement that Hitler and Stalin had evil goals does not concern anything real: it is just as fanciful as when we say that unicorns have a single horn. Hitler and Stalin did not have evil goals, according to error theory, because evil is fictional. In terms of good and evil, then, error theory cannot distinguish between Mother Teresa and Hitler.

Moral Disagreement

Despite these weaknesses, error theorists do not readily discard their view. They think it has much in its favor. They claim, for instance, to be able to explain the endless disagreements people have when they discuss moral concepts such as right and wrong (Mackie 1990).

Moral disagreements are not hard to find. Some societies maintain that monogamy is the right marital arrangement and that polygamy is wrong; other societies maintain that polygamy is morally right. Some Indian societies maintain that killing cows is morally wrong; many other societies say that killing cows can be morally acceptable. Some societies prohibit cannibalism, while others have practiced it regularly.

These moral disagreements provide a stark contrast to the unanimous agreement over the color of snow. Indeed, they offer a contrast with other areas of widespread agreement, such as the scientific agreement that material things are composed of atoms.

Widespread moral disagreement makes sense within error theory, at least according to its advocates. In morals (according to error theory), we are not talking about what is real; rather, we are talking about fictional ideas. Consequently, different people form different ideas of these imaginary qualities, leading to continual disagreements. In contrast, science does not talk about fictional ideas; rather, it talks about what is real. This focus upon a common reality leads to agreement rather than disagreement.

We should not readily accept this argument of error theorists. The link they forge between fictional ideas and disagreement is problematic. Human beings are rather prone to disagreeing, even when the terms being discussed are clearly real. Consider the debate over evolution. There remains widespread disagreement over the origins of new life forms. Different accounts of origins may indeed be incorrect, but the terms involved—mutation, variation, natural selection, genes, and so on—express real things in the world. Nevertheless, people disagree. They don't need fictions in order to disagree. They have a knack for disagreeing.

Nor should we suppose that agreement necessarily reflects some grasp of the truth of reality. Through most of human history, people have agreed that the earth is at the center of the universe. Furthermore, they have agreed upon matters that most error theorists would consider fictional. Throughout history, for instance, many people have agreed that some spiritual beings exist, such as angels or demons. On the error theorists' own terms, such agreement should never have arisen.

Careful consideration reveals that people are apt to disagree—but not on account of fictional terms. Their disagreement typically arises from two sources (*ST*, I-II, 94, 6). First, our human minds are limited. While we do have the ability to discover truths about the world, this ability is hampered by many inadequacies. Indeed, when we reach agreement, it is not (typically) because we so clearly understand the matter involved.

Consider the rotundity of the earth. Most people, while inclined to agree that the earth is round, would be hard-pressed to give any solid evidence for their belief. It is sometimes falsely claimed that before 1492 unenlightened human beings believed that the earth was flat. In fact, the belief in a round world has been widespread for a long time, well before Columbus sailed the ocean blue. Furthermore, disagreement remains even today. The so-called Flat Earth Society provides arguments that the earth is flat. Few people would be prepared to respond to their arguments and give cogent reasons for believing the world is round.

The point of this discussion is not to question the shape of the earth. Rather, it is to point out the weakness of our minds. We can indeed discover the shape of the earth, but the task is not easily achieved. We should not be surprised, then, when we find disagreement over this issue and over others as well.

Morals are no different. In order to generate disagreement, moral terms like "right" and "wrong" need not be fictional. Human beings might indeed have the ability to understand these terms and even to identify them in concrete instances. This ability, however, might be obscured by difficulties and by confusing counterarguments (*ST*, I-II, 94, 6). We should not doubt our ability to recognize the real evil of rape just because we are unclear over questions of capital punishment or euthanasia. Indeed, we should not be troubled even though we cannot give some exact or systematic account of what we mean when we say that rape is evil.

People are prone to disagree for a second reason as well, a reason that applies most especially to morals: our desires get in the way. The point is evident at a personal level when we are tempted to do some wrong action (*ST*, I-II, 77, 2). Consider the following situation. Christine and Kenny are at a dinner together. After the main course, a tray of chocolates is set upon the table. After Christine has finished eating two chocolates, she sees that the tray is almost empty. She knows that Kenny has not yet had a chocolate; she knows that she should leave some chocolates for Kenny. Nevertheless, she loves chocolate, and she cannot get her mind off having yet another piece. She begins to tell herself that Kenny is not really interested; she tells herself that she has had a rough day and that she deserves the comfort of some extra chocolates. She takes the remaining two, leaving none for Kenny.

Christine has become confused over what is right for her to do. Her confusion, however, does not arise because the issue at hand is so very complicated that she cannot figure it out. Indeed, she initially recognizes that she should not take the extra chocolates. Her confusion, then, does not arise from any limitation or defect in her understanding. Rather, it arises on account of her desires. She talks herself into taking the chocolates in order to satisfy her desires.

The same sort of thing can happen at a societal level. Whole societies can justify the satisfaction of their desires. Societies might justify slavery, in part, because the continued institution of slavery satisfies a multiplicity of desires. We end up with moral disagreement over the question of slavery. From where does the disagreement arise? According to error theory, it arises because the evils of slavery are a mere fiction, a fantasy that some people make up. Is it not more realistic to suppose that the disagreement arises on account of desire? People want to believe what satisfies their desires.

The bewitching force of our desires is especially active in the domain of morals because both desires and morals touch upon the question of how we should behave. Even in other areas, however, the force of desire is far from inactive. Diverse views about the existence of God, for instance, might arise in part on account of desires. Atheists often accuse theists of simply believing in something that will comfort them, but the atheists themselves are not immune to the lure of desires. Some atheists, for instance, might find the idea of God repugnant because God places restraints upon their behavior.

Whenever we find people passionate over some topic—from the existence of God to the question of evolution—we should not be surprised to find strong desires lurking directly below the surface. Perhaps people are more prone to disagree over morals than over other topics, but only because morals press more immediately upon the nerve of their desires.

The following table portrays different areas of disagreement. The second column suggests what might be the source of the disagreement. The

Table 2-2. Disagreement

Area of disagreement	Cause of disagreement	Is there something that is true and false in reality?
Shape of the earth	• Weakness of the human mind • Human desires	Yes
Possible evolutionary origins of human beings	• Weakness of the human mind • Human desires	Yes
Existence of God	• Weakness of the human mind • Human desires	Yes
Moral matters	?	?

third column suggests that all these areas concern something in reality, which may be true or false. In no case does the disagreement arise because there is no truth to the matter. Notice that for moral matters, the boxes have been left empty. Realism and error theory disagree over what should be placed in these empty boxes. Realists claim that moral matters are just like the other areas: morals concern something real and disagreement arises from weakness of the mind and human desire. Error theorists claim that disagreement in moral areas is different from all these other areas: morals (they claim) do not concern reality, and for this reason (rather than because of mental weakness and human desire), we have disagreement in morals.

The Oddity of Moral Terms

The case for error theory, then, finds little support from observations of disagreement. Its advocates, however, claim it has other strengths. They claim, for instance, that error theory can explain the oddity of moral qualities (such as right and wrong) that are endorsed by naïve realism (Mackie 1990). When we say that snow is white, the meaning is quite straightforward. We comprehend the quality of whiteness. But when we say that rape is wrong, we have a difficult time explaining what we mean. The "wrongness" of rape seems rather strange.

The oddity of moral terms, however, hardly provides an open-and-shut case for error theory. As we have already noted, fictional ideas, such as unicorns and leprechauns, are often quite straightforward, having no mystery about them. We clearly understand what they are, and we also understand that they are not real. On the other hand, some terms that clearly concern realities are rather odd or mysterious. Jerry is the father of Michael, but we cannot find—in Jerry—some quality of fatherhood that is as straightforward as the whiteness of snow. We can give an account of what it means to be a father, but as an aspect of Jerry, this causal relation remains rather strange.

These odd aspects of reality include some uses—outside the domain of morals—of the words "right" and "wrong." Imagine the following situation. Kirsten and Giuseppe are driving to the grocery store, which they are now approaching on their right. Giuseppe suddenly tells Kirsten to turn left. Kirsten then responds, "That action (turning left) is wrong."

Is Kirsten's statement true? It would seem so. We can judge that she makes a correct statement, even if we cannot spell out exactly what the word "wrong" means.

Consider another situation. Jonathan is sick with a bacterial infection of the lungs. He consults Dr. Teresa, who gives the correct diagnosis but then prescribes an antacid. We do not need to know the exact meaning of the word "wrong" to recognize that she has given the wrong prescription. The meaning of the word might be odd, at least in comparison to the whiteness of snow, but an antacid really is the wrong prescription. The case involves no fictional term.

In these two cases, the use of the word "wrong" is not a moral use. Rather, the first case seems to involve what could be called a directional use of the word "wrong." The second case seems to involve a medical use. In these two contexts, the word "wrong" does not have a fictional character. At the same time, its meaning is not straightforward. We cannot point to the wrongness of prescribing an antacid in the way that we can point to the whiteness in the snow. We may be unable to define "directional wrongness," and we may be unable to define "medical wrongness." Nevertheless, the word "wrong" is (in these cases) referring to something real.

We should not suppose that the same word suddenly takes on a fictional character within the moral context. We should not suppose that when we say, "Rape is wrong," we have made a statement parallel to "A unicorn has a single horn." We should not suppose that the wrongness of rape is fictional just because we cannot point to it in the way that we can point to the whiteness of snow.

In fact, an explanation of the words "right" and "wrong" is not that difficult to discover (*ST*, I-II, 21, 1). The nonmoral uses clearly involve some goal and some proposed action. When the proposed action moves us toward the goal, we call it "right"; when it conflicts with the goal, we call it "wrong." Kirsten, for instance, has the goal of getting to the grocery store. The statement "Kirsten should turn left to get to the grocery store" is wrong because the proposed action conflicts with her goal. The statement "Kirsten should turn right to get to the grocery store" provides the right directions because the action moves her to the goal. Similarly, an antacid is the wrong prescription because it does not move to the goal of curing the bacterial infection. On the other hand, an antibiotic such as penicillin is usually the right prescription because it moves to the goal of health.

In these cases, we are evaluating proposed actions as right or wrong. We are not evaluating them for some fictional characteristic. Rather, we are evaluating their relationship to a certain goal.

We have no reason to think that the words suddenly take on a new or fictional meaning when we switch to the moral domain. Rather, we should expect a similar meaning. We should expect to find proposed actions relating positively or negatively to some goal. The statement "murder is wrong" must mean that murder fails to achieve a certain goal; on the contrary, it undermines the goal.

The meaning of "right" as involving an action that moves toward a goal and "wrong" as involving an action that opposes this goal is presented in the following table.

Table 2-3. The meaning of the words "right" and "wrong"

Agent	**Goal**	**Right action (moves you toward the goal)**	**Wrong action (opposes the goal)**
Doctor	Health	Prescribing an antibiotic for a bacterial infection	Prescribing an antacid for a bacterial infection
Traveler	Grocery store	Turning right into the grocery store parking lot	Turning left
Human being	Moral good	Kind actions	Murder

The Moral Goal

The moral goal will not be health or a destination (such as the grocery store). More likely, it will have something to do with human interactions. We have a goal about how human beings should interact with one another, and murder does not get us to that goal. In the case of morals, the word "wrong" might seem more mysterious than when used in the context of medicine, but only because we are less clear concerning the goal.

Within the modern context, the goal in the case of morals seems especially problematic. We are averse to the idea of a moral goal. We prefer to think that we can all choose our own goals and that morals merely place side constraints on the way that we pursue these goals. We can set the goal of being wealthy, for instance, but morals tell us that we should not steal in order to achieve this goal. But what if the statement "stealing is wrong" tells us something about a goal that we ourselves did not set? What if it tells us about a goal that was set for us? Many will have a hostile reaction to such a predetermined goal.

We abandon this moral goal, however, at great risk. Once the moral goal has been lost, then suddenly the meanings of the words "right" and "wrong" become very mysterious indeed. These words must take on entirely new meanings, meanings that have nothing to do with the relationship between an action and a goal. Perplexed by this difficulty, we might cast about searching for some new meanings. We might speculate that in the moral context, the word "wrong" refers to a command. The statement "murder is wrong" simply means "do not murder." Or we might speculate that it means "I do not like murder." Or we might speculate concerning some mysterious moral quality called "wrongness." In these three speculations, you probably recognize the views of prescriptivism, emotivism, and naïve realism.

After we have examined these speculations and found them wanting, our subsequent dissatisfaction might throw us into the arms of error theory. The word "wrong," we might conclude, is only fictional. It is something that people have made up, just as they have made up the idea of unicorns.

We are forced into this conclusion, however, only because we have taken the first step. We have begun by rejecting a moral goal. Without this goal, we are forced to twist the meaning of the word "wrong," divorcing it from any reality in the world around us. We are forced to conclude that the word "wrong" takes on a unique and special meaning in the domain of morals.

Aristotle suggests that we are like archers who have a target to hit (*NE*, bk. 1, chap. 2). All too often, however, we do not know where the target is. Consequently, we do not know the "right" direction to shoot our arrows, nor do we recognize the "wrong" direction. Becoming clear on this goal, then, is itself a goal well worth pursuing. This clarity demands that we first brush aside other confusions common in the modern era.

chapter 3

Skepticism

> Skepticism can never provide firm ground under a man's feet. And perhaps, after all, we need firm ground.
>
> —Aleksandr Solzhenitsyn, *In the First Circle*

The opposite of moral relativism is often described as moral realism. Moral relativism claims that moral statements, which include notions like good and evil or right and wrong, do not identify anything real about objects or actions. They might assert something entirely fictional, as error theory claims, or they might assert something about our feelings, as emotivism claims, or they might merely express commands, as prescriptivism claims. In any event, they do not assert a real characteristic of actions.

According to moral realism, on the other hand, moral terms like good and evil do identify something real about actions. Naïve realism, for instance, alleges special qualities, such as rightness or wrongness, that can be found in actions, just as whiteness can be found in snow. Not all forms of realism need be so naïve. They might reject the idea of special qualities but nevertheless affirm that moral terms do identify something real.

As suggested at the end of the last chapter, moral terms might name a relationship between an action and a goal. The statement that an antacid is the wrong prescription for a bacterial infection of the lungs does not assert a special quality of wrongness. It does affirm, however, a real relation (or perhaps the lack of a relation) between the act of prescribing an antacid and the goal of healing a bacterial infection.

Natural law ethics is a form of moral realism. Indeed, some people, when they speak of natural law ethics, mean nothing other than realism: a natural law ethics is simply an ethics founded in reality. This account of natural law ethics, however, is rather minimal. Natural law ethics is indeed a realist account, but it is much more than realism. Not every form of realism is also a natural law ethics. Unlike naïve realism, for instance, natural law ethics does not defend the existence of special moral qualities such as "wrongness."

Skepticism

Moral realism has more to it than its insistence, mentioned above, that moral terms identify something about reality. In addition, moral realism makes a claim about our minds. In particular, it claims that we are able to know the real moral aspects of the world.

In this regard, moral realism is opposed to a view called skepticism. This view can agree, in principle, that moral qualities are (possibly) found in reality. Some actions might indeed be truly evil (or wrong), and other actions might be truly good (or right). Despite this concession, skepticism is not a realist account, for it denies that human beings have the ability to know this true evil or true good. Murder might be truly wrong, but we will never be able to know this truth with any certainty. Our minds are simply unable to grasp such truths.

To clarify the point, consider three possible views concerning colors. First, color realism maintains that objects around us are really colored and also that we see these colors with our eyes. The leaves of a tree really are green, and we come to know that color with our power of sight. Second, color relativism maintains that objects are not, in fact, colored. Certain wavelengths of light reflect off objects such as leaves, but these wavelengths have no such thing as color—they simply have lengths and frequencies—and colors are only images in our minds. Finally, color skepticism maintains that objects are indeed colored (or at least they might be), but we have no way of knowing what the colors are. We have only our subjective experiences, which our minds create but which do not necessarily reflect the reality. I may see something as green, but you may see it as pink.

Our goal here is not to resolve the question of colors but simply to provide an analogy by which we might understand three different views concerning moral features of actions (Jensen 2018). First, moral realism maintains that these features are found in reality and that we have minds by which we can come to know them. Second, relativistic views (such as error theory) maintain that moral features of actions, like good and evil, are not at all found in reality: they are feelings or fictions or some such thing. Finally, moral skepticism grants that moral features might indeed be found in reality, but it denies that we have human minds by which we can come to know these features. Murder might really be wrong, but we will never be sure because we do not have the kinds of minds by which we can grasp the good and evil in things.

Moral Disagreement, Again

Relativism and skepticism are often lumped together, and indeed the same sort of arguments used in defense of relativism are also used for skepticism. The human capacity to know what is right and wrong, for instance, is called into question by way of moral disagreement. If we really could know what is right and wrong (so the argument goes), then we would not find such widespread moral disagreement between different societies.

We have already seen the inadequacy of this argument. Disagreement might arise not because we lack the capacity to know moral truths but from two other sources. First, our desires might give rise to disagreement because we prefer to satisfy our disordered desires rather than acknowledge the moral truths that we perceive. Second, our human minds are weak. While we have the capacity to know moral truths, we might have difficulty coming to know many of them.

Skepticism takes this weakness of the human mind to the extreme. Rather than acknowledge that we can know moral truths with difficulty, it claims that our minds are so weak that they cannot know moral truth at all. Skepticism has at least advanced beyond relativism. It has recognized that disagreement tells us nothing about reality; rather, it tells us something about our minds (that they are weak). Unfortunately, its conclusion concerning the weakness of our minds is too strong.

Skepticism, then, does not face exactly the same difficulties with disagreement as does relativism; nevertheless, it has its own problems with disagreement. Skepticism, for instance, may have difficulty explaining widespread moral *agreement*. In the present age, we often emphasize our human disagreements, but we ignore our agreements. Such agreements are in fact not that uncommon, although the agreement is sometimes mixed with disagreement over details (Lewis 1947). In general, for instance, human beings agree that killing innocent human beings is wrong. Any disagreement on this matter typically concerns the details of some special exceptions. Again, human beings agree about the importance of the family structure. Some societies may uphold monogamy and others allow polygamy, but all these societies agree that a fairly rigorous family structure must be maintained.

This widespread moral agreement suggests that human beings are perceiving certain fundamental moral truths. We may be perceiving them imperfectly, but we are grasping them nevertheless. Of course, the skeptic might insist that the agreement arises from other sources, such as social conditioning. This line of reasoning, however, effectively undermines the argument from disagreement. If skeptics insist that agreement might arise from something other than an ability to perceive the truth, then by parallel they must grant that disagreement might arise from something other than the absence of this ability.

Disagreements over Matters of Fact

For the moral skeptic, the argument from disagreement is plagued with another difficulty: moral disagreements often concern something other than the moral features of the action. Certain Hindu cultures, for instance, think that we should not kill or otherwise harm cows; in contrast, most other societies think that cows may be killed for human benefit, such as for food and clothing. As it turns out, however, this disagreement does not rest upon divergent moral principles. Rather, it arises from divergent conceptions of the nature of a cow. According to these Hindu societies, a cow is an elevated reincarnated human soul; in contrast, most other societies think that a cow is an animal with no human or rational soul.

Despite this factual disagreement, these diverse societies do maintain a moral agreement. They maintain similar attitudes, for instance, concerning individuals who have a human or rational soul. In general, they agree that such individuals should not be harmed. The diverse views on cows, however, lead to disagreement over how to apply this moral principle. The Hindu societies conclude that we should not harm cows (since cows have a human or rational soul); the other societies conclude that it is acceptable to harm cows (since cows do not have a human or rational soul).

In short, the different societies do not so much disagree over a moral principle as they do over what is typically called a matter of fact. They agree concerning the moral attitude toward individuals with a rational soul. They disagree over where precisely we find such individuals, in cows or only in human beings.

A similar point might account for some of the differences between cannibalistic and noncannibalistic societies. The moral principle that we should not eat other human beings finds widespread agreement, even in some cannibalistic societies. The disagreement arises, in these cases, over the identification of human beings. The victims of cannibalism are often identified as demons, pigs, or some other nonhuman being. Once again, the disagreement arises from what might be called a matter of fact: who is and who is not a human being.

This observation proves inconvenient for moral skepticism, although it poses no problem for what is called universal or global skepticism. A moral skeptic claims that our human minds can grasp some aspects of reality (such as color or shape or the natures of chemicals) but that they are unable to grasp moral realities. In contrast, a universal or global skeptic claims that our human minds cannot grasp any aspects of reality. The universal skeptic, then, should expect to find disagreement everywhere, while the moral skeptic should expect to find disagreement primarily in moral matters.

We have already seen that human beings are adept at disagreeing in many areas, whether concerning morals, evolution, or the shape of the earth. These disagreements pose a problem for the moral skeptic, who should expect to find widespread disagreement only in moral matters. As it happens, what appears to be moral disagreement turns out to be, more fundamentally, a disagreement over matters of fact. The disagreement about how to treat cows, for instance, is not a disagreement over moral principles; it is a disagreement over the nature of cows. Likewise, the disagreement about eating what we presume to be a human being is often a disagreement over whether in fact it is a human being.

Some Unpleasant Consequences

Widespread moral disagreement, then, provides no support for moral skepticism. Moral skeptics, of course, might have other arguments in favor of their view. The argument from disagreement, however, is typically considered the strongest argument in favor of skepticism. Since the strongest argument does not in fact hold water, we should be wary of other arguments as well.

Skepticism, however, faces problems besides weak supportive arguments. Moral skeptics must be willing to swallow some unpleasant consequences. If skepticism is true, then we do not really know that rape is wrong, we do not know that discrimination is wrong, we do not know that chattel slavery is wrong, and we do not know that being kind to others is good. If skepticism is true, then rape might be morally good and refraining from rape might be evil. These conclusions of skepticism are rather unpalatable. We might prefer to reject skepticism and hold fast to moral realism.

Still, it would be good to get beyond the bare conviction that certain moral propositions are true and to discover how we come to know these truths. In the following chapters, we will investigate how natural law accounts for our knowledge of moral good and evil.

chapter 4

Good and Evil

> Good and evil in actions—just as it is in other things—derives from the fullness of being or from a defect therein.
>
> —Thomas Aquinas, *Summa theologiae*, I-II, 18, 2

In the previous chapters we have focused upon moral terms such as "right" and "wrong." In this chapter, we will shift our attention to the ideas of "good" and "bad." Moral relativists and moral skeptics treat these ideas in the same way that they treat "right" and "wrong." Moral relativists deny that good and evil are really found in reality; moral skeptics deny that we are able to understand good and evil. In our efforts to overcome these two negative views, then, it will be worth our while to examine the concepts of good and evil (or bad) (Geach 1956; Thomson 1994).

Functional Things

We know that a good pen writes well, a good eye sees well, and a good doctor heals well. We are not troubled by skepticism in these areas. We may not be able to spell out in detail how we come to our knowledge of good and bad, but we do not doubt that we have it. Who could possibly deny that a good eye sees well or that a good doctor heals well? The certainty, however, should not dissuade us from pursuing the matter. The details are worth having. We must discover the precise manner in which we know good and evil.

Our idea of the good is intimately linked with a certain class of things, what might be called functional things (*ST*, I, 5, 4). A pen has the function of writing, a knife has the function of cutting, an eye has the function of seeing, and a doctor has the function of healing. Not only do these things *have* functions; we can even say that these things are defined in terms of their functions. A pen is a utensil for writing, a knife is a utensil for cutting, an eye is an organ for seeing, and to be a doctor is to have a profession with the function of healing.

Other things have no function. We do not suppose that a triangle has a function, nor are we inclined to say that a pebble or the moon has a function. Without functions, these things are neither good nor evil. We do not speak of good or bad pebbles, nor of good or bad triangles.

We could say that a flat pebble is good for skipping on the water, but then we have given the pebble a function (of skipping). Similarly, we might say that a drawing of a triangle is good. This statement, however, has shifted attention from a triangle to a drawing of a triangle. While the triangle does not have a function, a drawing does have a function (as well as the artist who makes the drawing). The drawing has the function of representing something, in this case, a triangle. In contrast, a triangle just by itself has no function. We can speak, then, of good and bad drawings, but we cannot speak of good and bad triangles.

Completion

Functional things, then, are good or bad in relation to their functions. Furthermore, they are complete or incomplete in relation to their functions (*ST*, I, 4, 1, ad 1). Suppose that you have a knife that lacks a handle or a pen that lacks ink. We call these items incomplete. Furthermore, their lack of completion pertains to their functions. The knife needs a handle to complete its function, and the pen needs ink to complete its function. A knife that lacks ink, on the other hand, is in no way incomplete, since ink has nothing to do with its function of cutting. More examples are easy to supply. An eye without a cornea is incomplete because the cornea helps fulfill the eye's function. Doctors without knowledge of illness are incomplete because they fulfill their function by way of such knowledge.

What about nonfunctional things like a triangle? A triangle with only two sides is not an incomplete triangle: it is no triangle at all. Triangles, it turns out, are always complete. Otherwise, they simply are not triangles. If Sarah is drawing a triangle and she stops short after having drawn only two sides, then we might say that her triangle is incomplete. We really mean to say that her drawing of the triangle is incomplete, for as we have seen, drawings of triangles do have a function. Drawings of triangles can be incomplete, but every triangle is a complete triangle.

For functional things, completion (as well as a lack of completion) depends upon their functions. This link between completion and function arises from an interesting feature of functional things: by way of their functions, they stretch beyond themselves to another being (*QDV*, 22, 1). By its function, for instance, a knife stretches beyond itself to the act of cutting. A knife is not an isolated being. By its very nature—its functional nature—it relates to other things. In contrast, a triangle, which has no function, is an isolated being: nothing in the triangle moves beyond itself.

A pen without ink still has the function of writing; in other words, it is still a pen. The pen stretches beyond what it currently has. It stretches to the act of writing, and consequently it stretches toward the actual possession of ink. Without the ink, then, it is incomplete; it lacks that toward which it is moving. The pen has something—for it has at least its function—but it lacks something else. It lacks what it is moving toward on account of its function.

A triangle is different. By having three sides, it is complete. It does not stretch beyond these three sides to something further. It has everything that belongs to a triangle as soon as it is a triangle. The bare minimum for a triangle is three sides. In contrast, the bare minimum for a pen is the function of writing with ink. Actually having ink adds to this bare minimum. Consequently, a pen (a bare minimum pen) can be incomplete. It can lack that to which it moves by way of its function. In contrast, a triangle either is (in which case it is also complete) or is not. It moves nowhere beyond its bare minimum.

This notion of moving beyond self allows us to recognize different senses of being complete or incomplete. First, as in the examples above, a functional thing is complete when it has all the parts needed to realize its function; it is incomplete when it lacks a part (or parts) needed for its function. A pen without ink lacks a part needed for its function. A pen with all its parts is complete.

Second, a functional thing can be complete or incomplete based upon certain properties that relate to the function. A dull knife, for instance, has something incomplete about it. It is not incomplete in the first sense, for it has all its parts (the handle and the blade). Nevertheless, it lacks something needed to fulfill its function. It lacks the property of being sharp. This knife, then, is complete insofar as it has all its parts. Nevertheless, it is incomplete in another and secondary sense.

The same might be said for a myopic (or nearsighted) eye. It does not lack any composing parts. Nevertheless, we call it defective. It lacks the proper relation between the lens and the retina, a relation that is needed to fulfill its function properly. A myopic eye, then, is in some way incomplete, but not quite in the same way as an eye without a cornea. In either event, however, the lack of completion is in relation to the function.

Continuing this reasoning, we can recognize yet a third manner of being incomplete. A knife sitting idly in a drawer is in some manner less complete than a knife that is actually cutting. The knife in the drawer has all its parts; furthermore, it is sharp and ready to cut. Nevertheless, it lacks something in relation to its function. It is not now realizing its function. A knife while actually cutting, then, is more complete than the same knife sitting idle.

The meanings of the words "complete" and "incomplete," of course, have been extended. First, the whole is complete when all its parts are present, such as a knife having handle and blade. Second, an agent (or the thing that acts) is complete when it has all it needs to perform its function well, such as a knife being sharp. Finally, something directed to a purpose is complete when it is actually fulfilling that purpose. All three of these meanings of "complete" are in reference to the function. We know when we have a complete knife—in any of the three meanings—only by knowing its function.

The Good as Completion

We readily recognize that the idea of being good is tightly linked to the idea of being complete. A good knife has both handle and blade, and a good knife is sharp. A knife is especially good when it is actually being used to cut. After all, that is what it is for. We might say that the idea of being complete overlaps with the idea of being good (*ST*, I, 5, 1).

Still, the ideas are not exactly the same. After all, we say that a triangle is complete, but we do not say that a triangle is good. The idea of being complete is not necessarily attached to a function, but the idea of being good is always attached to a function. A triangle (which does not stretch beyond itself) is complete by having all its parts. It is not, thereby, a good triangle, for there is no such thing as a good or bad triangle. We can conclude that the good is not just any completion: it is that which completes something with a function; it is the completion of something stretching beyond itself (*QDV*, 21, 1).

For this reason, we are most comfortable with the first meaning of "complete." This meaning applies both to the knife, which must have handle and blade, and to the triangle, which must have three sides. The other two meanings of the word "complete" belong only to the knife and not to the triangle.

In contrast, the term "good" is most associated with the second meaning of completion. A knife that is missing a part is certainly not a good knife. On the other hand, a knife that has all its parts is not thereby a good knife. In order to be good, it must be sharp. Mere completion of parts, then, does not make something good. A good knife must have more than its parts; it must also be sharp. In short, it must be complete by the second meaning of completion (that is, having the property or properties by which it performs its function well).

The third meaning of "complete" (the knife actually cutting) is less associated with a good knife because it involves an ephemeral or passing attribute—namely, the actual activity of cutting. A knife is good, we suppose, according to what it has in its stable existence (blade, handle, quality of being sharp, and so on). The activity of actually cutting is indeed what is most complete in a knife, but this activity is transitory. A good knife is *able* to cut well. Whether it is actually cutting well does not enter into our typical judgment of its being good.

Three Kinds of Goods

We have been focusing upon good functional things, such as good knives, good eyes, and good doctors. We commonly use the word "good" in this manner, but we use it in other ways as well. We not only speak of good doctors, for instance; we also speak of what is "good for" a doctor, or what is the "good of" a doctor. We might say that education and training, for instance, are good for a doctor, or we might say that knowledge of health and illnesses is the good of a doctor.

The phrases "good for" and "good of" are sometimes used interchangeably. The precise difference between the two need not concern us. What matters are the underlying philosophical ideas. All the diverse grammatical uses of the word "good" ultimately express one of three primary ideas (*QDM*, 1, 2). First, a functional thing is called good when it is complete. In this manner, we speak of good doctors and good knives. Second, that which completes a functional thing is described as "the good of" or "good for" the thing it completes. Knowledge is good for a doctor (or the good of a doctor) and being sharp is good for a knife. Finally, that which causes a completion can be called "good for" the thing. A knife sharpener is good for a knife, and education is good for a doctor.

This third meaning can be described as the "useful good." It does not concern what is essential to a complete functioning thing. Rather, it concerns that which may be used to bring about a well-functioning thing.

What belongs to a good knife is its quality of being sharp. A knife sharpener is merely useful for producing this quality.

The opposite of good is expressed by the word "bad." The opposite of a good knife is a bad knife, and the opposite of a good doctor is a bad doctor. Being sharp is good for a knife, but being dull is bad for a knife. The quality of being sharp completes a knife, but the quality of being dull makes the knife incomplete. Similarly, ignorance of health and illness makes for an incomplete doctor. Corresponding to the three meanings of "good," then, we find three meanings of "bad." A bad knife is an incomplete knife. Being dull is bad for a knife because it is the lack of a completion. Finally, rust is bad for a knife because it causes the lack of completion.

The word "evil" is also used as the opposite of good, but it is more restrictive. Usually, it is reserved for moral matters. A dull knife is not an "evil" knife. On the other hand, we might say that Hitler is "evil." Even in moral matters, not every bad thing is called evil. Being a drunkard may be a moral fault, but we are not apt to describe the drunkard as "evil." In short, the word "evil" is usually reserved for extreme moral depravity.

Good Actions

These claims about good knives, good eyes, and good doctors are straightforward enough, but you might be wondering what they have to do with the moral good. The good of an eye is what completes an eye. But what about the good of a human action? What makes the act of helping those in need to be a good action? What makes the act of murder to be a bad action? A bad knife lacks some completion. Can we say the same about a bad human action like murder? A good knife fulfills its function. Can we say the same about a good human action, like helping the needy?

In order to answer these questions, we might begin by considering domains outside of morals, such as medicine. What makes for a good medical act and what makes for a bad medical act? Dr. Teresa's act of prescribing an antacid for a bacterial infection is a bad medical act. In contrast, had she prescribed penicillin, it might have been a good medical act.

These cases seem to fit the pattern of functional things. Medical acts do indeed have a function: they are directed to the endpoint of health. In the case of a bacterial infection, a prescription of an antacid seems to lack something needed for its completion. Prescribing an antacid, then, is an incomplete medical act; consequently, it is a bad medical act. The act of prescribing penicillin, on the other hand, has what it needs to fulfill the function of a medical act; consequently, it is a good medical act.

These diverse actions of prescribing might also be viewed from the perspective of the function of the doctor who performs the action. Teresa has the function of healing, so she is good when she has what she needs to heal. But in this situation, the act of prescribing an antacid cannot fulfill her function of healing, so it is bad for Teresa (as a doctor); it makes her to be a bad doctor. In the same way, the quality of being dull makes a knife to be a bad knife.

Before we proceed, it is worth explaining the terminology of "end," "endpoint," and "goal." These words express the target toward which movements or desires are directed. Medical acts are moving toward the end or goal of health, a knife is moved (when used) toward the end of cutting, and so on. In what follows, the terms will be used interchangeably. Nevertheless, the term "endpoint" has some advantages over the others. The term "end" can refer to any stopping point, with or without a direction. Death is the end of life, for instance, but no one would say that life is directed toward death. In contrast, the term "endpoint" is more suggestive of a direction or movement toward a certain target. It also has advantages over the term "goal." We tend to reserve the word "goal" for conscious activity. We can say that the endpoint of a knife is to cut, but it is a bit awkward to say that the goal of a knife is to cut. Knives can have endpoints, but only human beings have goals. In the discussion that follows, we are concerned with any activities, whether conscious or not, that are heading to an endpoint.

One more thing about the endpoint. In an important sense, the endpoint precedes the movement. We first have the endpoint of written words, and only then do we have pens with which to write them. We first have the endpoint of health, and only then do we have doctors with the role of healing. The point to keep in mind is that pens do not make their own good by arbitrarily moving toward some endpoint. Rather, a pen has a movement precisely because there is an endpoint. In the same way, human beings cannot make their own good simply by moving toward some endpoint. This priority of the endpoint over movement will be examined in more detail in chapter 6.

Let us return to the question of good actions. The examples of medical actions provided above fit perfectly within the analysis of good and evil (*ST*, I-II, 18, 1). The good (according to the second usage described in the previous section) is that which completes a functional thing (as being sharp completes a knife); evil (or bad) is that which prevents this completion (like being dull). According to the first use of the word, a good functional thing has what is necessary to complete its function (as a good knife is able to cut well); a bad functional thing lacks something needed for its function. When we apply this analysis to medical actions, which have the function of bringing about health, we see that good medical actions have what it takes to heal well while bad medical actions lack something necessary to fulfill their function. In either event, good and bad medical acts depend upon function.

You probably noticed that in the domain of actions, "good" overlaps with "right" and "bad" overlaps with "wrong" (*ST*, I-II, 21, 1). Teresa's bad medical action of prescribing an antacid is also described as a wrong medical action; the good action of prescribing penicillin is also described as the right medical action. In short, right actions are good actions, and wrong actions are bad actions; the converse is also the case. The words "right" and "wrong" (unlike the words "good" and "bad") do not extend beyond the domain of actions. We do not describe a good knife as "right," nor do we describe sharpness (which is good for a knife) as "right."

The overlap between good actions and right actions is no surprise. In chapter 2, we saw that right actions relate appropriately to the goal of the action; in contrast, wrong actions undermine the goal. We now see that the goal can be linked to a function. The goal of medical acts is health because the function of medicine is to heal. Right actions, then, complete their functions, while wrong actions undermine their functions. In other words, right actions are good and wrong actions are evil.

The Moral Good

As discussed in chapter 2, many modern ethical theories reject the idea of a moral goal; consequently, they have difficulty applying the concepts of "right" and "wrong" to the domain of ethics (Anscombe 1958). Prescribing an antacid for a bacterial infection is the wrong action for Dr. Teresa because it does not move to the goal of health. Within the context of these modern ethical theories, however, the same meaning of "wrong" cannot apply to murder. The act of murder cannot be compared to a moral goal—either as promoting it or undermining it—because (according to many modern moral theories) there is no moral goal.

The same problem arises for the terms "good" and "bad" (or "evil"). These words make sense for knives, pens, eyes, and doctors because these things are directed to an endpoint by way of their functions. But morals are different, at least according to many modern ethical theories (Pigden 1990). Morals are different because human actions—within the context of the modern mindset—do not have a function. The good and evil of moral actions, then, cannot be defined in terms of a function. Morally good actions do not complete the movement to an endpoint found within a function. Morally evil actions do not lack this completion. It follows that the words "good" and "bad," in the domain of morals, must have a new and unique meaning.

We would be wise to hesitate before accepting this conclusion. We have no reason to suppose that the moral good is different from all other goods. We have no reason to believe that the moral good is esoteric. We have no reason to believe that the basic meaning of the word "good" suddenly shifts when we start talking about morality. We have no reason to suppose that the meanings of the words "good" and "bad" suddenly become mysterious in the domain of morals. In other areas, these words do not sit behind a veil, beyond which the human mind cannot penetrate. Rather, they are readily accessible. Why, then, should these words become strange and puzzling in the domain of morals?

Even when applied to morals, these words need not be puzzling. The mystery can be lifted, as long as we are willing to acknowledge a moral function and a moral endpoint. Those who insist upon denying this function should not invent new meanings for words. They should acknowledge that words, when taken from one area and then applied to another, retain the same meaning, or at least a related meaning. The words do not take on an idiosyncratic meaning.

Those who persist in denying a moral function should not turn to emotivism or prescriptivism with their peculiar meanings for "good" or "right." They are left with only one plausible option: they should adopt some version of error theory. For if in fact there is no moral function, then there can be no moral good. And if there is no moral good, then moral terms must be fictitious, like unicorns.

This version of error theory, however, is weaker than the standard version, which is generally connected to some variation of naïve realism. According to this standard version, the world is populated with strange and unusual properties—properties such as "rightness," "wrongness," and "goodness." We might be inclined to think that these curious properties are fictitious.

When faced with the good of knives, eyes, and doctors, however, we are much less likely to suppose that something fanciful has been fabricated. The goods of these things are not unusual properties. Furthermore, these goods are clearly real. The good, in these cases, is that which completes a movement to an endpoint. The oddity of naïve realism has been supplanted by something much more palatable.

Our Knowledge of the Good

The preceding discussion has not only eliminated the strange properties of naïve realism; it has also revealed the manner in which we come to know moral concepts such as the good. In other words, it has addressed the concerns of moral skepticism (as opposed to moral relativism). In order to explain how we come to know the unusual properties of "goodness," naïve realism has typically resorted to a kind of direct and immediate awareness of the good (Moore 1903). Our knowledge of the good becomes (for naïve realism) as mysterious as the special properties that we come to know. We either grasp the good or we don't. No further explanation is possible.

In contrast, this chapter has suggested that our knowledge of the good relies upon more basic knowledge, such as the knowledge of the movement to an endpoint found within a function. When we grasp something moving to an endpoint, we readily perceive the completion of this movement as good. When we recognize the function of an eye, we perceive the good of an eye.

Natural law ethics is neither relativistic nor skeptical. Moral features such as good and evil are real, and we can come to know these features of reality. In short, natural law ethics is a realist view. The same can be said for naïve realism, but naïve realism is not a natural law view. Not every realist account, then, is a natural law account. Unlike naïve realism, natural law maintains that good and evil are not special or unusual properties found in reality; they are simply the completion (or lack of completion) of a function. Unlike naïve realism, natural law maintains that we know good and evil not by way of some special immediate knowledge. Rather, by grasping some aspects of reality (such as functions), we also come to grasp the good.

chapter 5

Ought

A categorical imperative represents an action as objectively necessary in itself, without reference to any other purpose.

—Immanuel Kant, *Fundamental Principles of the Metaphysics of Morals*

This word "ought," having become a word of mere mesmeric force, [contains] no intelligible thought: a word retaining the suggestion of force, and apt to have a strong psychological effect, but which no longer signifies a real concept at all.

—G. E. M. Anscombe, "Modern Moral Philosophy"

As we have seen, many modern ethical theories lead to perplexity when they encounter words like "good" and "wrong." In the domain of morals, these words must take on a special and unusual meaning. This modern discomfort with moral terms converges emphatically over the use of the word "ought." Without doubt, the word "ought" is linked to ethics, as when we say that Melissa ought to help those in need. Not surprisingly, then, the word has proven an enigma for modern ethical theorists, who have been mystified more by ought-statements than by any other ethical terminology. Bewilderment surrounds not only the meaning of ought-statements but also their derivation or origin. As a result, the word "ought" becomes drained of all meaning, as G. E. M. Anscombe notes in the quote at the beginning of this chapter.

A Great Divide

These modern ethical theorists perceive a great divide between is-statements and ought-statements (Hume 1983). The philosopher David Hume, for instance, was perplexed—when reading about morals—to find is-statements mixed together with ought-statements. According to his thought, the domain of what is the case (is-statements) has nothing to do with the domain of what ought to be.

Others have suggested that the move from "is" to "ought" is a kind of logical fallacy (Moore 1903). We cannot begin with statements about the way the world is and logically conclude to statements about how the world ought to be. We cannot begin merely with statements about what Melissa is like (is-statements) and reach the conclusion that Melissa ought to help those in need.

This view insists that in order to conclude to a particular ought-statement, we must already have begun with a prior ought-statement in our premises. We might begin, for instance, by recognizing that we ought to be kind toward others. Since helping out someone in need is a way of being kind to them, we can then conclude that Melissa ought to help those in need. We have concluded to an ought-statement, but only because we began with a more general ought-statement. We did not start with an is-statement and conclude to an ought-statement. Rather, we started with one ought-statement and concluded to another ought-statement.

Discovering Ought-Statements

In previous chapters, we began by examining terms as they are used without reference to morals. We began, for instance, by considering right and wrong medical actions or good and bad knives. After we had analyzed these words without a moral context, we then proceeded to consider their uses within moral contexts. The same procedure will prove helpful for ought-statements.

Suppose, for instance, that as Giuseppe and Kirsten are driving to the grocery store, he says to her, "You ought to turn right." Giuseppe has made a true ought-statement that has nothing to do with ethics. Furthermore, Giuseppe's ought-statement seems to arise from various is-statements. Most importantly, it is based upon the idea that Kirsten is heading toward the grocery store. Other is-statements are also important, such as the location of the grocery store and the current location of Kirsten and Giuseppe. On the face of it, this ought-statement arises from is-statements.

Consider another example. Emma makes the statement that "lawnmowers ought to cut grass." Her statement is true because lawnmowers have the function of cutting grass. If, instead, Emma had said, "Scissors ought to cut grass," we would recognize that her statement is false precisely because scissors, although *able* to cut grass, do not have the function of cutting grass. Emma's true ought-statement concerning lawnmowers, then, arises from an is-statement. It arises from the idea that lawnmowers have the function of cutting grass.

Both of these examples involve a movement or a direction to an endpoint. Kirsten is moving to the endpoint of the grocery store; the lawnmower is directed (by way of its function) to the endpoint of cutting grass. Similar cases are not difficult to come by. Given that Matthew has the goal (or endpoint) of losing weight, for instance, we judge that Matthew ought to go on a diet or that Matthew ought to exercise. The progression from the is-statement (Matthew has the goal of losing weight) to the ought-statement (Matthew ought to go on a diet) is not at all mysterious.

Similarly, no mystery surrounds the judgment that a tree ought to put out roots in the direction of a source of water. Given that a tree has the endpoint of gaining nutrients (including water), the ought-statement follows naturally. We might say of a mouse, as it works its way through a maze, that it ought to turn right. This ought-statement is true based on the supposition (perhaps questionable) that the mouse is moving to the endpoint of getting through the maze.

All these cases involve something that is moving toward an endpoint. We should not be surprised, then, to discover that ought-statements are connected with a movement to an endpoint (*ST*, I, 82, 1). Sometimes the movement to the endpoint arises from human desire. Kirsten, for instance, desires to get to the grocery store, and Matthew desires to lose weight. In other cases, the movement to an endpoint does not arise from desire. The lawnmower, for instance, has no desire to cut grass, but it is moving to this endpoint on account of its function. Similarly, a tree has no conscious desire to gain nutrients, but it is moving to this endpoint by its nature.

Even in human affairs, individuals can be directed to an endpoint independently of their particular desires. Suppose, for instance, that Teresa is a doctor seeing her patient Sean, for whom she has a strong dislike. She is not inclined to heal him; on the contrary, she desires to harm him. Nevertheless, we recognize that Teresa, as a doctor, is directed—apart from her desires—to the endpoint of healing her patient Sean, and that consequently, she ought to heal him.

From where does this movement to an endpoint arise? Not surprisingly, it has something to do with the role or function of a doctor, which is to heal. If Teresa were a lawyer, we would not say that she ought to heal her clients. We might say that she ought to defend them or that she ought to advocate their cause. These ought-statements are connected to the function or role of a lawyer. Again, quite apart from desires, lawyers are directed to the endpoint of advocating the cause of their clients. Usually, of course, doctors desire to heal their patients, and lawyers desire to defend their clients. Even when these desires are absent, however, doctors and lawyers are still moving to these endpoints.

Human Deliberation

The move from is-statements to ought-statements is also revealed by examining human deliberations. Consider Anna, for instance, who must determine the kind of peg that will fit in a hole. She has various pegs: some round, some square, some triangular, some large, and some small. The hole is round; therefore, she determines that her peg needs to be round. The hole is also small; therefore, she determines that her peg needs to be small. Anna's procedure is simple. She compares her many pegs (her options) to the hole, eliminating those that do not fit. She thereby reaches the conclusion that her peg needs the attributes of being round and small.

Anna uses a similar process in other cases of deliberating. Suppose she wants to get from London to Paris as quickly as possible. Her problem might be expressed as parallel to the problem with the pegs. Previously, she was trying to determine what the *peg* must be like in order to fit in the hole. Now she is trying to figure out what *she* must be like (what kind of actions she needs to have) if she is to be someone who gets from London to Paris as quickly as possible.

Her reasoning is also parallel. She considers the various options, such as taking an airplane, taking a bus (with a ferry), and taking a train (through the Chunnel). She then compares these causes (of moving from London to Paris) and determines that the Chunnel is the quickest, thereby eliminating the others. She concludes that she must be someone who takes the Chunnel.

From beginning to end (in both examples), Anna's reasoning involves only is-statements. In the first case, it includes statements such as "This peg is square" or "This peg is round." In the second case, it includes statements such as "The bus takes nine hours" or "The Chunnel takes three hours." In the first case, the conclusion is an is-statement expressing a necessity: the peg *needs* certain attributes in order to be one that fits in this hole. In the second case, the conclusion also expresses a necessity: Anna *must have* certain attributes (or take certain actions) in order to be someone that gets from London to Paris as quickly as possible.

The same conclusions, however, might be expressed as ought-statements. The peg *ought* to be round and small. Those who want to get from London to Paris as quickly as possible *ought* to take the Chunnel.

In fact, ought-statements express a certain kind of necessity, sometimes called hypothetical necessity (*ST*, I, 82, 1). Given a certain end, a certain means is necessary, or at least most fitting. Insofar as Anna is someone who wants to get from London to Paris quickly, it is necessary for her to take the Chunnel; in other words, she *ought* to take the Chunnel. The change of expression—from "necessity" to "ought"—does not seem to introduce an entirely new idea. It simply looks at the same idea in slightly different ways.

The intellectual move from is-statements to ought-statements, then, is not a journey from one realm into an entirely disparate realm. An ought-statement is a specific kind of is-statement. It expresses a certain kind of necessity; it expresses what is the case.

This conclusion is supported by another aspect of ought-statements: they can be true or false. Given that Kirsten is going to the grocery store, it is true that she ought to turn right; on the other hand, it is false that she ought to turn left. In this regard, ought-statements are different from other sentences, such as requests. Daniela's request, "Please pass the salt," can be neither true nor false. It does not express the way the world is; rather, it expresses a desire to change the world. Ought-statements can be true or false precisely because they express the way the world is. They express a necessity found in the world. In short, ought-statements are a certain kind of is-statement.

Two Kinds of Imperatives

If ought-statements follow so readily from a movement to an endpoint, whether arising from a desire or from a function, then what fuels modern misgivings concerning a link between is-statements and ought-statements? Why do modern ethical theorists perceive a logical divide between is-statements and ought-statements?

The worry arises from a recurring theme in modern ethical thought: somehow or other, according to this idea, morals are different. The moral good, for instance, is radically different from the good of knives; right and wrong within morals is radically different from right and wrong in matters of direction; so also, moral ought-statements are fundamentally different from other ought-statements (Kant and Ellington 1993).

This difference is well expressed by the philosopher Immanuel Kant, who distinguishes between two different kinds of imperatives:

hypothetical imperatives and categorical imperatives. By an imperative, Kant means a command statement, like "Help the needy" or "Do not defraud your customers." Kant divides these command statements into two quite distinct categories. Some commands are moral commands, which fall under what he calls the categorical imperative; other commands are hypothetical or conditional commands. The command, "Help the needy," for instance, falls under the categorical imperative and is a moral command. In contrast, Giuseppe's command, "Turn right," is not moral but hypothetical.

These imperatives can be expressed in terms of ought-statements. We might say, for instance, that Melissa ought to help the needy. This statement expresses the same idea (although less forcefully) as the command (directed to Melissa), "Help the needy." Similarly, if Giuseppe says to Kirsten, "You ought to turn right," he expresses much the same idea as if he gave the command, "Turn right." What Kant says of imperatives, then, can equally be said of ought-statements.

According to Kant, hypothetical commands get their force only through the desire for some end to be achieved. Giuseppe's command has force for Kirsten, for instance, only if she desires to get to the grocery store. If she wants to go to the hardware store (which is on the other side of the road), then she should turn left. In other words, Kant agrees with the previously discussed analysis of ought-statements. They follow naturally from at least one kind of is-statement—namely, those statements that concern a movement toward some end.

According to Kant, however, moral ought-statements are different. Their force is not conditional upon some desire or movement to an endpoint; rather, it is unconditional (or categorical). Moral commands have force even apart from any goal that the person hopes to achieve. The command "help the needy" leaves no option. It applies to Melissa, for instance, even if she has no desire for the well-being of the needy. The force of the command does not depend upon any desire that Melissa happens to have. This same unconditional force remains even when the imperative is expressed in terms of an ought-statement, such as "Those who are well-off ought to help the needy." This ought-statement has force for those who are wealthy, even if they selfishly have no concern for the needy.

Within Kant's system, hypothetical ought-statements arise from a movement to an endpoint, but moral ought-statements do not. By recognizing that Matthew desires to lose weight, we readily move to the idea that he ought to go on a diet. The same move does not apply to Melissa, who lacks any desire for the well-being of the needy. For Matthew, we begin by recognizing an endpoint and we come to see how he ought to behave. In the case of Melissa, this same movement does not apply. We do not begin by recognizing an endpoint that Melissa is moving toward and then come to perceive how she ought to behave. For moral imperatives (in Kant's account), the move from is-statement to ought-statement has broken down. These imperatives must be discovered in a new way.

The precise details of this new manner of discovery need not detain us. Kant provides his own details, but other philosophers provide different avenues of discovering moral imperatives. What matters, for our purposes, is that moral commands are different from hypothetical commands. According to many modern ethical theories, moral commands are not discovered by way of is-statements. For morals, no bridge can span the divide between the way things are and the way things ought to be.

Conditional Ought-Statements

You may have noticed that Kant ignores one possibility. Ought-statements arise not only from the desire for some endpoint but also from the direction to an endpoint founded upon function. The idea that Matthew ought to go on a diet arises from his desire to lose weight; in contrast, the idea that lawnmowers ought to cut grass does not arise from any desire of the lawnmower but from its function. Similarly, the idea that Teresa (as a doctor) ought to heal her patients (even if she dislikes them) arises independent of her desires: it arises from her role as a doctor. In Kant's analysis, this possibility is missing. He recognizes only two possibilities: either ought-statements arise from an endpoint set by desire or they are categorical, arising from no endpoint. He misses the possibility of an ought-statement that arises from an endpoint set by function rather than by desire.

In a way, all the ought-statements that depend upon an endpoint (whether set by desire or by function) can be called hypothetical. They differ only in the kind of movement toward the end. Matthew's ought-statements arise from desire, which is one kind of movement to an endpoint. The ought-statement connected to the lawnmower arises from function, which is another kind of movement to an endpoint.

For convenience, we will designate a terminology that distinguishes between the two cases. When the movement to the endpoint is found in desire, then (following Kant) we will speak of hypothetical ought-statements. On the other hand, when the movement is found in a function or a role, then we will speak of conditional ought-statements. The statement that Matthew ought to go on a diet, for instance, is hypothetical, while the statement that a lawnmower ought to cut grass is conditional.

Both hypothetical and conditional ought-statements get their force from some endpoint. In the terminology mentioned above, they both express a certain kind of necessity, a hypothetical necessity. Given a certain endpoint, certain causes are necessary. Given the endpoint of fitting a peg in a hole, the peg must be round and small. Given the endpoint of getting to Paris quickly, a trip through the Chunnel is necessary. Similarly, given the lawnmower's endpoint of cutting grass (found in the function of the lawnmower), it is necessary for the lawnmower to cut grass. In other words, it *ought* to cut grass.

Despite the dependence upon an endpoint, conditional ought-statements (as opposed to hypothetical ought-statements) appear to be somewhat categorical. They are not so easily set aside. Matthew can set aside the hypothetical imperative to go on a diet simply by abandoning his desire to lose weight. In no way, however, can the lawnmower set aside the conditional ought-statement to cut grass. Nor does Teresa's change of desire in relation to Sean (that she does not want to heal him) release her from the conditional imperative to heal her patients. This imperative does not depend upon her desires but upon her role as a doctor.

Kant observes that moral imperatives are unconditional: we cannot simply opt out of them by changing our desires. He concludes that moral imperatives cannot get their force from an endpoint. Consequently, Kant

Table 5-1. Kinds of imperatives or ought-statements

Kind of ought-statement	Found in what domain	Where it derives its force from	Kind of necessity	How we come to know
Hypothetical	Nonmoral	Desired end	Hypothetical	From is-statements
Categorical	Moral	Itself	"Moral" necessity	Not derived
Conditional	Moral and nonmoral	The end of a function	Hypothetical	From is-statements

creates a new kind of imperative—the categorical imperative—that in no way depends upon an endpoint.

Unfortunately, Kant overlooks the possibility of conditional ought-statements (as opposed to hypothetical ought-statements). These conditional ought-statements get their force from an endpoint; nevertheless, we cannot opt out of them simply by changing our desires. Instead, we would have to change our function or our role. In order to opt out of the conditional imperative to heal her patients, for instance, Teresa would have to stop being a doctor. The lack of a desire to heal a particular patient (such as Sean) does not eliminate the imperative.

Kant's oversight, then, may have led him to a hasty conclusion. From the idea that we cannot opt out of moral imperatives, he concludes that these imperatives do not get their force from an endpoint. But he overlooked another possibility. From the idea that we cannot opt out of moral imperatives, we might conclude that they are conditional imperatives rather than hypothetical imperatives. These imperatives do get their force from an endpoint; nevertheless, we cannot so easily opt out of them. Changing our desires will not suffice. Perhaps, then, Kant should have concluded that moral imperatives are conditional imperatives.

A Human Function

The ancient philosophers Plato and Aristotle advocate this last possibility. Plato suggests that human beings have a certain function, and he concludes, not surprisingly, that human beings have a certain excellence or good, which is found in the completion of that function (*Rep*, bk. 1). He also recognizes certain hypothetical necessities that follow upon the endpoint of a function. He concludes, for instance, that in order to fulfill the human function, human beings must be just.

Similarly, Aristotle claims that human beings have the function of reasoning (*NE*, bk. 1, chap. 7). From this function follows the human good, which is realized in knowing the truth. Certain hypothetical necessities also follow from this function. Indeed, Aristotle thinks that the whole of ethics is a matter of doing what is necessary to attain the endpoint derived from a human function.

Plato and Aristotle avoid the great dichotomy of Kant. Unlike Kant, they think that all ought-statements express some kind of hypothetical necessity concerning some endpoint. This position does not lead them to conclude, as Kant might suppose, that we can readily opt out of these ought-statements. Sometimes we can; at other times, we cannot. We can opt out of the ought-statement if it concerns an endpoint set by desire, but we cannot opt out if it concerns an endpoint set by the human function. Moral ought-statements belong to this latter category.

Plato and Aristotle, then, have no need for Kant's categorical imperative. Melissa ought to help those in need, but not because of any special imperative that has nothing to do with an endpoint. Rather, she ought to help those in need because she has an endpoint that she herself has not chosen. She has an endpoint arising from her function.

This option, however, is repugnant to many modern ethical theorists, who scoff at the idea that human beings could have some function. To modern minds, this idea seems quaint at best. The idea that Melissa has some kind of function moving her to an endpoint simply must be rejected.

These modern theorists are forced into the dichotomy presented by Kant. Either moral ought-statements are hypothetical (depending upon an endpoint set by desire) or they are categorical (depending upon no endpoint whatsoever). Since our desires are rather fickle, differing from person to person and changing from moment to moment, the first option seems untenable. The remaining option is that ought-statements must be something like Kant's categorical imperatives, which do not depend upon an endpoint. In the domain of morals, then, the word "ought" must be unique. It cannot mean the same as when we say that a lawnmower ought to cut grass or that a doctor ought to heal. For morals, the word must take on a peculiar meaning of its own.

Kant's categorical imperatives still express some kind of necessity. They do not express hypothetical necessity, in which some cause is necessary for the sake of an end. Nevertheless, they express an uncompromising necessity. When we say that Melissa ought to help the needy, we mean that it is necessary (morally) for her to do so. This necessity, however, is not hypothetical. Instead, moral ought-statements express a kind of absolute or categorical necessity. The exact nature of this necessity is far from clear. As with other views typically found in modern ethical theories, this necessity seems to be peculiar to morality.

Ought-Statements within the Natural Law

We have seen that natural law theory rejects the great divide between the moral good and the good of knives; it rejects the divide between right and wrong in morals and right and wrong in medical acts. Likewise, it now rejects the great divide between moral ought-statements and hypothetical ought-statements.

Aquinas clearly states, for instance, that moral commands are conditional (*ST*, I-II, 99, 1). They arise from some movement to an endpoint. Just as Kirsten ought to turn right because she is going to the grocery store, so Melissa ought to help the needy because she has some endpoint.

For Aquinas, then, moral ought-statements are not drastically different from other ought-statements. Kirsten is moving toward the grocery store, and so she ought to turn right; similarly, human beings are moving to some shared good, and so they ought to help the needy. In other words, moral ought-statements express hypothetical necessity, a necessity that depends upon the movement to some endpoint.

In our ordinary usage, the words "good" and "bad," "right" and "wrong"—and now "ought"—all have some connection with an endpoint.

Because of Kirsten's endpoint, we can say that it is good for her to turn right, that it is (directionally) wrong for her to turn left, and that she ought to turn right. Relativist ethical views, from error theory to prescriptivism, insist that morals are different. In the case of morals, these words have a peculiar meaning. The common theme, in each case, is the rejection of a moral endpoint.

If the moral endpoint is rejected, then the use of these words, within morals, must have some esoteric meaning. Suppose, for instance, that Giuseppe claims that Kirsten ought to turn right, but at the same time he insists that Kirsten does not have the endpoint of getting to the grocery store. Indeed, he insists that the ought-statement (that Kirsten ought to turn right) has nothing to do with any endpoint whatsoever. In that case, Giuseppe's claim that Kirsten ought to turn right must have an unusual meaning. In the same way, modern ethical views deny the endpoint but insist upon using the same words. We should not be surprised, then, to discover that these words take on a peculiar meaning, far from our everyday usage.

Natural law theory rejects these peculiar meanings. When we say that Matthew ought to go on a diet, a lawnmower ought to cut grass, and Melissa ought to help the needy, we do not use three dramatically different meanings of the word "ought." In all three cases, the word "ought" expresses a hypothetical necessity in relation to some endpoint. The three uses do differ, but they differ primarily on account of the different endpoints in each case.

Natural law theory, then, finds no great divide—even in the realm of morals—between the way the world is and the way the world ought to be. These two domains are not so dramatically different after all. They are not separated by some insurmountable barrier. The move from is-statements to ought-statements is not mysterious. An ought-statement is simply a particular kind of is-statement, one that concerns a necessity for an endpoint.

Revisionism

We should note, before we proceed any further, that some thinkers identify themselves as natural law theorists even though they endorse the great divide between the realm of morals and other domains (Grisez 1983; Finnis 1980). Like modern ethical theorists, they endorse unique meanings (in the realm of morals) for the words "good," "right," and "ought."

Those who adopt this view are often called new natural law theorists, and the view they advocate is called the new natural law. This terminology, however, grants a questionable point. It concedes that this view is indeed a version of natural law. It may be wiser to withhold this concession and remain more circumspect in our use of the term "natural law."

Imagine that Robin, a proponent of Immanuel Kant, insists that she maintains a version of natural law. In your incredulity, you might point out that Immanuel Kant was likely not even a realist, which is the absolute minimum requirement for a natural law view. Robin says that she is a natural law advocate because she maintains a realist version of Kantian ethics (even if Kant was not a realist).

You persist in your incredulity. Even a realist version of Immanuel Kant, you point out, makes no connection between ethics and human nature. Robin, however, insists that it does, for ethics (in Kant's view) depends upon the nature of practical reason. Furthermore, it follows from this viewpoint that our knowledge of ethics is inherent to reason, which is another way of saying that we have natural knowledge of ethical truths.

Robin makes some valid claims about Kant's ethics. Does it follow that we should concede the point, granting her the title of a natural law advocate? If we do, we have unmoored the term "natural law" from its historical context, leaving it little substance beyond moral realism. Kantians themselves would find the designation odd, perhaps even objectionable.

The term is likewise watered-down when we speak of the "new natural law," a view that has many similarities with various modern theorists whom we have investigated, such as Immanuel Kant. Most dramatically, "new natural law" theorists accept the divide between is-statements and ought-statements. They accept the divide between human nature and ethics. They accept the esoteric meanings of "ought" and "good" in the domain of morals. For them, the role of human nature within ethics, especially for the fundamental principles of morals, becomes reduced to practical rationality, and the "nature" in natural law becomes nothing more than a kind of immediate or built-in (and hence "natural") knowledge of ethics. For them, the good—at least as we know it practically (as opposed to speculatively)—is not that which completes human nature.

When pushed on this point, some advocates of "new natural law" will insist that the separation between the human good and human nature (in their view) is not so complete (Finnis 1987). The separation between the two is only on the side of our knowledge; on the side of reality, they claim, the ethical good remains founded in human nature. This rather subtle position (which will be examined a bit more in chapter 8) still leaves "new natural law" far distant from human nature.

Furthermore, the significance of their concession—that the good is founded upon nature on the side of reality (but not on the side of our knowledge)—seems to have little bearing upon the thought of new natural law advocates. When they are presented with a connection between human nature and the ethical good, for instance, they often respond with perplexity, asking what on earth nature could have to do with ethics. One prominent advocate of the view has even described the argument linking the human good to function as an "erratic boulder," thereby suggesting that the intellectual association between nature and the good has been a destructive force in the history of ethics (Finnis 1983). If these thinkers really maintain the connection suggested in the last paragraph, they should not respond with perplexity or consternation; rather, they should openly embrace the connection between the good and human nature. They might quibble over the manner of the connection, or they might insist that our knowledge initially arises independent of the connection, but they should not question the connection itself.

For these reasons, it seems better to err on the side of caution, being more circumspect in our use of the term "natural law." We will reserve the term for those views that acknowledge—in practice and not merely in theory—a tight link between human nature and the ethical good. We will reserve it for those views that acknowledge the link between function and the good. Given the role of a doctor, we perceive that a doctor ought to heal. Similarly, given the human function, we come to perceive how human beings ought to behave.

On account of this deep divide between "new natural law" and natural law as it has historically been expounded, it is advisable to find a new term for this view, so that we might retain some real content—beyond realism—for the term "natural law." Consequently, when we encounter this view in subsequent chapters, we will give it the name "revisionism" (or the "revisionist view"), and we will give the name "revisionists" to its advocates.

We can identify natural law views—at least according to our designation—as realist views that include the following three features. First, the nature of the ethical good is clearly founded upon our human nature; second, our knowledge of this good is dependent on our knowledge of what we are as human beings; third, our knowledge of the good is itself in some way natural. This third point we will examine in subsequent chapters.

chapter 6

Emotivism

A system of morality based on relative emotional values is a mere illusion, a thoroughly vulgar conception which has nothing sound in it and nothing true.

—Plato, *Phaedo*

According to the relativistic view called emotivism (mentioned earlier), moral terms like "right" and "wrong" are simply ways of expressing our own personal wants and desires (Ayer 2014). "Murder is wrong" means "I don't like murder." This same analysis applies to words like "good" and "bad," and indeed to all evaluative terms. "Pizza is good" means "I like pizza" or "I want pizza."

As we have seen, this account renders disagreements (over evaluations) nonsensical (Lewis 1947). Jim and Patti might argue heatedly over a movie they have watched. Jim thinks it was excellent; Patti thinks it was pathetic. If emotivism is true, then they are not actually disagreeing over anything. Jim is merely saying that he likes the movie, and Patti is saying that she does not like the movie. These two statements are completely consistent with one another and imply no disagreement.

Jim and Patti, however, think they are disagreeing. Indeed, while arguing, Jim is fully aware that he likes the movie and that Patti does not. He is not arguing over this point. Rather, he supposes that he is saying something about the movie, not about his preferences; when Patti responds, she also supposes that she is saying something about the movie. Emotivism, then, can make no sense of our everyday interactions.

A Problem of Priorities

Besides this problem, emotivism suffers from an even more fundamental flaw: it is unable to explain a common feature of our emotions or desires. Our emotions—and all our likes and dislikes—follow upon some prior judgment concerning the good or evil of the object desired. Allex desires pizza, for instance, only because he has first judged that pizza tastes good, that pizza is nutritional, or some such thing. This observation poses a difficulty for emotivism, because emotivism flips this order. According to emotivism, Allex does not desire pizza because he thinks it is good. Rather, he calls pizza good because he desires it.

The difficulty for emotivism is a kind of chicken and egg problem. Which came first, the chicken or the egg? Which came first, Allex's desire for pizza or his judgment that pizza is good? According to emotivism, the desire comes first, and only then does Allex call the pizza good. According to Aquinas, the judgment comes first: only after Allex has judged that pizza is in some manner good can he desire it (*ST*, I, 59, 1; *ST*, I, 80, 1; *ST*, I-II, 26, 1; *ST*, I-II, 30, 1, ad 3). In either account, desires and judgments concerning what is good are intimately linked. The two views differ on the question of priority.

Knowing and Desiring Powers

For Aquinas, the problem can be clarified by examining two different kinds of powers: knowing powers and desiring powers (*ST*, I, 78, 1; Jensen 2018). With our knowing powers, we are aware of the world around us. The sense of sight, for instance, knows the colors and shapes of the objects in our surroundings; the sense of hearing knows sounds; and so on (*ST*, I, 78, 3). We also have a memory (or imagination) by which we can know objects that are not present, as when we recall what someone looks like or where we last placed our keys (*ST*, I, 78, 4). Finally, we have the power of reason, by which we know the natures of things and their causes (*ST*, I, 79). By way of our reason, for instance, we can know that a rock is composed of atoms or that the sun causes us to become warm.

With our knowing powers, we sometimes become aware of our very selves. John can be aware of a pain in his back, and Helena can be aware that her heart is beating quickly. We can also become aware of our emotions. Allex, for instance, can be aware that he desires pizza. These cases do not contradict what we said earlier concerning knowing powers—namely, that with our knowing powers we are aware of the world around us. Sometimes, the world that we can know includes our own bodies and our own minds.

In contrast to knowing powers, which take in the world around us, desiring powers move us to act (*ST*, I, 80; *ST*, I, 81, 1). Because of his desire for food, Allex buys pizza and begins to eat; because Maria is angry at John, she scowls at him; and so on. The word "desire," when used most properly, refers to a very particular movement to act—typically the movement to acquire or attain something, as with Allex's desire to attain pizza (*ST*, I-II, 25, 2). When we speak of "desiring powers," however, we are using the word "desire" loosely, so that it includes all sorts of movements to act. In this manner, Maria's anger can be classified as a kind of "desire."

Our desires (in the broad sense) are what might be called conscious movements toward an endpoint. They move toward what is good and away from what is bad. A lawnmower also moves to some endpoint, for through its function it is directed to cut grass. The movement of the lawnmower, however, is not conscious, for lawnmowers have no consciousness at all. Similarly, a tree moves to put out roots and gain nutrition, but it does not do so consciously; rather, it is moved by its biological nature (*ST*, I-II, 26, 1). On the other hand, Leo the dog consciously moves to eat steak. He is aware of the steak and has a conscious desire for the steak (*ST*, I-II, 26, 1).

Clearly, Leo needs some awareness of the steak. If he does not sense it in any way whatsoever, he cannot possibly desire it. According to Aquinas, however, an awareness merely of the existence of the steak is also insufficient to give rise to desire. Leo's awareness must include a judgment that the steak is good to eat (*ST*, I-II, 9, 1, ad 2). Otherwise, he might have a desire to eat putrefying steak, or he might have a desire to eat rocks. He is aware of rocks, but he does not desire to eat them because he does not estimate that rocks are good to eat.

Leo sees a rock, a steak, and a tree insofar as each of them is colored. If they had no color (like air), he could not see them. When he hears the rock fall, the steak sizzle as it is being cooked, and the leaves of the tree rustle in the wind, he does not hear these objects insofar as they are colored. Rather, he hears them insofar as they make sounds. The power to see and the power to hear, then, perceive the very same objects, but they perceive them on account of different aspects, either on account of being colored or on account of making noise. We can distinguish between the object perceived (a rock, a steak, and a tree) and the aspect or formality under which it is perceived (as colored or as making noise) (*ST*, I, 77, 3).

When Leo recognizes that the steak is good to eat, a new formality is introduced. He sees the steak insofar as it is colored, he smells the steak insofar as it has odor, but now he knows something further about the steak. Beyond its color and odor, he knows that the steak is good to eat. With his power of sight, he knows the color of both the steak and the rock, but only with a further power—with what Aquinas calls the power to make estimations (or the estimative power)—does he know that the steak is good to eat while the rock is not (*ST*, I, 78, 4). Only with this further awareness does desire arise. Awareness by itself—of colors, sounds, odors, or other such things—is insufficient to give rise to desire. Only awareness of some kind of good gives rise to conscious desire.

According to Aquinas, then, awareness of the good definitely precedes conscious desire. The egg (of awareness of the good) must come first, and the chicken (of desire for the good) must come second. In contrast, emotivism claims that conscious desire comes first. Only when we desire something do we then judge it to be good. Indeed, our judgment

Table 6-1. Diverse powers

Power	Kind of power	Formality under which the object is known
Five senses	Knowing	Sensible qualities
Imagination	Knowing	Sensible qualities as absent
Estimative power	Knowing	Sensible qualities as good or bad
Emotions	Desiring	Sensible things as good or bad

(that it is good) is simply a judgment that we desire it. When Helena calls the act of studying good, she simply means (according to emotivism) that she desires it; her judgment of the good, then, cannot possibly precede her desire.

Avoiding a Circle

Like any chicken and egg problem, Aquinas's chicken and egg priority raises a further question. Where does the first item (the egg of awareness of the good) come from? It cannot come from the chicken, or we would have a circle. The egg would come first, but the chicken would then come before the egg.

It might look like Aquinas falls into this error. He says that awareness comes before desire. Someone might insist, however, that when asked what comes before the awareness of the good, Aquinas would be forced to answer that desire must precede awareness.

Why might someone suppose that Aquinas falls into this circle? Because of what we have already seen concerning the notion of the good. Allex is aware, for instance, that being sharp is good for a knife only because he is first aware that the knife is moving (through its function) to the endpoint of cutting. Allex is aware of the good, then, only by first being aware of a movement to an endpoint. We have just said, however, that the desire for the good is itself a movement to an end.

Concerning the pizza, then, Allex seems to have the following three steps:

(1) Allex is aware of his movement to the endpoint of eating pizza.

(2) Allex judges that fulfilling this movement (by actually eating the pizza) is good.

(3) Allex desires to eat the pizza.

Since Allex's desire is itself a movement to the endpoint of eating pizza, it seems that we have ended up (step 3) where we began (step 1). Step 1 and step 3 seem to be exactly the same thing.

Fortunately, Aquinas is not forced into this trap. Step 1 might look like step 3, but the two are not exactly alike, or at least they need not be. In the presentation above, the difference between the two has been obscured. Both step 1 and step 2 involve a movement to an endpoint. Indeed, they involve a movement to the same endpoint (of eating pizza). It does not follow that the two movements are one and the same. All rats are mammals, but it does not follow that all mammals are rats. Similarly, a conscious desire is a movement to an end, but not every movement to an end is a conscious desire. As we have seen, a function is a movement to an end, but it is not a conscious desire. Likewise, the biological makeup of a tree, apart from any conscious desire, moves it to the end of gaining nutrition.

In step 1, Allex is aware of his movement toward the endpoint of eating pizza. Is Allex, in this step, aware of his emotional desire for pizza? No, for that emotional desire does not arise until step 3. Then what movement to an end is he aware of in step 1? He must be aware of some nonconscious movement to an end, such as a function or a biological movement. He might be aware, for instance, that pizza fulfills his biological need for nutrition and that consequently eating pizza is good. He knows that pizza is good (as a form of nutrition) not from his desire for pizza. Rather, he knows it from the movement of his biological nature toward nutrition. Just as Allex can recognize what is good for a tree based upon its biological movements to an end, so he can recognize what is good for himself on account of similar movements.

We are left with the following series:

(1) Allex has some nonconscious movement to an end, such as his body's movement to nutrition.

(2) Allex is aware of this movement.

(3) Allex is aware that what completes this movement is good for him.

(4) Allex consciously desires the nutrition of pizza.

(5) Only after step 4 can Allex become aware of his conscious desire for pizza.

Emotivism has a different series:

(1) Allex emotionally desires pizza.

(2) Allex becomes aware that he desires the pizza.

(3) He judges that pizza is good, which is nothing other than to say that he desires it.

In this latter series, Allex must have an emotional desire that does not depend upon any awareness of any good.

Another example might help clarify the proper ordering of our knowledge concerning the good. Young children often persistently ask the question "why?" These children have discovered their own minds. They know that with their minds they can understand the world around them. Coming to know the causes of things is, for them, a great human good (*ST*, I-II, 3, 8). They recognize that this knowledge completes their minds, which have a capacity—a movement—to discover the causes in the world around them. So hungry are they for this good that parents (regrettably) sometimes want to suppress their persistent questions.

In relation to the thought of Aquinas, this example suggests the following series for a child named Bernardita:

(1) Like other human beings, Bernardita has a mind with the capacity to grasp the causes of things; it naturally moves out to understand the world and its causes.

(2) Bernardita becomes aware of her own mind and its capacity to know causes.

(3) Bernardita recognizes that the completion of this capacity is good for her.

(4) Bernardita consciously desires to know the causes of things.

(5) Bernardita is aware that she desires to know the causes of things.

Bernardita does not begin by recognizing her conscious desire to know the causes of things. Rather, she begins by recognizing that she has a mind capable of knowing. She recognizes that her mind is made complete only by attaining something beyond itself, only by attaining knowledge of the causes of things. In short, she recognizes that her mind is stretching beyond itself; it is moving toward knowledge of the world. The good she perceives is precisely a completion of her mind and its movement (*ST*, II-II, 1, 3, ad 1). If she began with steps 4 and 5, then she would misidentify the good. If she began with her own conscious desire, then she would conclude to a good that completes this *conscious* movement to an endpoint. She would not conclude to a good that completes her mind and its movement.

The good of emotivism must always be satisfaction, which is the completion of conscious desire. It must leave unanswered the question, "Satisfaction in what *good*?" Bernardita seeks satisfaction in the good of her mind. If she were an emotivist, she would seek satisfaction just by itself, a satisfaction that is connected with her mind but only by the brute force of her desire. No awareness of the good makes the connection.

The Sovereignty of the Good

We have emphasized that the natural law is concerned with the real good, not with a subjective assertion of the good. Furthermore, this real good can be grasped and understood by human beings. We can now add a further detail: this real good is not founded upon our emotional desires. On the contrary, our conscious desires follow upon the real good and our awareness of it.

As we have seen, modern ethical theorists typically reject the notion of a human function as unworthy of consideration. Consequently, they must explain the human good in terms that have nothing to do with a function. Emotivists (those espousing emotivism) succeed better than others. At least they attempt to link the notion of the good with a movement to an endpoint; they link the good to our emotional desires. In contrast, advocates of naïve realism assert that the good is an attribute like being yellow or being red, an attribute that appears disconnected from a movement to an endpoint (Moore 1903).

Ultimately, however, emotivists miss the mark. They recognize that the good is linked to a certain movement to an endpoint, but they fail to recognize the basis for this link. The real basis has to do with the nature of the good, which is that which completes a movement to an endpoint. For emotivists, however, the good is not that which completes a movement to an endpoint. Rather, the good is simply a name we apply to things that we happen to desire. Emotivists fail to recognize that these very desires are themselves dependent upon our perception of the good. For them, the good becomes linked with arbitrary emotional desires.

As a result, the good of emotivism is not a good found in the world; it is not a good that we discover. Rather, it is a good that we assert, a good that we impose upon reality. Our desires become sovereign. They do not *follow* the good but *define* the good. The good of a rapist is found in the act of raping; after all, that is what he desires. The good of Hitler was to kill certain peoples; after all, that is what he desired.

Natural law theory rejects this subjective good. For natural law, desire is not sovereign; rather, the good is sovereign. Our desires must follow the good and submit to it.

Consider the act of rape, for instance. According to natural law, we first recognize that rape is evil because it opposes the completion of some movement to an endpoint. The movement involved will be explained further in subsequent chapters, but for now we can simply observe that human beings are directed to a shared endpoint. They are not solitary beings. The good perceived, then, is a shared good, a good possessed together. The act of rape is not an act of sharing the good; on the contrary, it undermines sharing between the perpetrator and the victim. Consequently, the act of rape is an evil rather than a good. Once we recognize that rape is evil, then we can have the appropriate emotional response: we should feel repugnance to the idea of raping.

The rapist does not follow this pattern. He does not have repugnance toward the act of rape; on the contrary, he has desire. From where does his desire arise? According to Aquinas, it must arise, like every desire, from his judgment that rape is good. In the act of rape, for instance, he might perceive some pleasure, which provides at least a limited fulfillment of his capacities (which include the capacity to feel pleasure). For this limited good, he throws away the shared good. His particular desire, he decides, must override the good that completes his nature. He hands himself over to a good that he himself defines, a good that his desires assert. He follows the pattern of emotivism rather than the pattern of natural law.

chapter 7

Human Nature

> Human excellence consists in the fact that God made him in His own image by giving him an intellectual soul, which raises him above the beasts of the field.
>
> —Augustine, *A Literal Meaning of Genesis*

> The gods implant reason in men, the highest of all things that we call our own.
>
> —Sophocles, *Antigone*

This chapter, which dwells upon human nature and human mental capacities, may appear to have little to do with natural law ethics. This appearance is deceptive. We have seen that our knowledge of the good depends upon our knowledge of nature. For instance, we know what makes for a good eye only by knowing what an eye is. The human good is no different. If we are to know what makes for a good human being, we must know something about human nature. Indeed, no discussion of ethics can do without some discussion of human nature.

We discover the nature of a thing, at least of a functional thing, by coming to know its activity (*ST*, I, 77, 3). We know the nature of an eye, for instance, by knowing its activity of seeing; we know the nature of a doctor by knowing the activity of healing. Similarly, only by understanding human activity will we come to understand human nature.

Fortunately, we need not examine every detail of human nature. For the purposes of natural law, we need discover only those natural movements that give rise to the human good. Just as the good of an eye is found in the completion of its movement to the activity of seeing, so also the human good will be found in the completion of some natural movement to an endpoint. Just as the function of an eye is realized in the activity of seeing, so the human function will be realized in activity. Our focus, then, will be upon human activities (Jensen 2018).

Within human activities, we have already explored the important distinction between knowing and desiring. We will examine this distinction in greater detail, beginning with knowing powers.

Knowing Powers

Our knowing powers can be divided into three general categories (*ST*, I, 78, 1). First, we have the five external senses, to which might be added a kind of sense knowledge of our internal states (*ST*, I, 78, 3). We are sensibly aware, for instance, of our aches and pains, of the different positions of our bodily parts, of the tensing of our muscles, and so on.

Second, we have what Aquinas calls internal senses (*ST*, I, 78, 4). He calls them senses, in part, because they are tightly linked with the external senses. They start with the external senses, and their knowledge concerns many of the same things as the external senses; nevertheless, they go beyond the external senses. With her power of sight, for instance, Helena knows a red rose. With her power to remember, which Aquinas categorizes as an internal sense, she also knows the color of the rose, for she can remember that it was red. Her memory, however, goes beyond the external power of sight. With her memory, for instance, Helena knows the rose even when it is absent.

Like the memory, the imagination (another internal sense) also gets beyond the five senses. With her imagination, Helena takes in what she has already sensed, and she puts it together in new ways. She has seen a mountain before, and she has seen the color gold before, but with her imagination she puts them together, imagining a golden mountain. In a similar fashion, she imagines a 10-headed monster.

The internal senses also include other powers by which we go even further beyond the senses. Animals (including human beings) make instinctive judgments, as when a bird judges that it should make a nest. It also judges that twigs are helpful for this purpose; it judges that some insects are good to eat and others are not; and so on. As we have already noted, Aquinas gives the name "estimative power" to the capacity that makes these instinctive judgments.

While the external and internal senses are common to human beings and animals, the third kind of knowing power—reason—is found in human beings alone (*ST*, I, 78, 1). With our reason, we know the causes of things, the relations between things, and the natures of things. With the power of sight, Helena perceives that a rose is red, but with the power of reason, she comes to know the chemical makeup of the rose or the nature of color or the nature of light rays.

Reason extends far beyond both the external senses and the internal senses. As noted earlier, Helena's memory goes beyond her sense of sight: it knows the rose even in the rose's absence. Nevertheless, her memory does not go far beyond the external senses. Even the instinctive power is intimately connected with concrete sensible items. A bird, for instance, does not form a propositional judgment, such as "I ought to gather twigs." Rather, it simply recognizes something fitting about gathering this twig.

In contrast, reason is aware of an entirely new domain. Suppose that Joe decides to build a house (as a bird builds a nest). Joe first recognizes that certain actions—such as laying bricks and pounding nails—will cause the house to come together; he recognizes that certain materials—such as lumber, bricks, and sheet rock—have important properties needed for the construction of his house. Furthermore, he recognizes the very nature of the house, that it has the purpose of providing shelter. In contrast, the bird perceives only that a nest is fitting.

In human beings, we find all three levels of knowing powers: external senses, internal senses, and reason. These diverse knowing powers sometimes know the very same object, but they identify different aspects or formalities. With her power of sight, for instance, Helena knows a rose as red. With her power of smell, she knows the same rose as fragrant. With her memory, she knows the rose as absent. A bee might similarly know the same aspects of the rose, and in addition it might have an instinct that the nectar of a rose is fitting to eat, but the bee will never know what Helena knows with her reason. It will never know, for instance, the nature of a rose as a kind of flower.

Desiring Powers

Just as Aquinas identifies diverse kinds of knowing powers, so also he identifies diverse kinds of desiring powers (*ST*, I, 80, 2). And just as some knowing powers are common to both human beings and animals while reason is peculiar to human beings, so also some desiring powers are shared with animals and some are peculiar to human beings. The emotions, which we discussed in the last chapter, are shared with animals. In addition to the emotions, Aquinas recognizes the will as a kind of desiring power peculiar to human beings.

We have a wide variety of emotions, including (but not limited to) the following: desire, anger, envy, love, hatred, aversion, anxiety, enjoyment, fear, hope, despair, and displeasure (*ST*, I-II, 23). Not all of them are "movements" in a straightforward way. It is not clear, for instance, that enjoyment moves us to act. Aquinas, however, recognizes resting in something as a kind of movement (*ST*, I-II, 31, 1). When Allex enjoys his pizza, he is resting in it. This enjoyment moves him to act, at least insofar as he does not continue—while enjoying the pizza—to pursue other foods. Enjoyment keeps us in the activity in which we are engaged. When Helena enjoys a sunset, she continues to gaze upon it. Without the enjoyment, she might go on to do other things instead.

The emotions are our most obvious desiring powers, but as far as Aquinas is concerned, they are not our only desiring powers, nor indeed are they our most important desiring power. That honor goes to the will (*ST*, I, 81, 3). In our day, we typically associate the will with free choice, which certainly is a movement to some endpoint. On account of his choice, for instance, Jerry moves himself to get in the car and drive to church.

What we choose to do is what finally moves us to act. When Maria is angry at John, for instance, she might desire to yell at him. In the end, however, she decides that it is better not to yell. Her choice to control herself is what finally determines her action. Maria has two movements: an emotional movement of anger propelling her to yell and a movement from her will to refrain from yelling. With her choice, Maria overrides her anger. Of course, she might give in to her anger, but that is also a choice she makes. Maria is ultimately moved to act by her choice, even if sometimes her choice is made under the influence of heated emotional passions.

In the modern era, many thinkers dismiss the will as a mere figment of the human imagination (Skinner 1971). They adopt a view called determinism: they claim we are not free but determined in all our actions. While we might imagine that we make choices, in reality we simply follow whatever happens to be our strongest desire. When Maria "chooses" not to yell, it just happens that she has a stronger desire to refrain from yelling.

A defense of free will does not fall within the purview of this book. In our discussions of ethics, we must take free will as a given, for without free will, natural law ethics—and indeed all of ethics—would make no sense. It is worth noting, however, that the argument in support of determinism suggested previously (according to which we always "choose" that for which we have the strongest desire) is circular. If Maria yells, so the argument goes, then her strongest desire was to yell. If she refrains from yelling, then her strongest desire was to refrain from yelling.

Such reasoning is no evidence at all. How do we know what Maria's strongest desire is? By looking at what she chooses to do. And what does she choose to do? That for which she has the strongest desire (so claims determinism). By definition, then, whatever Maria chooses to do is what she most of all desires. In other words, determinism excludes, before any discussion, the possibility that Maria had a stronger desire to yell but then—despite her strong desire—restrained herself with her free choice.

To the modern mind, the will is nothing other than a choosing power. Choice exhausts its possible movements. For Aquinas, the will is much more. Just as emotions come in a wide variety, from fear to anger, so acts of the will come in a wide variety, including but not limited to choice. In the will, as with the emotions, we can find desire, love, hate, enjoyment, envy, and so on (*ST*, I, 20, 1, ad 1). In each of these acts of will, the fundamental movement is similar to the emotions. Both in the will and in the emotions, for instance, enjoyment is a resting in a good; both in the will and in the emotions, desire propels us to attain some good; and so on.

This similarity between the will and the emotions should be no surprise. After all, both the will and the emotions are conscious desires. In this respect, they differ from what might be called nonconscious movements to an endpoint. A tree, for instance, moves to put out roots and to gain nutrition, but it has no conscious desire to do so. In contrast, Maria, with her anger, is consciously inclined to seek vengeance upon John. Similarly, with the enjoyment in her will, Helena consciously rests in the good of the sunset that she beholds.

The will and the emotions are conscious desires in two respects. First, they arise from some awareness of the good (or bad); second, in the very act of desiring, we are conscious of our desire. Maria's anger at John, for instance, arises from some awareness of the good of taking revenge on John for some perceived injustice. At the same time, Maria is conscious of the anger within her, even if sometimes she may have difficulty pinpointing the exact cause of her anger. Similarly, Jerry's choice to go to church arises from an awareness of the goods he can achieve; furthermore, he is aware that he makes the choice.

Differences between the Will and Emotions

Although the will and the emotions have these similarities, ultimately they are profoundly different. For our purposes, it is sufficient to consider three important differences.

First, although we are conscious of both our emotions and our will, we are conscious of them in different ways. The emotions are sometimes also called feelings, because we do feel our emotions. Maria, for instance, feels her anger. She might feel herself becoming warm, or she might feel her heart beating faster; perhaps she might say that her blood is boiling. Similarly, when Beth is afraid of an intruder, she feels her muscles tensing.

According to Aquinas, the will is different. It is not felt. Maria does not "feel" her choice to refrain from yelling. She feels the anger, but she does not feel the choice. Certainly, she is aware of her choice, but she is not aware by way of feeling a bodily change.

Aquinas thinks this difference derives from a fundamental difference between the will and the emotions. The emotions are constituted, in part, by a bodily change, which is a kind of preparation for action (*ST*, I, 20, 1, ad 1). For instance, when Beth is afraid, her heart beats faster and her muscles tense. In contrast, acts of will are not constituted by any bodily change. They are solely mental, without the corresponding bodily preparation for action (*ST*, I-II, 9, 5; *ST*, I-II, 17, 7; *ST*, I, 77, 5).

Bodily changes do often accompany choices (and other acts of will) but only because our choices are typically accompanied by emotions, which themselves involve a bodily change. Suppose, for instance, that Maria chooses to yell at John. Various bodily changes (such as an increased heartbeat and tense muscles) accompany this choice. They are not part of the choice, however. Rather, they are part of the emotion of anger, which motivated Maria's choice.

The second difference between the will and the emotions concerns the awareness that precedes the movement and gives rise to it. Before Beth is afraid, she must have some judgment of an evil to be avoided; before Helena enjoys the sunset, she must have some judgment that it is good. Both the emotions and the will require this prior awareness. Nevertheless, each arises from a distinct kind of awareness (*ST*, I, 80, 1). The will, says Aquinas, arises from reason, while the emotions arise from the internal senses, in particular from the power of making instinctive judgments.

This second difference between the emotions and the will is as profound as the difference between the instinctive power and reason. While the instinctive power knows something as fitting, only reason fully understands the good. Only reason can recognize function or other movements to an end. Only reason knows that the good is that which fulfills or completes these movements. The true meaning of the good, then, is understood only by reason.

As we have seen, different knowing powers know objects under different formalities, even as the power of sight knows a rose as colored and the power of smell knows a rose as fragrant. The same sort of difference appears in our knowledge of something good. Reason knows the good under its proper formality. It knows the good as that which completes the movement to some endpoint. In contrast, our instinctive awareness of the good recognizes only this or that particular fittingness of an object, such as the fittingness of twigs for a nest. The bird does not know the good (such as the gathering of twigs) precisely as good for itself as a bird.

Both acts of the will and acts of the emotions, then, arise from some grasp of the good, but they do so in different ways. The will arises from reason, which fully grasps the nature of the good. The emotions arise from a kind of instinctive knowledge of an internal sense power, which grasps this or that particular object as fitting.

In human beings, this portrayal of the emotions must be qualified. When human beings perceive the world around them, reason interacts with senses. When Max perceives the oak tree before him, for instance, he uses his senses, his imagination, and his reason—all intertwined with one another. He knows it as an oak tree (with his reason) precisely because he perceives certain features (with his senses), which he recalls (with his memory or imagination) as similar to other trees. Given this profound interaction, his perceptual estimations of good and bad are imbued with reason, or at least they can be (*ST*, I, 78, 4). A bird recognizes a twig as fitting only through instinct and conditioning. In contrast, Allex recognizes pizza as fitting through an estimation shaped by reason. In human beings, then, the emotions can be influenced, to varying degrees, by reason (*ST*, I, 83, 3).

This second difference between the will and emotions (that is, the different knowing powers from which they arise) gives rise to the third and most profound difference. Just as knowing powers grasp the same object under different formalities, so also desiring powers move toward an endpoint under different formalities. The will, following reason, moves to the good under the proper formality of being good. The emotions, following instinct, move to the good as fitting for some particular thing (*ST*, I, 82, 5). The will truly moves to the good in general; the emotions move toward this or that particular completion.

The will, then, is far more encompassing than the emotions. With his emotions, Allex desires some particular object fitting for some particular end, as pizza is fitting for pleasure and nutrition. With his will, he desires what is good for himself as a whole. Unfortunately, Allex might think that a partial good—which is in fact detrimental to him—is good for him overall. He might think that gorging upon pizza is good for himself as a whole, when in fact it merely provides a partial fulfillment, the satisfaction of his emotional desires.

Consequently, we most properly identify ourselves with our will and not with our emotions. With her emotions, for instance, Anna might feel envy toward Michael, but with her will she wants his good. The emotion of envy is an unfortunate distraction for Anna, but what matters most in her relation to Michael is the movement of her will. Perhaps Maria feels anger toward John, but in her will she desires mercy for John. The anger may prove a constant temptation, but what matters most in her relation to John is the movement found in her will. A person is most identified, then, not by her emotions but by what she wills (*ST*, I, 48, 6).

Nonconscious Powers

As we have seen, human beings have some powers shared with animals, such as the senses and the emotions, and they have other powers peculiar to human beings, such as reason and will. We can add a third category—namely, powers shared not only with animals but also with plants (*ST*, I, 78, 2). Human beings—like trees—have the power to take in nutrients and thereby to keep themselves alive. The power to reproduce is also shared with plants and animals.

Like the emotions and will, these powers move toward some endpoint. The power of nutrition moves to the endpoint of keeping alive. The power of reproduction moves to the endpoint of a new individual, and ultimately to the endpoint of maintaining the species. Unlike the emotions and will, these powers are not conscious desires. The tree moves to put out roots and take in nutrients apart from any awareness of the good. It also develops seeds and reproduces apart from consciousness.

In human beings, of course, these powers are typically exercised in conjunction with some conscious activity. Allex takes in nutrients, for instance, by consciously eating. Once he has eaten, however, his body processes the nutrients without any conscious input. Similarly, sexual intercourse is typically a conscious activity, but the actual reproduction and development of the baby in the mother's womb occur without conscious effort on the part of the mother or father. The mother does perform various activities that assist in this development, such as eating healthily, but she thereby provides only the materials by which her body continues the gestation.

In a way, the knowing powers (such as reason and the senses) have something in common with these nonconscious moving powers. Clearly, the knowing powers are not shared with plants. Clearly, they are also conscious (indeed, they are conscious by definition). Nevertheless, the knowing powers can themselves be viewed as moving to an endpoint (*QDV*, 25, 2, ad 8; *ST*, I-II, 56, 3, ad 2). The power of sight, for instance, moves to the activity of being aware of colors; similarly, the power of reason moves to the activity of being aware of the natures of things; and so on. Precisely because these powers involve a movement to an endpoint, we come to recognize various goods as completing these powers. It is good for the power of sight (residing in the eyes) to see; it is good for the power of reason to engage in reasoning; and so on (*ST*, I, 82, 4).

As movements to an endpoint, the knowing powers are in one way conscious and in another way nonconscious. As we have seen, the will and emotions can be called conscious desires in two ways. First, we are conscious of them, even as Maria feels her anger. Second, a conscious judgment of the good gives rise to these desires, even as Allex's awareness of the good of pizza gives rise to his choice to eat pizza. Knowing powers such as reason are clearly conscious in the first way. We are aware of our acts of reason and our acts of sensing, and we are thereby aware of our movement to these endpoints.

But knowing powers—as movements to an endpoint—are not conscious in the second way (*ST*, I-II, 30, 1, ad 3). The power of sight moves out to the activity of seeing, and it does so independently of any prior judgment that seeing is good. Of course, we sometimes choose to look at things, and this choice depends upon some judgment concerning the good. Jerry chooses to look at the traffic around him, for instance, and in that sense his act of seeing follows upon his judgment that it is good to know about the traffic. More accurately, his act of looking—his act of directing his seeing power upon this or that object—arises from a prior judgment concerning the good. The very act of seeing is itself spontaneous. Jerry opens his eyes, and his power of sight moves out to the act of seeing.

Good eyes see well. We recognize this basic truth on account of the function of the eye. In other words, we know what is good for an eye based upon the movement of the eye to the activity of seeing. Unlike the emotions, this movement does not presuppose a prior awareness of the good. Rather, the fulfillment of this movement, which is itself the good of the eye, can be a good that gives rise to conscious desire. Helena can recognize that seeing the sunset is a specific good; it is the fulfillment of a nonconscious inclination. Only then does Helena choose (with a conscious desire) to gaze upon the sunset.

A Reasoning Animal

This brief survey gives us a picture of the many capacities and activities that constitute human nature. We should not suppose, however, that human beings are a hodgepodge collection of diverse capacities. We fully comprehend human beings not simply by understanding these many diverse capacities; we must, in addition, recognize that these capacities are ordered to one another into a unity.

An analogy might clarify the point. We can speak of many "capacities" or activities of a car. It has the capacity to move about. It has the capacity to wipe water off the windshield. It has the capacity to heat or cool the interior air. It has the capacity to play the radio. It has the capacity to honk. And so on.

We do not identify a car, however, simply as a collection of these activities. Rather, we identify a car primarily in terms of one activity. A car has the function of moving people (and other items) around. This one activity provides the purpose for all the others. A car that is wonderful at honking but cannot move about is not a well-functioning car. On the other hand, a car that can move about but cannot honk has at least the essential function, even if the car could be improved by adding a horn. All the other activities contribute to the well-functioning of the car only insofar as they support or enhance the chief function of transportation. In short, a car is a functional thing; it is defined in terms of its function. Its function is that activity toward which all the others are directed.

Similarly, human beings have many capacities and activities, but they are defined (as functional things) in terms of one chief activity, an activity that provides the purpose for all the others. This activity, says Aquinas, is reason (*SCG*, III, chap. 37, no. 7).

Aquinas looks at all our diverse powers—from sensing, imagining, willing, reasoning, and so on—and asks which is the most important. Which is the most central? Which serves as the unifying function of the whole person? We have the power to take in nutrition and the power to reproduce, but these powers are not as elevated as our knowing powers, nor are they as significant as our conscious desiring powers. Among our knowing powers, reason far exceeds the senses, both external and internal. Among our conscious desiring powers, the will far exceeds the emotions. Between the will and reason, which are the powers peculiar to human beings, Aquinas concludes that reason is the most central: it is our defining power. The nature of functional things, we have seen, is found in their functions. Most essentially, then, human beings are reasoning animals.

A well-functioning human being will engage in many activities, but all will be guided by reason and directed toward reason. Suppose, for instance, that Maria gets angry in opposition to the guidance of reason. Then she is like a car that can honk but cannot move about. The car is not a well-functioning car, and neither is Maria a well-functioning human being. In a well-functioning car, the activity of honking contributes to the central activity of moving about. Similarly, in a human being, the activity of being angry should contribute to the central activity of reasoning. The function of the emotions in human beings, when fully understood, includes their role as a part within a rational animal. As such, emotions truly complete the whole only when they are ordered to the overall activity of the whole, which is to reason.

The Human Good

Several ethical implications follow logically upon the reflections in this chapter. As we have seen, the good is the completion of some movement to an endpoint. For functional things, the good is the completion of their functions, even as the good of a knife is to cut and the good of an eye is to see. Similarly, the human good is found in the realization of the human function.

The human good is not found most of all in our emotions and senses; rather, it is found in reason and the will (*ST*, I-II, 3, 3). The emotions and senses, and other powers shared with the animals, are not irrelevant to our human good. On the contrary, our good is intimately bound up with these activities. The good is not divorced from our animal nature. Nevertheless, our good is not found merely in animal activity. It is found in our animal nature as elevated by reason and will. It is found in the capacity of reason as embedded within our animal nature.

Modern ethical theorists do not typically err by misidentifying the human function. More often, they deny any human function at all. Without a human function, the human good ceases to be, at least as the word "good" is commonly used. Human beings without a function are like triangles, which have no good or bad features because they have no function. Moral relativism follows as a matter of course. If we continue to speak about a human good or human evil, we must be misapplying the terms. As error theorists would have it, we must be creating a kind of fiction.

Ultimately, when we have denied the human function, we will be forced to make up some special meaning for these words. We might mean, as emotivism claims, that what is good is simply that which we desire. Or we might mean to express a command, as prescriptivism would have it. In any event, we cannot mean by the word "good" what we mean in all other domains, from knives to doctors. We cannot mean that human beings are good by fulfilling their function, for the function has been denied.

Naïve realism is another alternative. It claims that the good—in the case of human beings—is some special quality like being yellow. Unlike colors, however, this quality is not grasped by any observations. It cannot be identified in terms of any observable qualities. Rather, it is grasped by some kind of immediate apprehension of the mind, by a kind of intuition.

Natural law theory rejects all these views because it accepts the importance of the human function. It recognizes that human beings are functional beings and that the human good is the completion of our human function. In short, the human good is what fulfills our nature.

chapter 8

Intuitionism

The intuition of the moral sentiment is an insight of the perfection of the laws of the soul.

—Ralph Waldo Emerson, Harvard Divinity School Address, July 15, 1938

One modern ethical view, which we (with reluctance) will call "intuitionism," agrees with Aquinas and the natural law—although not in every respect (Ross 2003). Intuitionism agrees with Aquinas's realism. Furthermore, it agrees (up to a point) with Aquinas's answer to the chicken and egg question: it agrees that the egg of awareness of the good must precede the chicken of desire for the good. Finally, this view agrees that our good, and our awareness of the good, is linked to nature, at least in some sense.

Despite these many agreements with Aquinas, intuitionism parts ways with Aquinas on two important points. First, regarding the chicken and egg, it differs over the follow-up question, "What came before the egg?" Second, it differs over the notion of human nature that is relevant to the good.

On account of the first difference, intuitionism also falls into the peculiarity of nearly all modern ethical views: it divorces our ethical knowledge of the good from all other knowledge of the good. Our knowledge of the ethical good is unique, distinct from our knowledge of the good of a knife and the good of an eye.

Before we proceed to examine the differences between intuitionism and natural law, it is worth pausing to explain our reluctance over using the word "intuitionism." As it is used today, both in philosophical and common parlance, the term has a much broader scope than the view we will be investigating. Intuitionism as commonly understood, for instance, does not need to be an ethical realist view; it can be relativistic. Most accurately, then, we are investigating one particular kind of intuitionism, not intuitionism in general. The term is worth retaining, nevertheless, since a more precise term is hard to find. Besides, to the extent that intuitionism engages with natural law, it is apt to take on these more particular features, such as moral realism.

Intuitions of the Good

As suggested above, intuitionism both agrees and disagrees with Aquinas on the question of the chicken and the egg. It agrees that awareness of the good must precede desire for the good. It disagrees on the follow-up question: what precedes our awareness of the good? As we have seen, according to Aquinas we are aware of the good only by first being aware of some movement to an end. We know what is good for an eye only by first knowing that an eye has the function of seeing; similarly, we know what is good for a human being as a whole only by knowing the function of a human being.

If intuitionism rejects this answer, then what answer does it provide? It claims that no prior awareness precedes our awareness of the good. Rather, we know the good by some direct intuition. After all, for any series in which one thing comes before another, we must always come to something that is first, something that has no prior foundation. Aquinas pushes beyond our knowledge of the good and looks for a foundation of this knowledge. He finds it in our knowledge of human capacities and function. In contrast, intuitionism stops with our knowledge of the good; that knowledge is first, with nothing prior.

The difference can be spelled out with greater precision. Aquinas claims that before we are aware of the good, we must be aware of some movement to an endpoint, such as a function. Allex, for instance, (1) is aware that his biological nature is moving toward nutrition, (2) then becomes aware that nutrition is good for him, and (3) finally desires to eat, and this desire is itself another—and separate—movement to an end. Intuitionism, on the other hand, claims that no knowledge precedes our awareness of the good. Rather, we have a direct intuition of the good. As far as intuitionism is concerned, step 1 is skipped, and Allex begins immediately with step 2.

This account of intuitionism agrees with natural law in several key points. It agrees that the human good is an objective reality to be perceived. It also agrees that our desires follow upon an awareness of the good. It disagrees only concerning the antecedent (or lack thereof) of this awareness.

Furthermore, we can add another similarity between intuitionism (as portrayed here) and natural law. Intuitionism insists that the good, and our perception of it, is connected with nature. Our intuition of the good, it claims, is inborn or built into our nature. Furthermore, the desires that arise from this natural knowledge can also be called inborn or natural. We have a natural desire for the true human good that we perceive naturally—that is, by intuition.

In its defense, intuitionism can point out that the analysis (in chapter 6) of Allex's reasoning has an oversight. The analysis explains one way in which pizza is good to eat; it is good as a form of nutrition. Unfortunately, the analysis leaves unexplained another way in which Allex recognizes pizza as good to eat: he judges that it tastes good. Pizza could be good for nutrition but taste bad; on the other hand, it could taste good but be horrible for nutrition. The two judgments, then, are not one and the same.

The first judgment—that pizza is good for nutrition—derives from an understanding of the movement to the endpoint of staying alive. But what about the second judgment? What movement to an end helps Allex to recognize that pizza tastes good? No movement at all. At least, so claims intuitionism. Allex simply has a kind of intuition, an immediate perception, by which he judges that the pizza tastes good. Of course, this judgment presupposes previous experiences of eating pizza. It does not presuppose, however, an awareness of any movement to an endpoint. After eating pizza, the judgment arises on its own.

Our earlier investigation into the difference between kinds of knowing powers reveals that Aquinas can agree, in part, with intuitionism. He recognizes that not all knowledge of the good is a complete knowledge of the good. Recall that we can know the good with our reason, but we can also recognize the fittingness of some good by way of our estimative power or instinct, even as a bird recognizes the fittingness of straw for a nest. Between reason and instinct, only reason fully grasps the nature of the good. Reason recognizes the good as the completion of the movement to some endpoint. In contrast, instinct does not fully understand the good. It grasps fittingness, but it does not understand any prior movement to an endpoint. The bird, for instance, does not recognize some biological movement toward reproduction, nor does it recognize that this movement can be completed only by way of a nest. It simply perceives that a nest is fitting.

In the case of the internal sense power of instinct, then, awareness of the good fits the pattern suggested by intuitionism: it has no antecedent. Since the desires of the emotions can follow upon instinct, they can arise without any awareness of a movement to an endpoint. Allex's emotional desire to eat the tasty pizza can arise from instinct, without any prior awareness of some movement to an endpoint.

Problems with Intuitionism

Aquinas, then, agrees with intuitionism to a limited extent. Some knowledge of the good is by way of a kind of intuition (or instinct); it presupposes no prior awareness of a movement to an endpoint. The internal senses, with their incomplete grasp of the good, become aware of particular goods without any prior knowledge of movement and without any prior knowledge that the good is that which completes a movement to an endpoint.

At the level of reason, however, Aquinas parts ways with intuitionism. Reason fully grasps the nature of the good. Since the good is the completion of the movement to an endpoint, it follows that knowledge of this movement is inseparable from rational knowledge of the good (*ST*, I-II, 94, 2).

Despite the measure of agreement, intuitionism is inadequate as a foundation of natural law. For one thing, instinctive judgments can differ from person to person. What tastes good to Allex might not taste good to Anna. The instincts of our sensing powers, then, are subject to the most common criticism of intuitionism—namely, that intuitions sometimes conflict. Allex's intuitions may not be Anna's intuitions. In that case, whose intuitions are we to follow?

Second, Aquinas thinks that our instincts at the sense level are an unreliable guide for human behavior. Animals must be guided by such instincts, since they do not have reason. Human behavior, however, can—and should—be guided by reason. Indeed, even the very instincts themselves—and the emotions that follow upon them—should be guided by reason, to the extent that they can be (*ST*, I-II, 24, 2).

As we have seen, the will follows upon reason and the emotions follow upon the internal senses. Nevertheless, reason has the capacity to shape and guide our emotions (*ST*, I, 81, 3; *ST*, I-II, 17, 7). It does so by way of the internal senses, which are to some extent subject to reason. Maria, for instance, can try to remember where she left her keys; similarly, she can choose to imagine a 10-headed monster. With her reason and will, then, she shapes her imagination. As a result, she can also shape her emotions. When she is angry at John, for instance, she can use her reason to calm and modify her anger. She can rationally consider the situation, recognizing that her anger is not justified (Jensen 2013). She does not thereby have complete control over her emotions, but she can have at least some measure of control (*ST*, I, 81, 3, ad 2).

The third and most important inadequacy of our instincts derives from the very nature of the human good. The human good is not found most of all in our emotions and senses. Rather, it is found in reason and will (*ST*, I-II, 3, 3). As we have seen, the will is a much more important desiring power than the emotions. Furthermore, reason is a much greater knowing power than any of the senses, whether exterior or interior. Our human good is not found solely in our animal nature. More important are the powers peculiar to human beings (reason and will), which are not shared with the animals. The human good is a good of reason.

All the activities of a well-functioning car are ultimately directed to the activity of transportation. Similarly, the activities of a well-functioning human being are guided by reason and directed to the good of reason. Consequently, if Maria's anger is contrary to reason, then it does not support the human good but undermines it. In general, emotions that follow instinct but oppose reason do not fulfill human beings. A good human life does involve emotions, but only insofar as these emotions are shaped by reason and directed to the central function of human beings, which is to reason.

Our instinctive knowledge of the good, then, is inadequate as a guide for our behavior. Indeed, Aquinas thinks that these intuitions are sometimes disordered and require the restraining power of reason. The guidance provided by the natural law, then, cannot be founded upon our instincts; it must be founded upon the knowledge of reason.

Natural and Unnatural

A final inadequacy of instincts concerns their link with human nature. In a sense these instincts, and the emotions that follow upon them, can be called natural. After all, they are to some extent inborn. We might also say that they follow necessarily upon our nature. These two meanings of natural (what is inborn and what is necessary), however, do not capture the link between natural law and human nature.

We should be wary of referring to whatever is inborn as natural. A congenital birth defect might be called natural in this regard. If Helena is born with only half a heart, then we could say that this defect is natural to her. More profoundly, however, the defect is unnatural. It is opposed to human nature. Similarly, inborn emotions can be called natural, but it might happen that some inborn emotions are opposed to our human nature; they might be defective and unnatural. Perhaps Maria was born with a particularly irascible temperament. The inborn nature of her anger does not make it good any more than Helena's inborn birth defect is good.

This misunderstanding of human nature (that what is inborn is natural) is often coupled with a closely related misunderstanding: what is statistically common is sometimes mistaken for what is natural. Killing other human beings (especially in warfare) has been common throughout human history. We might conclude that killing is natural. Similarly, theft has occurred with some regularity in human history, so it also might be considered natural to human beings. According to this reading, human nature is nothing other than what human beings do with regularity. We can discover human nature, then, simply by tabulating instances of behavior.

For human beings, regularity fails as a standard on account of free will, by which we can—and do—regularly choose to violate the natural law. The practice of lying, for instance, is almost universal among human beings; nevertheless, it is contrary to the natural law. Regular behavior by itself, then, can provide no standard for discovering the natural law.

Natural law theory uses neither of these mistaken notions of human nature. Rather, it uses the standard of function. The nature of a functional thing is found in its function, as the nature of an eye is to be an organ for seeing. Even a defective eye—an eye that cannot see—still has this nature. Even if a large percentage of people need corrective lenses to see well, the nature of an eye is still found in the power of vision.

Most essentially, then, human nature is found in the human function, and this human function, we have seen, is reason. Natural law guides human behavior in relation to the human good. Since the human good is realized in our function, natural law is concerned with our nature as functional beings. If Teresa (as a doctor) harms one of her patients, then she is not acting according to the nature of a doctor. Similarly, a murderer is not—while murdering—acting in accord with his human nature.

The multitude of murders throughout human history does not make the action natural. An inborn desire to murder would still be an unnatural desire, despite its origin at birth.

Intuitions in Reason?

Some intuitionists might claim that intuitions of the good are not limited to the sensing power of instinct. Reason itself has some intuitions of the good (Grisez 1965; Grisez 1983). In other words, we do not begin—even at the level of reason—with the recognition of a movement to some endpoint and only then come to a recognition of the good. Rather, we begin with a recognition of the good as immediately grasped by reason.

Once again, the three steps found in Aquinas's account are truncated to two steps. According to Aquinas, we begin with (1) an awareness of some movement to an endpoint, from which (2) we recognize the good as the completion of this movement, on account of which (3) we desire the good. Intuitionists wish to eliminate the first step. At the level of the internal senses, this first step is indeed absent, but some intuitionists claim that this first step is absent even for reason.

Aquinas himself, they might claim, provides support for their position (Grisez 1965). Thomas insists that fundamental human goods are "known per se," which means that the knowledge of these goods does not derive from other knowledge (*ST*, I-II, 94, 2). In other words, the knowledge of step 2 is independent of other knowledge. It cannot depend (the intuitionists claim) upon the knowledge of step 1. Aquinas himself, then, seems to be endorsing intuitionism.

Revisionists, whom we encountered in chapter 5, make precisely these claims. They reject the label of intuitionism, but their view is not distinct from intuitionism as we have used the term here. They maintain that our knowledge of the good does not essentially depend upon prior knowledge; at most, observations of our inclinations provide a kind of occasion for us to recognize the good. Furthermore, they make this claim using Aquinas himself, with his account of per se knowledge.

Unfortunately, they distort his account. Aquinas, with his account of per se knowledge, is not denying all dependence upon prior theoretical knowledge; rather, he is denying a particular kind of dependence. He is not, for instance, denying the importance of understanding definitions. Imagine the following conversation between Tony and Suzie.

> Tony: What makes for a good hygrometer?
> Suzie: I have no idea.
> Tony: But why not?
> Suzie: I don't even know what a hygrometer is.
> Tony: Oh, you don't? It is something that measures the humidity in the air.
> Suzie: Then a good hygrometer will measure humidity well.

When Suzie does not know what a hygrometer is, then neither does she know what makes for a good hygrometer. When she learns the definition of a hygrometer, then she knows at least the very basics of what makes for a good hygrometer. Note that a hygrometer is defined in terms of function. In other words, a hygrometer is a functional thing, and when Suzie knows the function, then she knows the good of a hygrometer. Suzie's knowledge of good hygrometers, then, is not entirely independent of all other knowledge. It depends upon her knowledge of the definition of a hygrometer, which is also knowledge of the function of a hygrometer.

For per se knowledge, Aquinas does not deny this kind of dependence. Consider one of his favorite examples of per se knowledge: a whole is greater than its part (*ST*, I-II, 94, 2). By saying that this proposition is known per se, Aquinas is not supposing that Suzie can know its truth if she does not know what a whole is, what a part is, and what it means to be greater than. He acknowledges that kind of dependence.

Aquinas thinks, then, that our knowledge of the human good depends upon our knowledge of what a human being is. He thinks that human beings are functional things that are defined in terms of their activity. Ultimately, then, he thinks that we know the human good precisely by knowing that to which human beings are directed.

An Inverted Order?

Those who wish to extend intuitions even to reason fall into the well-worn pattern of modern ethical theorists. They make the moral good (or the human good) different from all others. According to these intuitionists, we know the human good—even with reason—by some kind of immediate knowledge, without a prior awareness of the human activity or function. In this regard, however, the human good must be different from all other goods.

Some revisionists acknowledge that the human good is, in fact, connected to our human nature, but they deny the connection in our knowledge (Finnis 1987). They claim that we do not know our human nature first and then come to know the good. On the contrary. According to their position, we first of all know the human good, and only thereby do we come to know our nature.

This inverted order (knowing the good and then knowing the functional nature) does not appear in any domain outside of the human good. Suppose we discover some ancient machine and are perplexed concerning its function or purpose. In 1901, for instance, divers discovered an ancient Greek shipwreck in which they found a mechanism that has since been identified as an Antikythera mechanism, a mechanism used to predict the movement of astronomical bodies. Initially, however, scholars puzzled over the purpose of the mechanism. In their inquiries, they did not think for a moment that they must first discover some good—independently of knowing the function—by which they then might come to discover the function. Instead, they reasoned in the reverse. By discovering the function, they could discover what good the ancient Greeks found in it.

Suzie knows the good of a hygrometer precisely by knowing its function. In similar fashion, we know the good of a knife, the good of an eye, and the good of a doctor. For triangles and for pebbles, we recognize the absence of any good or bad. Why? Precisely because we recognize that these things have no function or endpoint. But now—when it comes to knowledge of the human good—the intuitionists insist that our knowledge is not based upon an awareness of the human function. Rather, it is immediate, with (at most) a kind of incidental or occasional connection to any prior knowledge.

Why, when it comes to human beings, should the process be reversed? Why should we first discover the good and, by way of this knowledge, come to understand the human functional nature? We have every reason to suppose that our knowledge of the good operates in the same manner in the case of human beings as in the case of all other functional things. We have no reason to suppose that our knowledge of the human good is peculiar.

Realism and Natural Law

As we have seen, not every ethical realist view is a natural law view. Rather, natural law ethics is a particular kind of realist view. Intuitionism (as described above) is an ethical realist view. Nevertheless, intuitionism downplays the role of human nature—our functional human nature—with regard to the human good. Natural law ethics recognizes the human good as the completion of our human function. Our knowledge of the human good rests upon our knowledge of the human function. In short, natural law ethics is a realist ethical view that considers our functional nature as integral to the moral good.

The intimate link between natural law and human nature finds another point of contact in what can be called "natural" knowledge. Our knowledge of the most fundamental human goods, and the moral rules that follow upon these goods, can be called natural knowledge. What does it mean to call knowledge natural? It means one thing to the intuitionists and another thing to Aquinas.

For the intuitionists, natural knowledge involves no essential dependence upon any other knowledge. For Aquinas, our knowledge of the human good can be called natural even when it depends essentially upon understanding the functional nature of a thing; it is natural just so long as it does not depend upon prior argumentation. Suzie does not need an argument to grasp the rudimentary basics of a good hygrometer. Rather, when she recognizes the function of a hygrometer, she immediately grasps its good, or at least the most basic features of its good. Similarly, once we recognize movements to an endpoint in human beings, we also grasp corresponding goods that complete these movements. We need no argument, but we do need to recognize functional movements within human nature.

chapter 9

The Shared Good

No man is an island,
Entire of itself;
Every man is a piece of the continent,
A part of the main.

—John Donne, "For Whom the Bell Tolls"

Aristotle observes that "without friends no one would choose to live, though he had all other goods" (*NE*, bk. 8, chap. 1). And Cicero says that if you take away friendship, nothing pleasant is left in life (*De Am*, 22). They both capture a fundamental truth concerning the human good: it is not solitary. We can acquire all that people consider good, but our life is empty if we do not have friendship. Boundless wealth, extensive power, profound knowledge, and vast expertise in a multitude of fields, all together with a collection of any other goods, will leave us discontented if we are alone, having no one with whom to share these goods.

The human good is a shared good (*DR*, bk. 1, chap. 1, 4). If we have the good alone, only by ourselves, then we do not fully possess it. It is something like the good of an orchestra playing symphonic music. No single individual possesses this good. Rather, all the members of the orchestra possess it together. Most intimately, we possess the good together with our close friends and family. More removed, we share it with colleagues or acquaintances. More distant yet, we share it even with strangers. We might, for instance, strike up a conversation with a stranger on an airplane or at a street corner.

The description of human nature provided in chapter 7—as an animal with the function of reasoning—does not immediately capture this social aspect of the human good. Good human beings perform their functions well, and if that function is to reason, then it seems that good human beings will reason well. On the face of it, the action of completing our function does not require other people: it looks like an isolated good rather than a shared good.

This question concerning the human good—whether it is isolated or shared—is central to the natural law (De Koninck 1997). Its importance is difficult to overemphasize. All of the natural law (that is, all of morality) stands or falls upon the answer to this one question. Every law, including the natural law, must be directed to the common or shared good (*ST*, I-II, 90, 2). If the human good is not shared, then the natural law is an empty concept. Without a good common to all human beings, the natural law does not exist.

Common by Predication and Common by Causality

Someone might easily misunderstand the idea of a good common to human beings. After all, the human good of reason (or the good of knowing the truth) is clearly common to all human beings. All human beings are animals with the capacity to reason, even if some people (on account of brain damage) have difficulty exercising this capacity. All human beings, then, have a natural movement to grasp the truth. Without a doubt, then, this good is common to all human beings.

This line of reasoning is certainly correct insofar as the word "common" is used. Unfortunately, it does not settle whether or not the human good is a common or shared good. Or rather, it does not settle the question in the right way. It does not answer the question in a way that addresses the concerns of Aristotle and Cicero. Nor does it address the concerns of the natural law.

Aquinas distinguishes two ways in which a good might be common to all human beings (*ST*, I-II, 90, 2, ad 2). On the one hand, it might be found in all human beings. On the other hand, it might be the singular goal toward which all human beings are ordered. Aquinas gives a name to each of these. The first meaning he calls "common by predication"; the second he calls "common by causality." The natural law requires a good that is common by causality, but the opening paragraph of this section presents an argument suggesting that the human good is common by predication.

This distinction needs clarification. Consider two ways in which two biologists might have a common pursuit of the truth concerning a certain cellular structure—say, the protein structure of mitochondria. On the one hand, Patti and Jim might pursue this truth independently. Patti is seeking this truth and Jim is also seeking this truth, but the two of them have nothing to do with one another. Indeed, they do not even know one another. Patti pursues the truth on her own, and Jim pursues the same truth on his own. The good of this truth is common to both Patti and Jim, but it is common only by predication; in other words, it is found in each of them.

On the other hand, Louis and Anna pursue this truth through a united effort. They work in the same laboratory, for instance, and they try to help each other understand the protein structure of mitochondria. Louis does not pursue the truth merely as his own, and Anna does not pursue the truth merely as her own. Rather, they pursue the truth as "our" good. The good of this truth is common to both Louis and Anna not only by predication but also by causality.

Aquinas gives the name "common by causality" because the singular good *causes* Louis and Anna to work together to achieve the good. This one good, we might say, causes a single movement to an endpoint, a movement that is realized in the united activity of Louis and Anna. For

Patti and Jim, in contrast, the truth concerning mitochondria causes two separate movements to an endpoint, one found in Patti and the other found in Jim.

For Patti and Jim, these movements are "common" in the way that the color red is common to two roses; it is found in both of them. The movement to the truth about mitochondria is found both in Patti and in Jim. Louis and Anna, however, have something more in common. The movement to the truth about mitochondria is indeed found in both of them, but the two of them do not have entirely separate movements. Rather, a single movement to the truth is realized both in Louis and in Anna. Louis's movement to the truth of mitochondria is part of a greater movement that belongs also to Anna. Likewise, Anna's movement to the truth is part of the same greater movement.

A United Subject

We can approach the distinction in a slightly different manner. Every good involves two elements: the completion and the subject it completes. The good of being sharp, for instance, is the completion of a knife. It is not a completion just in and of itself. It is no completion, for instance, of a hammer (which must be dull). The good of being sharp, then, is always the completion of some subject or other. As we have seen, a good is the completion of a subject that has a movement to an endpoint. A knife (through its function) is moving to cut, and being sharp helps to fulfill this movement.

The difference between the two common goods (by predication and by causality) might be explained in terms of the subject of the good. Patti and Jim are two separate subjects for two separate goods. These goods happen to be the same in kind (knowing the truth about mitochondria), but they are numerically distinct, in the way that two roses belong to the same kind of thing (roses) although they are numerically distinct. Patti is the subject of her coming to know the truth of mitochondria, and Jim is the subject of his coming to know the truth of mitochondria. These two goods are separate. They belong to two separate subjects, although they are the same kind of good. In the same way, the red found in a rose is numerically separate from the red found in a car, although they are the same kind of color.

In contrast, Louis and Anna form a united subject. They are moving to the truth of mitochondria together. Consequently, they have numerically one completion that fulfills them both. They have only one good, a good that is shared by both of them.

The idea of a united subject is not unusual. An orchestra, for instance, is the united subject of the symphonic music they play. The symphonic music is played not by any single individual but by the group as united. Similarly, a soccer team is the singular subject of the victory achieved over its opponent. Many members play separate parts, but their united efforts form the play of the whole team. Similarly, Louis and Anna move to the truth concerning mitochondria by way of a united activity.

A good common by predication, then, has separate subjects. What is common is the *kind* of good found in each subject. The goods themselves are numerically distinct, residing in numerically distinct subjects. In contrast, a good common by causality has a single subject that is composed of many members. The good itself is numerically one, residing in the numerically united subject.

Possessing and Producing Parts

The distinction can be further clarified by introducing another distinction made by Aquinas. He says that a movement to an endpoint might be united in two ways. On the one hand, several individuals might work together *to produce* a numerically singular good. On the other hand, several individuals might unite in order *to possess* a numerically singular good together (*SCG*, III, chap. 112, no. 3).

The two are not inconsistent with one another. An orchestra, for instance, works together to produce the sound of the music. At the same time, the members work together so that they might, as a group, play the music. Each member possesses the good of playing symphonic music together with the other members of the group.

Sometimes, however, these two movements are not united. The members of the stage crew, for instance, set out the chairs for the orchestra members; they move the piano when needed; and they open and close the curtains. As such, they are part of the united movement to produce the music. None of the stage crew, however, actually plays the music. They do not share in the act of playing symphonic music together. They only *produce* the good; they do not *possess* it as united.

Patti and Jim do not work together to produce the knowledge of mitochondria; each works entirely separately. In contrast, Louis and Anna work together to produce the knowledge of mitochondria. Louis and Anna, however, have something more than a productive union—or at least they might. They also want to possess the knowledge together. They want to talk it over, to share their insights with one another. They want to enjoy the truth as a team.

The contrast is made clearer by another possibility. Ariel and Sean are also two biologists working together in the same lab in order to achieve knowledge of mitochondria. Ariel and Sean, however, do not particularly care for one another; indeed, each sees the other as a rival. They work in the same lab, and as such they form part of a united movement to produce knowledge concerning mitochondria, but they have no desire to share the knowledge with one another. They see each other only through the lens of utility. Ariel supposes that Sean's insights might be helpful for her own insights, and Sean supposes the same regarding Ariel. What they want out of the other person is production of the good; they do not desire a shared possession. Many business arrangements have this purely utilitarian aspect.

Possessing the good, then, is something more than producing the good (although it may *involve* producing the good). A good is possessed by a subject insofar as it completes the subject. A knife sharpener produces the good of being sharp, but the sharpener does not possess this good. Instead, the *knife* possesses the good, for the knife is the subject that is completed by it. Similarly, many individuals might work to produce a good, but they possess it together only if it completes them as a united subject. For Ariel and Sean, the good, once produced, completes them separately. For Louis and Anna, the good, once produced, completes them together. They want to have it as a pair.

Most completely, then, a shared good is a good pursued together in order that it might be possessed together. A good produced by a united effort—if not possessed together—is not a shared good in the fullest sense. Consequently, one attribute often associated with shared goods is that they are not diminished when possessed. Brian's possession of the truth does not detract from Karen's possession of the truth. In contrast, if Brian and Karen share a single bowl of ice cream, then each bite that Brian takes (and thereby possesses) diminishes the good that Karen can possess, and vice versa.

We should not conclude that no material good can be a true shared good. As we have already suggested, the divide between producing and possessing is not absolute. Sometimes (as we will see more completely in chapter 23), individuals who already share a good—who are all possessing parts of a united group—can possess a good in the very production of it. Parents share a good with and in their children. Consequently, they can share a familial good by helping to bring about this good. The good of their child enjoying an ice cream cone, for example, can be shared in the very activity of bringing it about.

Different Ways of Sharing

Human beings share goods in a variety of ways. The orchestra members, for instance, share the good of symphonic music by a united and coordinated activity. Sports players do something similar. Even chess opponents share the good in this way (supposing they are playing for enjoyment and not simply to win a tournament).

Louis and Anna also coordinate their activities, each doing his or her part within the lab. These two, however, have something more. In addition to sharing the good by coordinated activity, they share their knowledge through conversation. They engage in what might be called mutual giving. Louis gives his knowledge to Anna (by telling her about it), and Anna reciprocates by giving her knowledge to Louis. Similarly, after two people watch a movie together, they share their enjoyment by conversing about the movie. Their separate possessions become united by their exchange of ideas.

Mutual giving often takes place by way of conversation, but it does not have to. Indeed, the very playing of symphonic music can be portrayed as a mutual giving. The cellists give what they have (their cello playing) to the violinists (and to other orchestra members), and the violinists give what they have (their violin playing). The giving is not through conversation but by the activity of playing with coordination.

Through these acts of sharing, we get beyond a commonality of predication. We get beyond merely having the same kind of good. We also get beyond merely producing numerically one and the same good. More than *producing* the good, we *possess* numerically one and the same good together. Through these acts of sharing, then, the good is shared in the fullest sense: it is common by causality.

The terms "common" and "shared" are both acceptable to describe such goods, but we will give preference to the latter term. The English word "common" tends to refer to a commonality of predication. On the other hand, the term "shared" has a tendency not to be interpreted in this way. When we hear that a good is shared, we are slightly less likely to think of two goods as the same in kind but possessed separately and individually.

Sharing the Good of Reason

We are now ready to ask whether the functional good of human nature is a shared good. The argument near the beginning of the chapter missed the point. Yes indeed, the good of knowing the truth is common to all human beings, since all have the function of a reasoning animal. This argument, however, concludes only to a commonality of predication. The same kind of good (the good of reason) is found in all human beings. The argument does not tell us whether the good is common by causality. It does not tell us whether the good of reason is possessed by human beings together.

On the face of it, such a shared possession seems implausible. Tim cannot (it seems) share the good of knowing the truth with every human being. He has no contact whatsoever with most human beings. Indeed, among the vast multitude of human beings, he knows only a fraction. Without the exchange that comes through contact, he apparently cannot share the good with them. Louis and Anna know one another, and they share the good by an exchange of ideas. In contrast, Tim does not know Flora, who lives on the other side of the world, and he cannot exchange any goods with her. Their separate goods, then, must remain isolated from one another, or so it seems.

This approach, however, takes too narrow a view of sharing the good. Actual contact, with actual conversation, is not the only way to share goods. Sometimes we share goods by coordinated activity, as Clare the cellist does within the orchestra, and sometimes this coordination involves complete strangers. In our day, for instance, many scientific projects are such coordinated unions. They involve international collaboration between a multitude of scientists, many of whom do not know one another.

The CERN project (the European Organization for Nuclear Research), which involves research using the world's largest hadron particle collider, is a good example. Of course, much of the coordinated activity involves what could be called the production of knowledge—that is, the tools needed to acquire new knowledge. A scientist within the project, however, is likely to have a sense that the knowledge acquired is shared by everyone involved.

Large universities, at least as originally conceived, might also provide a good example. Different individuals from many different fields each attain part of an overall comprehensive understanding of the world. Of course, much sharing of ideas occurs by way of conversation, as well as by publication, but many faculty members will not know one another. Nevertheless, even the coordination of activity itself is a kind of sharing.

In this picture, the university members set out on a shared project. Together with others, they hope to attain knowledge of the world. They recognize that they themselves have a very limited scope of knowledge.

Brian, for instance, might be an expert in history, but he knows very little about biology, which is Karen's expertise. Even within history, Brian knows only a tiny fraction. He is an expert in ancient Greek history but has only limited knowledge of Russian history. Brian realizes, then, that he cannot attain the ideal of understanding the world all by himself. He must unite with others. He and Karen together possess a more extended comprehensive knowledge than he does all by himself. When he and Karen unite with still others, then they begin to approach a group that understands the world.

Often, members within this group might help one another to come to understand various truths, even as Louis and Anna help one another understand mitochondria. Even apart from this productive help, however, members share the good by coordinating their individual acts of knowing the truth. Clare shares her musical talent with the other orchestra members simply by coordinating her activity, so that they play together. Clare does not teach Bridget how to play the violin, but she shares her playing with Bridget nevertheless; the two share by way of coordination. Similarly, even if Brian does not teach Karen about history and Karen does not teach Brian about biology, the two can share the good by way of coordinating their diverse knowledge. Brian desires his knowledge as also belonging to Karen, with whom he is united.

The coordination of activity does not require even the limited contact of proximity. Suppose, for instance, that Christopher and James belong to the same charitable organization, which seeks to save people from the evil of human trafficking. Christopher lives in Texas, but James lives in Minnesota. Furthermore, the two have never met. The one does not even know that the other exists. Nevertheless, their activities are coordinated within the group. They are working together for the same goal.

Their union does not need to be limited to a mere productive role in the way that the stage crew helps to produce the music of the orchestra. Christopher can truly desire to share a good even with someone he does not know. He has a sense of union with all those who belong to the charitable organization. He is working together with all these people, and together they possess a great good, the good of helping those in need.

Human Limitations

We typically unite with others for some goal when we recognize our own limitations. Clare recognizes that by herself she cannot play symphonic music, so she unites with the other members of the orchestra. Christopher recognizes that he cannot effectively free people from human trafficking all by himself, so he unites with others, who coordinate their activities to achieve this united goal. Clare is limited with regard to symphonic music. Christopher is limited with regard to helping those in need. On account of their limitations, they unite with others. They both know that they cannot alone possess the whole good. Each can possess it only together with others.

When Brian has the goal of attaining truth about the world, he finds a similar limitation (*DR*, bk. 1, chap. 1, 5–7). His knowledge is very limited. By itself, his rational capacity is quite expansive: he is able to know a myriad of diverse truths. With his concrete limitations, however, he is able to know only a fraction of these truths. If he wishes to understand the world, then he must understand it not only by himself but also together with others.

With regard to knowledge, Brian has two kinds of limitations. First, Brian is limited in that he cannot know all that can be known about the world, just as Clare cannot play all the parts of the symphonic music. Second, Brian is limited in that he cannot even attain his partial knowledge without the assistance of others. In the same way, Clare must have initially learned to play the cello from others.

In general, the mere production of knowledge requires coordination. We must make observations, we must tell others about them, we must reach logical conclusions, and once we have reached these conclusions we must once again tell others about them. Throughout all human history, human beings have developed ideas and passed them on to future generations. The idea of a so-called autodidact (a self-taught savant) can have only partial truth. An individual might lack formal training, but he relies upon others nevertheless. He certainly relies upon others as an infant, and he may well rely upon some who are now long dead by way of reading their writings. As the poet John Donne noted, "No man is an island."

Donne's poem accentuates another of Brian's limitations: he is mortal. Brian's life must come to an end. However much knowledge he attains in the short span of his life, Brian must ultimately give it all up with death. If limitations give rise to a sharing in the good (as we have seen), then we might expect this greatest of all limitations (mortality) to be the harbinger for another sharing in the good. The sharing in the human good is not only across space but also across time. We share in the knowledge that others have attained before us, and our sharing in the good will continue with those who come after us.

Donne's poem cautions us, "Never send to know for whom the bell tolls; It tolls for thee." In other words, when you hear that someone has died, do not ask who has died, for you yourself have died—that is, a part of you has died. For this reason, when we hear of the unexpected death of a stranger, we feel sorry for him. Likewise, when we imagine a world in which human beings become extinct, we have a sense of loss. In this science-fiction scenario, that project of which we are all a part has become extinguished.

We might continue reflecting upon the limited human condition for many more pages. The essential point, for our purposes, concerns the conjunction of two opposites. On the one hand, the human capacity of reason is directed to an almost unlimited object; the truth of the world extends far beyond our sight. On the other hand, all human individuals are severely limited, so that they can never attain, by themselves, the object of their capacity. By its very nature, then, the human function can never be realized alone. It must be realized together with others. It is inherently a shared good.

Two Special Communities

These ideas are summed up by Aristotle's observation that human beings are political animals by nature (*Pol*, bk. 1, chap. 2). By "political" he does not mean crafty, nor is he referring to the exercise of governmental intrigue. Rather, he implies that human beings are by nature social; they must unite into a community. He does not mean that all human beings are outgoing or particularly friendly. Rather, he suggests that all human beings are parts of a greater community. Their very functional nature—as beings directed to the endpoint of grasping rational truth—demands the union with others. In short, Aristotle conveys much the same as John Donne: "No man is an island."

Short of the communion of all human beings, two lesser communities stand out for their importance. First, the family is a community that shares in the good of bringing new human life to maturity. The members work together, coordinating their activities, to achieve a well-rounded, well-balanced member of society. Of course, every family has its defects, and some families have serious failures, but the point of the family, as far as Aquinas is concerned, is to bring new human beings to live virtuously. The family is not concerned merely with the physical well-being of children; in addition, it is concerned with their mental and spiritual well-being (*ST*, II-II, 154, 2). This good is achieved not individually but together.

Second, political communities are subsets of the overall human community (*DR*, bk. 1, chap. 1, 8). They are the union of many individuals and of many families in the effort to attain some measure of self-sufficiency. Most important, in this regard, is not material sufficiency, nor even intellectual sufficiency. Rather, the most important sufficiency is that of crafting and enforcing laws; it is the sufficiency of being a community that can direct itself to the good. Autonomy (being a lawgiver to oneself) applies only to the political community.

We should not confuse this political community with the modern bureaucratic state. The political community—as Aquinas understood it—is concerned with a shared good. It is not concerned with merely material wealth or worldly peace. Like other collaborations for a shared good, it is a kind of friendship. It need not be an intimate friendship, but within the political community citizens seek the good of one another—that is, they seek the human good as realized together.

The modern bureaucratic state is not concerned with a united effort to achieve some good. Rather, it is concerned with the micromanagement of the lives of isolated individuals, individuals who each have their own separate goals and goods but no single project that unites them all.

The Greatest Good

This brief discussion has hardly touched upon the myriad ways in which human beings share the good. We raise children together, we study together, we play together, we discuss our thoughts with friends, we run corporations together, and we relax together. Communicating by way of speech is essential to most of this sharing.

The need for a shared good is revealed in our spontaneous reactions. However much we attain, whether materially or spiritually, we dread the thought of having it all alone. A millionaire with no friends is a miserable man. An intellectual savant who hoards his knowledge as a private good—a good to be had by himself alone—is not to be praised but pitied. As Cicero says, friendship is "the greatest thing in the world; nothing so conforms with our nature; nothing is so exactly what we want in both prosperity and adversity" (*De Am*, 17).

What matters, as far as the natural law is concerned, is that the human good is indeed a shared good. Brian's good of knowing the truth is not his good alone. It belongs not only to himself but to others as well. It is a good possessed together with others. When Brian perceives that his rational capacity is directed toward the truth, he ultimately perceives that it is directed toward the truth as shared with others. Just as we know that doctors ought to heal their patients, so we know that rational animals ought to pursue the truth together with others.

chapter 10

Law

For when man is perfected, he is the best of animals, but when separated from law and justice, he is the worst of all.

—Aristotle, *Politics*

Our defense is not in our armaments, nor in science, nor in going underground. Our defense is in law and order.

—Albert Einstein, *New York Times Magazine*

We have, so far, shown how good and evil are not merely human fabrications. They are truly found in reality. We have also shown that human beings can come to know good and evil. Indeed, we have shown that this knowledge can arise from an awareness of our human function; furthermore, we have shown that human nature is identified through its function, which is to reason. Although the human good is complex, it is unified by the one function of reasoning. This human good, however, is not a good possessed in solitude. On account of our human limitations, we can attain the good of reason only by uniting with others.

We have not yet shown that this knowledge of good and evil is linked with something called a natural law. Making this link requires some understanding of what a law is. We are all familiar with human laws, so if we get a better understanding of human laws, then we might be able to determine whether the term “natural law” is appropriate.

Four Features of Law

Thomas Aquinas identifies four features essential to every law (*ST*, I-II, 90, 1–4):

(1) It is a directive of reason guiding human actions.

(2) It is directed to the common good.

(3) It is given by the proper authority.

(4) It is made known or promulgated.

Human laws clearly direct behavior. The law to drive on the right side of the road, for instance, directs people to drive on the right side of the road. Similarly, laws against theft direct people away from stealing. In each case, one group of human beings (the lawmakers) directs the behavior of another group (the members of the political community).

Something similar occurs when the word “law” is applied outside the domain of human law. Sometimes, for instance, we speak of the laws of nature. Gravity is a law of nature, as are the laws of electromagnetic fields. The idea of the laws of nature first arose within a clearly theistic context, for the early scientists—such as Newton—typically believed in God. These scientists used the idea of the “laws of nature” to express the direction that God gives to his creation. God directs bodies, for instance, to follow the rules of gravity. The theistic context has since been dropped, and consequently the term “law of nature” is now used to express merely a universal pattern of activity or an observed regularity found in nature. Such “laws” *describe* how things act; in contrast, laws for human behavior *prescribe* how we are supposed to act.

These “laws of nature” are sometimes expressed by the term “natural laws.” This practice gives rise to confusion over the subject of our inquiry.

The same term "natural law" is used to refer to regularities in subhuman nature and also to moral norms for human behavior. To avoid confusion in this book, we will reserve the term "natural law" for the latter usage and will use the phrase "laws of nature" to refer to the regularities in subhuman nature. The term "natural law" will always refer to moral directives that are connected—in a manner to be explained as we proceed—with our human nature.

Laws are not just any directive of human behavior. Many directives do not go by the name of "law," except in a very extended sense of the word. Bob, for instance, might direct himself to exercise three times a week, but we would not give the name of "law" to this directive. Similarly, when Giuseppe tells Kirsten to turn right, he is directing her behavior, but he is not making a law.

A law requires additional features beyond merely being a directive of reason. In the most proper meaning of the word, for instance, a law directs to the common or shared good. Laws about driving, for instance, are directed to the common well-being of drivers and of those living in society in general. In contrast, Bob's directive to exercise aims to achieve his personal health. The laws of nature (or scientific regularities) meet this requirement because these directives move natural things to the overall good of the universe.

We might give the name of a "rule" to those directives that aim at some good short of the common good. Even if they aim at a good that is in some way shared, they can be called rules rather than laws, as long as the shared good is less than the overall good of society. We might speak, for instance, of rules within a company, which aim at the shared good of the company. Similarly, rules within a particular family aim at the shared good of that family. Bob, then, has given himself a rule (and not a law) to exercise three times a week. Likewise, Ariel's company has a rule (and not a law) that workers cannot congregate around the coffee station.

A third feature of laws follows upon the second feature. Given that a law aims at the shared good, it must originate from those who have charge over directing the community to its good. As a private individual, Ariel cannot decide to make traffic laws. She might think that the speed limit for a road on which she commonly drives is set too low and that it should be 10 miles per hour faster. Nevertheless, she has no power to change the law. Even rules—not just laws—fit this pattern. Ariel cannot make rules for her company unless she is a manager or supervisor of some sort.

Laws have one final feature: they must be promulgated. In other words, they must be made known to those who are supposed to follow them. Imagine, for instance, that the legislators of a country decide that for the sake of safety, drivers should stop when the light is red, but the legislators also decide to keep this directive secret so that no one can know about it. This rule meets the first three conditions of a law, but it is not a law, for it does not meet the final condition. If a law is to direct human behavior, then the people involved have to know about it. As we have seen, knowledge precedes our choices. Ariel cannot choose to follow traffic laws if these laws have not been made known to her.

Is There a Natural Law?

These four features of laws apply straightforwardly to human laws, but Aquinas grants that the term "law" is sometimes used in an extended sense. In these cases, the features can themselves be somewhat reshaped or stretched. The law of gravity, for instance, merely describes how objects behave, but within a theistic perspective, it might be viewed as a directive toward certain behavior. As such, it does achieve the overall good of the universe. Furthermore, it arises from God, who has charge of the good of the universe. The directive operates, however, without knowledge on the part of bodies. Nevertheless, it is "promulgated" in a sense, for God gives bodies what they need to follow the directive.

Can these four features be extended to include what may be called the natural law (*ST*, I-II, 91, 2)? Suppose, for instance, that Jim comes to know his function as a reasoning animal. He then recognizes that he should seek to know the truth. Believing falsehood would thwart his function, and coming to know the truth would at least partially fulfill his function. Ultimately, he recognizes a certain directive for his behavior: try to understand the truth. Is this directive a law?

This directive readily meets the first condition of a law. It is indeed a directive of reason concerning human behavior. It directs Jim to a certain activity, just as traffic laws direct Ariel's behavior when driving. Jim's awareness of this truth is not something idle, disconnected from his own behavior. Given his knowledge of altimeters (a tool for measuring altitudes), for instance, Jim might be aware that a (certain kind of) good altimeter must be able to measure the barometric pressure. Since Jim himself, however, has nothing to do with making or using altimeters, this knowledge of the good of altimeters in no way provides direction for his own action. In contrast, his knowledge that a rational animal should pursue the truth has direct bearing upon his own action. This directive, then, seems to meet the first condition of a law.

When understood correctly, this directive also meets the second condition, which states that laws must concern the common or shared good. As we have seen, the good of reason is not a good possessed by isolated individuals. Jim must pursue the truth together with others. Therefore, if Jim thinks the directive to pursue the truth concerns his good alone, then he has misperceived the directive.

The third feature of law (that it arises from those who have charge over the community) is more problematic. Who exactly has charge over the whole human community? Perhaps nature itself does. Or perhaps God does. Or perhaps no one (or nothing) does. As we will see more completely in chapter 27, God does indeed have care over the whole human community. In some way, as well, it makes sense to say that nature has care over the human community. By "nature" we do not mean "mother nature" or the sum total of causes operating in nature. Rather, we mean human nature. Our human nature is a functional nature; as such, it moves us to the human good, which is by nature a shared good. We could say, then, that nature has care of the human community.

Does nature give rise to the directive that Jim understands (the directive to pursue the truth together with others)? In other words, can this directive meet the third condition, according to which a law arises from the one who has care over the community, which we have identified (at least tentatively) as nature? Our analysis in the earlier parts of this book suggests that it can.

Functional natures, we have seen, give rise to directives. A doctor, for instance, has the nature of someone with the role of healing. By understanding this functional nature, we come to recognize that doctors ought to heal their patients. We perceive that doctors are moving to the end of healing patients, and then we recognize, by a certain hypothetical necessity, that in order to achieve this endpoint doctors must (or ought to) heal their patients.

Similarly, on account of his nature, Jim is moving to the endpoint of understanding the world around him. When Jim becomes aware of this movement—when he becomes aware of his function—he then recognizes a hypothetical necessity. He recognizes that in order to achieve his function, he must try to understand the truth. Additionally, he recognizes that he must try to understand the truth together with others. This directive, then, arises from his nature. It arises from his nature in two ways. First, his nature provides the movement to the endpoint. Second, his nature provides him with reason, by which he recognizes the movement to the endpoint and his consequent need to pursue the truth.

If we suppose that nature has charge over the human community, then we can conclude that this directive of reason meets the third condition of law. It arises from the one who has care over the community.

The same conclusion follows if we suppose that God has charge of the human community. We should not be distracted by certain religious beliefs or religious revelations. It would be beside the point, for instance, to cite Jesus Christ as saying that the truth will set you free. As a Christian, of course, Aquinas fully believed that God has provided some directives to human beings in this manner. In the Decalogue (the Ten Commandments), for instance, God has revealed that we should not murder others. Such revelations, however, do not provide an origin for a natural law. Rather, they provide the source for what Aquinas calls the divine law, a special law that is in many ways beyond human nature. Even if God has revealed that we should pursue the truth, then, this revelation would not make him the source of the natural law; it would make him only the source of the divine law.

Nevertheless, God is indeed the source of the directive that Jim comes to understand. Since God has created the universe, he himself is the source of human nature. But nature, we have seen, is the source of the directive that Jim comes to understand. God, then, is the source of the same directive, because he is the source of the nature that gives rise to it. One and the same directive can arise from two different sources. It arises from God by way of nature.

For natural law, the fourth feature of law (its promulgation) is far from straightforward. In what way is the directive to pursue the truth promulgated? It is not written down, nor is it proclaimed by word of mouth. Nevertheless, it is made known to human beings. As mentioned previously, with our reason we become aware of the directives that follow upon the movements within our nature.

Reason is part of human nature. Indeed, it is the central part of human nature. Human beings, then, have been given—by nature—a mind by which they can understand their own functional nature. After all, with our reason we can grasp the natures of things. Furthermore, human beings have been given—by nature—a mind that can recognize directives arising from a function, for reason perceives the relations between things, including the relations that follow upon a function. In an extended sense, then, the directive to pursue the truth has been promulgated by nature. Through our nature, we have all that is needed to understand this directive.

As we have already noted, Aquinas grants that sometimes our understanding of natural directives can be confused because of either bad arguments or bad desires (*ST*, I-II, 94, 4). For the most basic directives, however, Aquinas thinks that this confusion is unlikely. We can say, then, that the directives that arise from nature—at least the most basic of them—are promulgated by nature.

The directive to pursue the truth, then, meets the four conditions of a law. First, it is indeed a directive of reason concerning human behavior. Second, it concerns a shared human good. Third, it arises from both nature and from God, one of which (or both of which) can be described as having responsibility for the human community. Finally, it is promulgated: it is made known to human beings by our natural power of reasoning.

In short, this directive meets all four conditions of a law—at least in some extended sense. This directive, then, is fittingly called a natural law. It is not a human law, since it does not arise from human authority, nor is it promulgated by human authority. On the other hand, it does arise from nature and it is promulgated by nature.

Precepts of the Natural Law

Besides the directive to pursue the truth, our functional nature gives rise to many other directives. As we will see, it gives rise to a directive prohibiting murder, directives concerning the raising of children, and many other directives as well. All these directives might fittingly be called natural laws.

To these directives, Aquinas typically gives the name of "precept" (*ST*, I-II, 92, 2). The norm to pursue the truth, then, is a precept of the natural law. So also are the norms that we should not murder others and that we should love others.

When discussing the precepts of the natural law, Aquinas divides them into three categories (*ST*, I-II, 94, 2). He bases the distinction upon the different categories of movements to an end found within our nature (which are sometimes called natural inclinations). First, some precepts concern inclinations (or movements to an endpoint) that are found in everything created. Everything, for instance, has a movement to preserve its own existence; even the elements, thinks Aquinas, maintain a stable existence and resist being changed into something else. Second, some precepts concern inclinations that are common to human beings and animals. The inclination to reproduce sexually, for instance, is common to human beings and many animals. Finally, some precepts concern inclinations that are peculiar to human beings, such as the rational drive to the truth. This threefold division seems to concern different goods that can be found in human beings, such as existence, the continuation of the species, and the truth.

As we have seen, all these precepts can count as laws only insofar as they concern a common or shared good for all human beings. Even the precepts having to do with preserving our own existence, then, do not aim at a singular and isolated good. Our own individual existences are not private goods to be possessed in solitude. Just as Clare's act of playing her small part is not only her good but a good that belongs to the whole orchestra, so also our individual existences are not our own private goods. They are goods that belong to all others, for we are possessing parts of the shared human good. What we have belongs to others, and what others have belongs to us. For this reason, Aquinas thinks that suicide is wrong, in part because it harms the human community (*ST*, II-II, 64, 5).

As mentioned previously, the importance of the shared good is hard to overemphasize. Consequently, precepts that clearly and immediately concern the shared good take on a special priority within the natural law. Aquinas identifies, for instance, two primary precepts of the natural law. First, we must love God above all others; second, we must love our neighbor as ourselves (*ST*, I-II, 100, 3).

These precepts should not be confused with the Gospel precepts, although they sound exactly alike. The precepts of the natural law and those of the Gospel differ in important respects. First, they differ in the way that they are known. The Gospel precepts are known because God has chosen to reveal them to us. In contrast, the natural law precepts are known through observations and through our natural capacity of reasoning. No special revelation from God comes into play. In this manner, we can perceive the golden rule as a natural law. According to our nature, we should do unto others as we would have them do unto us (*ST*, I-II, 99, 1, ad 3).

The Gospel precepts differ from the natural law precepts in another way as well. The precise meaning of "love" is not exactly the same. The love that Jesus proclaims is greater than the love to which the natural law urges us. This difference, however, need not detain us.

The precepts to love—at least the precept to love other human beings—follow naturally from what we have seen in the last chapter: the human good is not a private good but a shared good. We love those with whom we share the good. This point is most obvious for our close friends and family. We want to share our good with them, and we want their good to be also our own good. In precisely this way, we love our friends. We are certainly not close friends with every human being, but if we want to share the good with them, then we want our good to be theirs and their good to be ours. We do not have to love them intimately in the way that we love our friends and family, but we should have a basic love for them.

The precept to love God will also follow upon our function of reasoning, but we will make this point clear only beginning in chapter 27. Until then, we will focus on precepts relating to other human beings.

Quickly following upon the precept to love other human beings is a kind of opposite command, a prohibition against harming others. Aquinas says that "do harm to no one" is a basic precept of the natural law (*ST*, I-II, 100, 5, ad 4). In the next several chapters, this prohibition will require much clarification.

part II

Harm

chapter 11

Doing Evil

Do not say, as some slanderously claim we say, "Let us do evil that good may come of it."

—St. Paul, Romans 3:8

Aquinas distinguishes between two different kinds of precepts, affirmative precepts and negative precepts (*QDM*, 2, 1). The precept to love our neighbors as ourselves is an affirmative precept. The precept to do harm to no one is a negative precept (*ST*, I-II, 100, 7, ad 1; *ST*, II-II, 122, 6, ad 1). Not surprisingly, affirmative precepts tell us to do a good action while negative precepts prohibit us from committing an evil action. Through an affirmative precept, we are enjoined to do the good of loving others. Through a negative precept, we are prohibited from doing the evil of harming them.

Consequentialism

The prohibition against harming might seem problematic. Sometimes it seems like a good idea to harm others. Harming might appear good not just for our own advantage but even for the shared good. Consider the position of Traci in the case of *Holding Hostages* (mentioned in the introductory chapter). Killing Louis seems useful in order to save 20 other people, who are held hostage by Pat (who demands that Traci kill Louis). The common or shared good, then, seems to be better served by killing Louis than it would be by refraining from killing him. In the first case, only one person dies; in the second case, 20 people die.

As we will see, the natural law prohibits Traci from killing Louis, even though she might save 20 lives by doing so. This conclusion, however, will be clarified only in the course of several chapters. As we attempt to clarify the natural law, the best place to begin is with the opposite view, which urges Traci to kill Louis.

The ethical view called consequentialism provides a stark contrast to Aquinas's natural law approach (Mill and Sher 2002). According to consequentialism, we should always seek to produce the greatest amount of good for the greatest number of people. In Traci's situation, for instance, she should simply add up goods that result from her actions. Killing Louis results in one death and 20 saved lives. Deciding not to kill Louis results in 20 deaths and one saved life. Simple math resolves her dilemma. The idea upheld by natural law ethics—that we should not do evil in order that good might come of it—has no place within consequentialist ethics.

Harming and Not Helping

In the consequentialist calculation, Traci's options differ only in the quantity of the lives lost and the lives saved. Consequentialism overlooks another important difference. If Traci chooses to kill Louis, then she harms Louis. If she decides to leave Louis untouched, then she does not thereby harm the hostages. Pat harms them, but she does not.

The options differ in what Traci does or does not do. In the one case, Traci harms Louis—which is prohibited by the natural law; in the other case, she fails to help the hostages. The difference is more clearly depicted in a set of two contrasting cases, which we will call *Limited Linda* and *Deadly Deb*.

Limited Linda: neither Chris nor Norbert can swim, and both have fallen into the lake, far apart from one another. Linda can hurry to save Chris, but then Norbert will have drowned in the meantime. On the other hand, Linda can hurry to save Norbert, but then Chris will have drowned in the meantime. Linda chooses to save Norbert; Chris dies.

Deadly Deb: Norbert has fallen into the lake, and he is floundering, unable to swim. Deb cannot reach him, but Molly is near enough to be able to save him. Molly agrees to save Norbert, however, only if Deb holds Chris under the water and drowns him. Deb drowns Chris; Molly saves Norbert.

The two cases have many parallels. In both cases, either Norbert will drown or Chris will drown. In both cases, the agent involved (Linda or Deb) can determine, through her action, who will live and who will drown. In both cases, the agent chooses the action that results in Chris dying and Norbert living.

Despite the similarities, we judge the two cases differently. In *Deadly Deb*, Deb's choice to drown Chris (with the result that Norbert lives) seems morally objectionable. In *Limited Linda*, Linda's choice to save Norbert (with the result that Chris dies) seems perfectly acceptable.

What accounts for the different judgments? Not the quantity of lives lost and lives saved, which is exactly the same in either case. Rather, the two differ because Linda fails to do good to Chris while Deb positively harms Chris. Deb harms Chris in order to save Norbert. In contrast, Linda harms no one. Rather, she fails to do good to Chris; she fails to save him because she is saving Norbert instead. Harming and failing to do good, even when they have similar results, are quite distinct from one another.

The distinction between harming and failing to do good is one instance of a broader distinction within the natural law: the difference between doing evil and not doing some generally good action. Telling a lie, for instance, is a case of doing evil; failing to tell some truth is a case of not doing what is generally good. The natural law always prohibits doing evil, and it certainly encourages us to do good actions. Not doing what is generally good, however, is sometimes acceptable. Obviously, for instance, we do not have to be telling all of the truth all of the time; by following that directive, we would never stop talking.

This contrast rests upon a difference between the two kinds of precepts: affirmative and negative. The prohibition against lying is negative. It tells us what not to do, and it is expressed by the negative command "do not lie." Similarly, the command "do harm to no one," is a negative precept. On the other hand, the rule to help those in need is an affirmative precept, as is the command to love one's neighbor as oneself.

Aquinas says that negative precepts hold always and in every situation. In contrast, affirmative precepts hold always but not in every situation (*ST*, I-II, 71, 5, ad 3; *QDM*, 7, 1, ad 8). It is always the case, in every situation, that we should not harm. On the other hand, it is always the case that we should help those in need, but we are not always able to help in every situation. Linda, for instance, is not able to help both Norbert and Chris.

As we might expect, the difference can be explained through function, which underlies the human good. Failing to do good is at least sometimes consistent with the human function. In contrast, doing evil always opposes the human function.

Failing to Do Good

The first point is easiest to see. It follows upon the conjunction of two features: an expansive or broad function and a limited agent. Functions are typically directed to a rather broad endpoint. Reason, for instance, might be described as the capacity to know the truth about the world. The truth, however, is nearly endless. It includes truths about mathematics, biology, chemistry, history, geography, literature, and so on. Human agents, however, are severely limited. They can know only a fraction of the possible truths. Furthermore, by choosing to learn certain truths, an agent limits the possibility of learning other truths. If Chuck chooses to study geography, for instance, then he has less time to study literature. If he studies geographical knowledge of Europe, then he may not have the time to learn much about North America. Chuck is a limited agent who cannot completely fulfill the extensive function of reason. By choosing to fulfill it in one way (geography), he thereby precludes the possibility of fulfilling it in other ways.

Consider another analogy. Let us limit the function of a pen to the writing of words or the writing of letters (as opposed to drawing pictures, scribbling, and so on). Even this restricted function is still fairly broad. The agency of the pen, however, is severely limited. While writing one letter, it cannot also be writing another. While writing the letter "o," for instance, it cannot also be writing the letter "p." When achieving part of its good (writing the letter "o"), the pen fails to achieve other parts of its good. This failure is completely consistent with the function of the pen; indeed, the failure to fulfill the function in one way occurs in the very act of fulfilling the function in another way.

The human shared good clearly meets the two conditions: an expansive or broad function and a limited agent. While the human function is expansive in multiple ways, our immediate concern is the wide scope of individuals with whom to share the good. On account of her function, Linda is directed to share the good with all human beings. Because of her limitations, however, she can share the good immediately with only a tiny subset of human beings, those with whom she has some kind of contact.

Just as Chuck must limit his studies, deciding to learn some things rather than others, so also Linda must choose to share her good with some individuals, which precludes her from sharing it (immediately) with others. In the situation of *Limited Linda*, for instance, she can share herself through the act of saving Chris or through the act of saving Norbert, but her limitations prevent her from engaging in both acts of sharing (*ST*, II-II, 31, 2, ad 1). By fulfilling her function in one way (saving Norbert), she fails to fulfill her function in another way (saving Chris).

Linda, then, is like the cellist Clare, who fulfills her function of playing symphonic music by playing her small part within the whole orchestra. Similarly, Linda fulfills her function of sharing the good with other human beings by playing her small part within the whole. Like all human beings, she is limited. She must share the good by particular actions, which are directed to particular persons. By sharing the good with some members of the community, she thereby gives herself to the whole community. Her failure to do some good (for example, save Chris) is completely consistent with fulfilling her human function in another way, by doing some other good (such as saving Norbert).

Doing Evil

What about harming? Is it consistent with the human function or is it opposed to the human function? Once again, a few analogies will help us answer this question.

Suppose that Chuck, while studying geography, comes to think that the capital of Germany is not Berlin but Frankfurt. He now has gone beyond merely a failure to know certain truths. He has positively distorted the truth; he has fallen into an error. The failure to know certain truths (because he is knowing others instead) is completely consistent with fulfilling his function; in contrast, believing error is in opposition to his function.

Unlike a human being, a pen has no free will by which it can oppose its function, but let us imagine (for the sake of analogy) an anthropomorphic pen with free will. Suppose that the pen "decides" not to write letters but to erase. This action would be a kind of positive opposition to the function of the pen. To make the analogy tighter, we will suppose that the pen writes the letter "H" with only the vertical lines and not the crossbar. The defect is not merely the absence of the crossbar (which then might look like a failure to do good). Rather, it is a positive attempt to write the vertical lines without the horizontal line. In other words, the pen does not "aim" to write the complete letter (but then fail to accomplish this goal on account of limitations). Instead, the pen "aims" to write the vertical lines without the crossbar. The lack of the crossbar is part of the good it aims to achieve. It thereby positively opposes its function (to write letters). Like Chuck, who positively errs in his false belief, the pen positively errs in writing.

Or imagine a car that has free will, by which it can decide to fulfill one capacity or another capacity. This car is rather enamored with its stereo system, so that it continually seeks to play music. That is fine, just as long as the playing of music can still be ordered to transportation. But now let us suppose that the car wants the music together with the absence of transportation. This car is fulfilling a partial capacity (playing music) while it is positively opposing its overall function.

These examples do not concern a broad function with a limited agent (as was the case for the failure to do good). Rather, they concern the order of an action. Chuck's function is ordered to the truth of geography, but his erroneous belief (that the capital of Germany is Frankfurt) is directed to falsehood instead. The pen's function is ordered to write letters, but the defective action is directed to a maimed letter. The function of the car is ordered to transportation, but the car directs itself toward what excludes transportation. Other examples are not hard to imagine. On account of her function as a doctor, Teresa is ordered to the health of her patients. If she deliberately makes Sean sick, then her action is directed not to health but to illness.

In cases of failing to do some good, we do not find the same conflict of direction. When Chuck limits his geographical studies to Europe, for example, he is still directed to geographical truth; he is simply directed to a limited subset of the possibilities. Similarly, when Linda saves Norbert, her action is directed to share the good. Because of her limitations, she cannot actively share the good also with Chris. Like Chuck, she must direct herself to a subset of the possibilities.

Deb is different. She does not simply share the good with a subset of the possibilities. She positively provides a contrary order. With her function, she is directed to share the good with other human beings, which includes Chris. In her action, she directs herself to take the good from him. She may seek the good of Norbert, but she seeks it by excluding the good of Chris. Linda performs a limited good; in contrast, Deb does evil.

Deb views Chris's evil as positively good. His death is usefully good in order to produce Molly's act of saving Norbert. As far as Deb is concerned, then, Chris's death is a positive goal to be achieved. Chris's good is no longer part of her own good. In fact, his evil is part of her perceived good. Linda has no such thought. She does not want to achieve Chris's death for any useful good. Rather, she regrets her limitations, which prevent her from saving both Norbert and Chris. Linda does not perceive the death of Chris as a kind of good.

Harming Others

Deb's attitude toward Chris is best understood by recognizing that both Chris and Deb are parts of a greater whole. Within the whole, each has his or her part to contribute. Within the whole of the orchestra, for instance, the cellist Clare has her own part to contribute. She would do no service to the orchestra if she decided that she was going to play all the parts: the violin, the cello, the bass, the percussion, and so on. As a part, she must recognize her limitations. Because she is limited, she shares the good with the other members by keeping to her role. She also receives the good from others by accepting the parts that they have to contribute. She accepts the good of Bridget the violinist, for instance, by recognizing that Bridget is herself a part, who has her own contribution to the whole.

The members of the orchestra do not contribute to the whole by acting upon one another. Clare, for instance, does not attempt to change Bridget; she simply plays her own instrument. In this regard, the human shared good is different. We sometimes contribute to the whole by acting upon other members. The part we have to play involves helping others play their part. Linda, for instance, contributes to the human good by acting upon Norbert, saving him from drowning. Clare shares the good simply by playing her instrument, without acting upon Bridget. Linda shares the good by actively changing Norbert. We will explain the underlying reason for such helping actions later in this book (chapters 22 and 23).

For now, we need to observe only that the order of these actions has two aspects. Since the actions aim to share the good with another human being, they are ordered or directed toward some good and to some person (or persons). Linda's action, for instance, is directed to the good of life and to the person of Norbert, who is a fellow member of the human community. Deb's action fails in both of these directions. She directs her action not to the good of Chris but to his evil. Consequently, she does not direct herself and her action toward Chris as a subject of her good. Her action is not directed toward Chris as a member who has a part, a share in the good. On the contrary, Deb excludes his part.

Linda does not actively share the good with Chris because she is occupied with the action of saving Norbert. She does not thereby direct herself to the evil of Chris. Nor does she exclude him from the shared good. In fact, her action is not directed upon Chris at all. Because of her limitations, she directs her action only upon Norbert. In contrast, Deb directs her action precisely upon Chris, seeking to bring about his death.

Even Clare (in the orchestra) directs herself toward the other members. She does not act upon them the way that Linda acts upon Norbert. Nevertheless, by playing her part, she gives what she has to Bridget and the other members. She treats them as fellow parts by contributing her own part and by accepting their parts as goods belonging to her. In the same way, Linda still includes Chris within her shared good. In the action of saving Norbert, she contributes her part, which she seeks as a good belonging to others, including Chris.

Deb cannot have the same attitude toward Chris. She cannot seek her action as a good belonging to Chris. Nor can she accept his part as belonging to herself. She acts contrary to this order. She acts precisely so as to exclude Chris's part. Her action may be explained in terms of the distinction, discussed previously (in chapter 9), between possessing parts and producing parts. If she were to accept his part, she would view him as a possessing part of the community (as the musicians are possessing parts of the orchestra). As it is, she views him as a producing part (as the stage crew are producing parts for the music of the orchestra). By her action, she directs Chris to a useful good outside himself. Indeed, she directs him to a useful good that excludes his own good.

Deb's action, then, fits the pattern of the erroneous geographical knowledge. It also fits the pattern of the pen that aims at defective letters. Finally, it fits the pattern of Teresa the doctor making her patients ill. In all these actions, the agent has a function directing to some good, but the action provides a contrary direction, thereby excluding the function. Deb is directed (by her function) to Chris as a possessing part of the human community. By her choice, however, she directs herself to his evil. By her action, she directs herself to Chris as a producing part. In two ways, then, she refuses to play her part. First, she directs herself to Chris's evil rather than to his good; second, she treats him (in the direction of her action) as a producing part rather than as a possessing part. Consequently, she herself has ceased to be a member of the greater community. She has set herself above the community.

Whenever we are directed to a shared good, we must be careful to contribute our part. We should not act like the pen, which aims at a part of a letter to the exclusion of the completed letter. We should not seek our own part to the exclusion of the whole. Imagine, for instance, that Bridget decides that her part is better than all the rest, so she plays it loudly, over the others. She thereby abandons the good of the whole, which is ruined by her playing. She seeks her own part, but no longer as a part; she seeks it as an independent good. Similarly, as a soccer player, Payton decides that she is better than all the other players; she hogs the ball when she should be passing it to teammates. Like Bridget, Payton is no longer seeking the shared good. She wants her part independently of the good of the whole. She seeks only a damaged good of the whole.

In the same manner, Deb refuses to play her part. She refuses to treat Chris as a possessing part, who has his own role to play, his own good to contribute. Instead, she treats him as a producing part, who has no share in the good. She goes against the precept of the natural law, which warns her to do harm to no one. By doing evil, she excludes her own contribution and the contribution of Chris.

Wrongful Failures

We have been drawing a strong contrast between doing evil and failing to do good. By killing Chris, Deb does evil, which is never permitted. By saving Norbert, Linda (acceptably) fails to do the good of saving Chris. The strong contrast, however, might give rise to a misunderstanding. We might lose sight of an important truth: failing to do good is sometimes reprehensible.

Consider the following situation.

> *Garrulous Gary*: Libby has fallen into the lake and is unable to swim. Gary is nearby and can save her. At the moment, however, he is chatting with his friend David (himself unable to swim and therefore unable to help Libby). Gary decides to continue chatting; Libby drowns.

Gary has not positively done evil to Libby; he has simply failed to help her. Nevertheless, we judge that he is morally to blame for his failure.

Gary might protest that he is a limited human being; he cannot be sharing the good with everyone at once. He has chosen to share the good with David (by talking with him). He cannot at the same time share the good with Libby (by saving her). In the end, he insists that he has not rejected the shared good. He has simply chosen to share the good in one way rather than another.

We do not accept such reasoning. But why not? It seems precisely parallel to the reasoning by which we judge that Linda can decide not to save Chris (because she is saving Norbert instead). How exactly do the two cases differ?

Sometimes a function, even a broad function, requires one particular action. Clare's role within the orchestra, for instance, requires her to play particular notes at particular times. Her role, of course, is nearly the opposite of an expansive function, but we might view her as having the broad function of playing music, which now requires very particular acts of playing music. Again, Beatrice's function as a mathematician is to know mathematical truth, and by studying some mathematical truths, her limitations prevent her from knowing other mathematical truths. At some times, however, she is required to know very particular truths. Normally, she does not need to be aware that the square of 89 is 7921, but when she is working through a particular problem, this knowledge may be needed. The absence of this knowledge is not typically opposed to her function, but in this situation, it is.

Let us return to the difference between Linda and Gary. Linda chooses between two seemingly equal options. Saving Norbert is on par with saving Chris. In contrast, Gary's options seem grossly unequal. On the one hand, he can save Libby; on the other hand, he can share some pleasantries with David. By choosing to chat with David, Gary seems to regard Libby as having little worth, as almost insignificant. Her great good (continued living) is placed below the slight good of David.

This comparative difference between goods, no doubt, plays some role in our contrasting judgments. Linda's choice to save Norbert is acceptable, even praiseworthy, although she thereby fails to save Chris. Gary's choice not to save Libby is objectionable, even reprehensible, although he thereby manages to chat with David. Linda pursues one good and thereby sets aside a similar good. Gary pursues one good but sets aside a much more important good.

At this point, however, it may seem as if we have thrown ourselves into the arms of consequentialism. We are judging Linda and Gary simply based upon whether they produce the greatest amount of good. In this situation, Linda produces as much good as she possibly could. In contrast, Gary could have produced a much greater good but has chosen otherwise.

If we apply this same standard (of producing the greatest good) to the case of Traci, then we reach the conclusion, it seems, that Traci should kill Louis. After all, she thereby saves 20 lives. Saving 20 lives is a greater good than saving one life. If Gary is to blame for choosing the lesser good (talking with David rather than saving Libby), then it seems that Traci should be blamed if she refuses to kill Louis. She thereby chooses the lesser good of saving one person, in contrast to the greater good of saving 20.

Appearances, however, can be deceptive. By killing Louis, Traci does not in fact choose the greater good. Indeed, even the contrast between Linda and Gary is deceptive. The standard of producing the greatest good is not present even in this case. Dispelling these illusive appearances, however, must wait for the next chapter.

chapter 12

The Greater Good

> Of all tyrannies, a tyranny sincerely exercised for the good of its victims may be the most oppressive. It may be better to live under robber barons than under omnipotent moral busybodies.
>
> —C. S. Lewis, "The Humanitarian Theory of Punishment"

While examining Traci's options in the light of consequentialism, which recommends that she kill Louis in order to produce the greatest good for the greatest number of people, we have discovered that consequentialism focuses only upon results and ignores the important distinction between doing harm and failing to do some particular good. Consequentialism, however, insists that this distinction is irrelevant. The results are all that matters. After all, by killing Louis, Traci is doing some good to the hostages. Her choice, then, is really a choice between two different goods. On the one hand, she can help Louis by refusing to kill him; on the other hand, she can help the hostages by killing Louis. Consequentialism claims that ultimately, her options are similar to Linda's, who must choose to save either Norbert or Chris. When faced with such alternatives, we should choose based upon the importance of the goods, and 20 lives are certainly more important than one.

A Common Defense of Consequentialism

On the face of it, the emphasis upon the "greater good" is linked with the shared good of many people. This appearance, however, will prove to be illusory. In fact, consequentialism abandons the shared good. What it calls the greater good is not the human shared good but merely a collection of individual goods.

This last point is revealed in a common defense of consequentialism, in which consequentialists use an analogy between individual deliberations and the common good (Hare 1981). In our individual pursuits, we are typically unable to achieve everything that we want, so we must choose between possible options. Bruce, for instance, must decide between two job offers. The first job is in a city that he likes, but it does not pay well. The second job would involve moving to a city that he finds unpleasant, but the pay is excellent. Because the situation prevents him from having everything that he wants, he must choose between a city he likes and good pay. When faced with such decisions, consequentialists note, we choose the option that ultimately brings us the greatest good. If money is more important to Bruce, then he will choose the second option; if a pleasant environment is more important to him, then he will choose the first option.

Similar limitations, with similar decisions, apply to the common good. Rarely is a shared good achieved to absolute completion or perfection. The orchestra, for instance, does not play perfectly, so its music has some defects. The human good, as well, is fraught with imperfections. Tom and Brenda, for instance, are married with children, but now Brenda develops cancer and is suffering greatly. The good that they share, which includes the good of Brenda, falls short of the ideal for which they hope.

When we pursue the shared good, then, we must often choose between possibilities, none of which perfectly realizes the good. Traci is in just such a situation. On the one hand, she can choose to kill Louis, and then the hostages will be saved; on the other hand, she can refuse to kill Louis, and then the hostages will die. In either event, the shared good will fall short of the ideal, which includes both the good of Louis and the good of the hostages.

In this situation, consequentialists advise Traci to follow the pattern of Bruce as he decides between two jobs. Just as Bruce should choose the option that brings his greatest good, so should Traci choose the option that brings about the greatest good of those who share the good. In short, she should kill Louis. Thereby, the greater part of the shared good—20 lives as opposed to one—is preserved.

The Unity of the Individual

This argument in defense of consequentialism reveals an inadequate notion of the unity of the good. Consequentialism fails to understand the unity of the good because it fails to understand the subject of the good, which is either the individual (for the good of the individual) or the community (for the shared good).

As we have seen, the unity of an individual can be compared to the unity of a car. A car has a variety of capacities, such as the ability to move from place to place, to play music, to cool the interior air, and to honk a horn. The car is not, however, a hodgepodge collection of capacities. These multiple capacities are all united by the overarching function of transporting from place to place. Completing other capacities, such as the capacity to honk or to play music, is good only by contributing to this one chief capacity.

The same applies to an individual human being, such as Beatrice. She has a multiplicity of capacities. She has the ability to maintain her existence, to see, to remember, to get angry, to reproduce, to reason, and so on. These multiple capacities, however, are united by her overall function of reasoning.

Each of these capacities is a kind of movement to an endpoint, which is completed by some good. Beatrice's capacity to maintain her existence, for instance, is a movement to the endpoint of her continued existence. Ultimately, this good—as well as any other completion—is truly good for Beatrice only if it is directed to her chief capacity of reasoning. With her free will, however, Beatrice can reject this chief capacity. She can pursue a partial good, such as pleasure, to the exclusion of her overall good. She can seek the pleasure of sweets to the exclusion of her overall good. Then she would be like an anthropomorphic car that becomes enamored with its stereo system; consequently, it chooses to play music to the detriment of transportation.

Consequentialism employs a different conception of the unity of the person. It recognizes the many capacities with their many completions, which make for many partial goods. Within consequentialism, however, the only unity for the person is the sum total of these partial goods. According to consequentialism, we pursue the greatest sum total of goods, as does Bruce when choosing between the two jobs. The consequentialist individual is a collection of capacities together with a will—or some source of desire—that seeks the greatest fulfillment of these capacities. The individual has no overall function—no chief movement to an endpoint—that unifies all the other capacities.

We have before us two accounts of a unified person. According to natural law, a person is unified through one chief function or purpose. According to consequentialism, a person is unified only by a desire for the collection of the greatest sum total of goods.

The two accounts differ in their manner of evaluating which goods are greater. With a unified function, we can rank goods in relation to the one chief good. For a car, for instance, we can rank the importance of air-conditioning, a stereo system, a horn, and a blinker. Having a blinker is more important for transportation than having a stereo system. Having a horn is more important than having air-conditioning. A car that lacks some of these completions is better or worse based upon the importance of its various capacities in relation to the one chief good of transportation.

But what if the car has no chief capacity, no overriding function? What, then, would make for a better or worse car? It would be difficult to say. We might rank the various capacities based upon our own personal desires. Perhaps Randy likes a stereo system so much that he would prefer a car with a good stereo system, even if it cannot move from place to place. Perhaps Anita likes to keep cool, so she would prefer a car with no stereo system and no movement from place to place, but with a very effective air-conditioner.

Clearly, such personal rankings have little to do with a good or bad car. Indeed, at this point it is unclear that we are even speaking of a "car," since we have lost sight of—and even discarded—the chief function of transportation. Rather, we are speaking only of a collection of possible capacities. We have no unity.

Similarly, if the individual person has no overriding function, then he is nothing more than a collection of capacities. Furthermore, these capacities can be ranked based only upon the personal whim or preference of desires. In itself, reason is not more important than anger, and anger is not more important than the urge to satisfy an itch by scratching. Randy might decide to scratch, eliminating his itch, even if he thereby gives up his reason. His only standard is his desire.

As we have seen, however, desire demands a standard of its own. We must first know the good before we can desire the good. Before we have greater or lesser desires, then, we should—most fittingly—know which goods are better than other goods. Randy should first recognize that reason is better than satisfying an itch; then he should more intensely desire that which is a greater good. Desire itself, then, should not be the standard of what is greater or lesser.

The Unity of the Community

These two standards of unity can also be applied to a group of individuals. The orchestra, for instance, has many members, each with his or her part to play. Each member has a function or movement to some endpoint. Violinists have the function of playing their part; cellists have the function of playing their part; and so on. These diverse roles are all unified by the overall function of playing the symphonic music. The part of the cellists is a good of the orchestra, but only if it is ordered to the overall function.

When Bridget chooses to play her part louder than all the rest—and even at times when she should be silent—then she opposes the good of the orchestra. She does not even complete her own role, since that role supposes her further direction to the whole.

Within consequentialism, the individual is simply a collection of capacities, with no overriding function. Similarly, the greater good of the community, within consequentialism, has no overarching function. Rather, the community is just a sum total of individuals, and the good of the community is the sum total of individual goods. Each person, with his or her diverse capacities, supplies a collection of diverse goods. These goods are not judged in relation to any overall purpose of the community. Rather, they are judged simply as a quantity within a sum total. In Traci's situation, for instance, the good of the group is simply the addition of individual goods. The lives of 20 hostages are weighed against the life of Louis.

The Greater Sum Total Is Not a Shared Good

This sum total is not a shared good (*ST*, II-II, 58, 7, ad 2: *In Pol*, bk. 1, chap. 1, 16). As we have seen, shared goods must be possessed together, through acts of giving the good to one another. A sum total of individual goods, however, is not possessed together. The goods remain individual. They do not belong to any unified community. The life of Louis is the good of Louis; the life of Krystyna (one of the hostages) is the good of Krystyna; and so on. These goods have no unifying subject. In contrast, the victory of the soccer team is the good of the team; it is the good of the members as united. Similarly, the symphonic music is the good of the whole orchestra, of the members as united.

Suppose that Sarah owns a laptop and Sam owns a bicycle. To whom does the sum total of the laptop and the bicycle belong? Unless Sarah and Sam have joint ownership, then the sum total belongs to no one. The laptop belongs to someone and the bicycle belongs to someone, but the combination belongs to no one. Similarly, the sum total of the goods of the hostages belongs to no one. The good of the orchestra belongs to the whole orchestra because the members are united by an overall function. As we have seen, however, a sum total has no inherent unity; it can be united only according to the whim of desire.

By killing Louis, then, Traci is not really seeking the greater good. She seeks only individual goods that complete individual persons. She seeks no good of the community that completes the individuals as united. The sum total of goods makes sense only if we forget that every good is the completion of some subject, a subject that has a movement to an endpoint. If we suppose, together with naïve realism, that the good is some special quality that applies to things independently of any subject, then we can tally a sum total that belongs to no one. But if (as we have seen) the good is the completion of some subject having a movement to an endpoint, then the sum total is nonsense.

The greater good of the community makes sense only when there is a united community. We can speak of the greater good of the soccer team because the members are united by an overall function. When we make judgments about what is better—what is the greater good—we do not add up individual goods. If the team were forced to give up one player, then it might choose to keep the goalie rather than the center forward. This judgment, however, has nothing to do with a sum total of individual goods. It has everything to do with the importance of the members for the overall function.

Imagine that Don, in order to satisfy his desire for a good car, starts adding up the different completions of different capacities. He includes the ability to transport as just one among others. None of the cars available to him have all the possible capacities, and several lack the capacity to transport from place to place. Don treats these immobile cars like all the others, simply adding up the completions of different capacities. He settles on a car that has good air-conditioning, a good stereo system, and a sunroof, but that cannot move from place to place. Clearly, Don has missed the point of a good car. By coming up with a sum total, he has not achieved the greatest good for a car.

Similarly, Beatrice—supposing she seeks great pleasure to the exclusion of her overall good—has not achieved her greatest good. By following the consequentialist suggestion to add up individual goods, while setting aside any thought of her overall function or purpose, she has lost sight of her overall good. By accumulating individual goods, she has lost her true good. Whatever great pleasure she gets from eating sweets, it cannot add up to something better than her chief overall good.

Why, then, does Bruce add up various good features of his job? Because he is not simply adding up goods. Rather, he is considering each good insofar as it relates to his overall good. If he were to include, within his considerations, the job of being a hit man or the job of being a drug dealer—both of which exclude the good of reason—then he would lose sight of his overall purpose. He would be left only with the sum total of pros and cons, to be weighed based upon the whim of his desire.

The same reasoning applies to a shared good. The overall good of the orchestra is not simply the sum total of the goods of its individual members. These individual goods must be united through coordinated activity, so that the individual goods can all be possessed together. The good of the cellist must not remain simply the good of the cellist; it must become the good of the percussionist and the good of the violinist. A sum total that eliminates this sharing is not the greatest good of the orchestra.

If Traci makes her decision by focusing upon a sum total of individual goods, then she also loses sight of the shared good. Just as the sum total of the laptop and the bike belongs to no one, so also no one possesses the sum total of the good of Louis and the good of the hostages. If Traci really seeks the good of the community, then she seeks a good that belongs to everyone involved. When she kills Louis, she excludes him from the good. Rather than share the good with him, she takes the good from him. A car without the function of transportation is not good *as a car*; it lacks the very good that makes it to be a car. Similarly, by excluding the good of Louis and seeking a good alien to him, Traci attains nothing of the shared good. She eliminates the very union needed for the shared good; she eliminates the foundation of any shared good.

Excluding Members from the Community

A consequentialist might object that Traci eliminates the shared good by either of her options. By killing Louis, she excludes the good of Louis, but by refusing to kill Louis, she excludes the good of the hostages. Traci (the consequentialist insists) is forced to make a choice. She must exclude either Louis or the hostages. In either event, the shared good is damaged. At least by killing Louis (so the argument goes), she retains the greater part of the shared good.

This argument, by continuing to judge in terms of sum totals, has not understood what it means to exclude Louis from the shared good. A pen that writes the letter "o" and does not (at the same time) write the letter "b" still retains its broad function of writing letters. In the concrete, some of this function is realized and some is not. In contrast, our imaginary pen that directs itself to a misshapen "H" has taken on another function. Its good, whatever it is, is not the good of the pen. It is a good alien to a pen and its function.

As we have seen, Linda (in *Limited Linda*) is like the pen that writes "o" but does not write "b"; on the other hand, Deb (in *Deadly Deb*) is like the pen that writes the misshapen "H." When she chooses to save Norbert, Linda retains her broad function of sharing the good. She even shares the good with Chris, although indirectly. In contrast, when Deb drowns Chris, she substitutes a new order, opposed to the direction of her role within the whole. By using Chris as a productive part, she refuses to accept him as a member that possesses the good with her. Linda makes no such rejection. She accepts the role of Chris as a possessing part, but on account of her limitations, she chooses to fulfill the shared function by helping Norbert instead of Chris. The good of Chris, then, is still her good, and her good still belongs to the whole; it still belongs to Chris who is a member of the whole.

Similar reasoning applies to Traci. By refusing to kill Louis, she retains the broad function, which aims to share the good even with the hostages. Given her limitations, she can contribute only part of the shared good. She can preserve Louis's life. In contrast, by choosing to kill Louis, she directs herself to a new endpoint, thereby excluding the order of her role within the community. She directs Louis as a productive part to a good that excludes his own. She rejects Louis as a possessing member of the community who has his part to play. What she wants from Louis is utility, a utility that excludes his own good. His evil has become her good. Just as Don, in seeking a sum total of automobile capacities, fails to seek a good car, so also Traci, if she were to seek a sum total, would fail to seek the shared good of the community. In this scenario, whatever good she seeks does not include Louis as a possessing part.

Net Results Versus Acts of Sharing

What about the contrast with which the last chapter ended? *Garrulous Gary* is like *Limited Linda*. He chooses not to save Libby (who is drowning) because he prefers to share the good with David through conversation. Nevertheless, we judge Gary differently than we judge Linda. The good she pursues (saving Norbert) is similar to the good that she forgoes (saving Chris). In contrast, the good that Gary pursues (conversation with David) is insignificant compared to the good that he forgoes (saving Libby). Our differing judgments appear to rely upon consequentialist reasoning. Gary is condemned because he fails to pursue the greatest good.

This appearance will prove faulty. What we are comparing (for both Linda and Gary) is not a sum total of resulting goods. Rather, we are comparing different actions that might be performed. We are not comparing the resulting death of Libby to the pleasure that David derives from conversation. Rather, we are comparing the act of saving Libby to the act of conversing (or sharing the good by way of conversation). Likewise, we are not comparing the life of Chris to the life of Norbert. Rather, we are comparing the act of saving Chris to the act of saving Norbert.

This point becomes clearer if we add a detail. Norbert is Linda's brother, but Chris is a stranger to Linda. Part of Linda's decision, then, depends on her ties to Norbert. She is not just adding up the lives. She is considering what she owes to her brother as opposed to what she owes to a stranger.

Within the natural law, says Aquinas, we owe more to those who are closer to us (*ST*, II-II, 26, 6). We owe more to our family and friends, for instance, than we owe to strangers. We should not look simply at sum totals; rather, we should look at our acts of sharing the good. Since we share the good more completely with those who are closer to us, we should give greater importance to these acts of sharing than to others.

Another example clarifies the difference between net results and actions of sharing.

> *Altruistic Anna*: Anna gives money to various charities that support people in Third World countries, providing them with enough food to survive from day to day. Her son Gil goes without a bicycle, without new clothes, and even without a healthy diet. Anna reasons that the money spent on a bicycle, clothes, and good food will go much farther in the Third World, so that many lives can be saved. She is producing a greater good by contributing to charity rather than by taking care of her son.

Perhaps Anna should be described as misguided in her altruism. In seeking a sum total, she has lost sight of those who are close to her. If she were to focus not on effects but upon acts of sharing, she might recognize that even buying a bicycle for Gil can be a greater act than saving the lives of many strangers. A life focused upon net results is an empty life. A life focused upon sharing the good is a full life, and we share the good most of all by personal acts of friendship with those who are close to us.

The natural law is not recommending that Anna neglect the poor. On the contrary, the natural law requires that we help out those in need. Anna should indeed be giving to charity. It does not follow that she should be neglecting her son (even if this neglect might save some lives). The sum total of good effects is not what matters; rather, sharing the good is what matters. The human shared good is the interaction of many people who share the good with one another. The sharing is most fully realized with those close to us.

Figuring out what is wrong with Gary's behavior, then, is not simply a matter of a net total of effects. Many factors come into play. The significance of the goods involved (the life of Libby as opposed to conversation with David) is certainly important, but not because of the effects by themselves. Rather, it is important because sharing a greater good is a greater act of sharing.

The good involved, however, is not the only factor. As we have seen, the union we have with others also affects our acts of sharing. Gary is closer to Libby (although she is a stranger) than he is to people far away that he might help by way of charity. Circumstances have placed her in his life. The urgency of this particular act of sharing can also play a role. Libby is in an urgent situation and needs Gary's help now. Those starving in remote places are not in need of Gary's particular help. Ideally, they should be helped most of all by those who are close to them. Other factors as well may be significant. Gary might have a special obligation to Libby. Perhaps, for instance, he is the lifeguard on duty.

Aquinas, it seems, reduces all these factors to two (*ST*, II-II, 26, 7). On the one hand, we must ask how important, within the shared good, is the good involved. On the other hand, we must ask how close we are to the person involved. Special obligations (such as being a lifeguard) fall into the second category because they give us a special union with those involved. The urgency of the situation seems to fall in the first category.

The Difficulty of Applying Affirmative Precepts

None of this gives us a magic formula by which we can definitively determine when we should be engaging in one act of sharing as opposed to another. Fortunately, most situations in life are not too complicated. It takes no formula to figure out that Gary should save Libby rather than converse with David. Our days bring us in contact with many people, and for the most part we are asked to share the good with those presented to us in the moment. In general, we should structure our lives so that we can share the good with those close to us. We should not become workaholics, for instance, who neglect our family or friends. At the same time, we must structure our lives to allow for some sharing with those who are more remote. We should organize our spending, for instance, so that we have something available for charity.

These general rules guide us in the application of affirmative precepts of the natural law. Recall that affirmative precepts hold always but not in every situation. For Linda, for instance, the precept to help out those in need applies to Norbert but not (given her limitations) to Chris. How do we know the situations in which the affirmative precepts apply? By way of the general guidelines suggested above. For the most part, no rocket science is needed to recognize the application of affirmative precepts.

Absent from the guidelines is any reference to a sum total of goods. Some people have suggested that adding up goods is one small part of natural law ethics, a part that can be overridden by other aspects of natural law. In fact, summing up goods plays no part within natural law. Rather, what matters is the importance of acts of sharing. Some actions are more important because they are directed to a more important good. This factor should not be mistaken for a calculation of net effects produced.

When we begin looking at effects produced, we lose sight of the shared good. We become like Don who has no conception of the overall function of a car. He simply adds up the various capacities that he finds in cars and considers the capacity to move about as only one among many. By focusing upon production rather than sharing the good, we also lose sight of the overall function of the human community. This function is realized not in effects but in acts of sharing.

A Concluding Complication

It seems that we may have resolved Traci's dilemma. The act of killing Louis is, for her, an act of rejecting the shared good. In contrast, by refusing to kill Louis, she does not actively harm the hostages. On account of her limitations, she is not rejecting the shared good, even though she does not fully realize the shared good in her action. The shared good is not found in a sum total of individual goods: it is found in acts of sharing. Traci, then, should not aim to add up individual goods but to share the good insofar as she is able.

This solution to our dilemma will prove to be substantially correct. Nevertheless, the situation might prove to be more complicated than has been suggested. Throughout our treatment of the negative precept, "do harm to no one," we have presumed that it applies to all human beings. This presumption, however, may be incorrect. After all, according to Aquinas the natural law does permit some harm to some human beings. Soldiers, for instance, are allowed to harm the enemy in a just war (*ST*, II-II, 40, 1). Similarly, the state may harm wrongdoers by way of punishment (*ST*, II-II, 64, 2). Again, if someone is attacking us, we might be allowed to harm him in self-defense (*ST*, II-II, 64, 7). If harm is allowed in these cases, then perhaps it can be allowed in Traci's case as well. In the next chapter, we will see under what conditions harm is allowed.

chapter 13

Punishment

> Those who hold the humanitarian theory of punishment think that it is mild and merciful. In this I believe that they are seriously mistaken. I believe that the "Humanity" which it claims is a dangerous illusion and disguises the possibility of cruelty and injustice without end. I urge a return to the traditional or Retributive theory not solely, not even primarily, in the interests of society, but in the interests of the criminal.
>
> —C. S. Lewis, "The Humanitarian Theory of Punishment"

The natural law enjoins us to do harm to no one. After making this observation, Aquinas notes (in the very next sentence) that the natural law also enjoins us to punish evildoers (*ST*, I-II, 95, 2). Punishment, however, is a certain kind of harm. Indeed, capital punishment seems to inflict the greatest harm, yet it is allowed under the natural law (*ST*, II-II, 64, 2). Aquinas seems to be contradicting himself. He says that we should do harm to no one, but in the next breath he says that we should harm evildoers.

We need not conclude that Aquinas—or the natural law—is inconsistent. We need only clarify the precept "do harm to no one." It might be rephrased as follows: as a private citizen, do harm to no one. Again, it might be rephrased in another way: do harm to no innocent person (*ST*, II-II, 65, 2). Either one of these clarifications would make Aquinas consistent. In the case of punishment, evildoers are not innocent but guilty of some offense. Furthermore, punishment cannot be carried out by private citizens (*ST*, II-II, 64, 3; *ST*, II-II, 65, 2). It must be carried out by government officials, and it must include fair trial proceedings.

While these clarifications allow for punishment, they both seem problematic. The second clarification ("do harm to no innocent person") seems especially problematic. The precept against harm is founded upon a shared good, for we should not harm those with whom we share the good. According to the second clarification, then, we share the good only with innocent human beings; we do not share the good with the guilty. As we have seen, however, the human good is a shared good. Therefore, it seems to include all human beings, not just the innocent.

Perhaps the guilty have excluded themselves from the shared good. In that case, we need no longer share the good with them. But then it becomes unclear why punishment should be reserved to public authorities, which is the detail provided by the first clarification.

These difficulties suggest that we have inadequately understood punishment and the harm it involves. This chapter hopes to fill in some of the gaps in our understanding.

Anger and Repentance

The nature of punishment is related to our emotions of repentance and anger. Consider the following case:

> *Selfish Sebastian*: Last week, Clare gave Sebastian a ride when his car broke down. Now Clare is in need of a ride, but Sebastian, feeling lazy, says that he is too busy.

In this situation, Clare might naturally feel angry. But perhaps a few days later and upon reflection, Sebastian recognizes the error of his ways and apologizes to Clare. If he apologizes in words alone and does not try to make it up, Clare might think that his apology is insincere. With a true apology, Sebastian will recognize that he has created an imbalance, placing himself above Clare, and he will seek to restore the proper balance. He does so by putting himself down (the apology itself is a kind of humiliation), and putting Clare back up, which he does through some kind deed.

But what if Sebastian does not apologize? Clare is angry. She feels that Sebastian has treated her as insignificant, as someone that he can use for his own benefit. Clare now wants to get back at him. She decides to give Sebastian the cold shoulder and refuses to talk with him when they meet.

We might suppose that Clare, in her anger, aims primarily to harm Sebastian. Aquinas insists, however, that anger is first of all concerned with good (*ST*, I-II, 46, 2). Her anger aims to restore the proper relationship between her and Sebastian. Through his action, Sebastian has upset the proper balance. He has put Clare down as insignificant and has thereby elevated himself above her. Clare wants to restore her proper place. She will do so by putting Sebastian back down into his place. In a way, then, Clare aims at Sebastian's harm. More fundamentally, says Aquinas, she aims at the good of restoring the proper order.

Clare's goals are not much different from those of the repentant Sebastian. He wants to set things right through his apology and through his recompense. Likewise, Clare wants to set things right through her punitive action. Ideally, she even wants to restore the friendship. She hopes that her action will bring about a change of heart in Sebastian. He will recognize the error of his ways and give Clare her proper due.

The Goals of Punishment

Punishment by the state has similar goals. Suppose that Ben has stolen Louisa's car and has now been given a one-year prison sentence. In this act of punishment, the government (like Clare) aims to restore the proper order. Ben has created an imbalance that must be set right. He has rejected Louisa as a fellow member with whom he shares the good; he has treated her as a productive part, as someone he can harm for his own goals. Ultimately, he has placed himself above Louisa. Indeed, he has placed himself above the whole community. He thinks that he can disregard his fellow members of the community, as well as the rules of the community.

The punishment aims to restore the proper order (*ST*, I-II, 87, 1; *ST*, I-II, 87, 6). It puts Ben back down, so that he becomes subject to the community. Louisa herself is thereby lifted back up. The community recognizes her as someone who cannot be trampled upon, as someone who shares in the good. Like Clare's anger, the punishment also aims at a change of heart (*ST*, I-II, 87, 3, ad 2; *ST*, I-II, 87, 7; *QDM*, 2, 10, ad 4). Perhaps while sitting in prison, Ben will learn his lesson. He will recognize that he should not steal cars, and he will mend his ways.

The goals of punishment, then, are parallel to the goals that Clare hopes to achieve in her anger. Indeed, these goals parallel those that Sebastian hopes to achieve through his apology and recompense. All these actions—repentance, anger, and punishment—aim at a restoration of the proper relationship; all of them aim at the restoration of the shared good.

In one important way, anger and punishment differ from repentance. By its very notion, Sebastian's repentance includes a change of heart. In contrast, both the punishment and the anger hope to achieve a change of heart, but they might not succeed. After being given the cold shoulder, Sebastian might continue in his selfish ways, unconcerned about Clare. After his prison sentence, Ben might return to a life of crime.

Suppose that Clare recognizes that Sebastian is unrepentant. She thinks it unlikely that he will change. Nevertheless, she continues in her punitive behavior: she still refuses to talk to Sebastian. The two goals at which she aims, then, can be separated. She can seek the goal of restoring her proper place but abandon the goal of changing Sebastian's heart. The latter goal is not essential to her anger.

The same separation can occur in punishment. Even if Ben is a hardened criminal who is unlikely to change his ways, the government still aims to punish him (*ST*, II-II, 25, 6, ad 2; *ST*, II-II, 108, 4). Even if it cannot achieve the goal of reforming Ben, it can at least achieve the goal of restoring the proper order.

Aquinas distinguishes two goals of punishment. First, the goal of retribution aims to restore the proper order. Second, the medicinal goal seeks to change hearts. Between these two, retribution is most essential to punishment, although Aquinas says that human punishment always includes a medicinal element (*QDM*, 2, 10, ad 4).

Modern theories of punishment include other goals besides retribution and the reform of the criminal (Tadros 2011). Deterrence, for instance, is the goal of discouraging other people from wrongdoing. On account of his prison sentence, for instance, Ben himself might not change his ways, but perhaps other people will see his punishment and consequently will decide not to steal cars. Aquinas actually includes this goal under the medicinal element (*ST*, I-II, 87, 7). Punishment is medicinal, he says, either to the wrongdoer or to other people who are tempted to wrongdoing. It might reform the wrongdoer himself, but it might also reform others.

Before seeing how punishment is consistent with the precept to do no harm, we should make one last observation. Suppose that Ben regrets his action. He even goes so far as to return the car and apologize to Louisa. Nevertheless, the government might still punish Ben. The goal of reform is no longer relevant, since Ben has already reformed. Nevertheless, the punishment still makes sense, both on account of the goal of deterrence (just mentioned) and on account of the goal of retribution. Even though Ben has repented, the balance must still be set right; Ben must still be put down by the community, so that he can take his proper place as a part.

Punishment and the Shared Good

We are now prepared to see why punishment makes sense within the shared good. Why can the state put Ben in prison, although imprisonment is a kind of harm? More dramatically, why can the state go so far as capital punishment for more serious crimes such as murder? Since the ultimate human good is a shared good, it seems that we should take the precept "do harm to no one" quite literally. We should not narrow its scope, so that it applies most fully only to the innocent.

In fact, the narrower scope makes perfect sense. It follows upon the very choice of the wrongdoer (*SCG*, III, chap. 144, no. 4). Through his serious offense, says Aquinas, Ben has chosen to reject the shared good. As a possessing part, Ben shares in the good by seeking himself and his own good precisely as a part. He seeks his good as belonging to himself, but he also wants it as belonging to others. Viewing himself as a part, he directs himself to the whole. By stealing the car, however, he does the exact opposite. He rejects his role as a part and places himself above Louisa; indeed, he places himself above the whole community (*ST*, I-II, 87, 6). He does not see himself as a part who must share his partial good with others. Rather, he sees himself as above Louisa. He subjects Louisa to himself and to his goals. She is a kind of tool who can be directed, as a useful good, to a goal that is alien to her own good.

As we have seen, Aquinas distinguishes between two different kinds of parts within a community: possessing parts (called primary parts by Aquinas) and producing parts (called secondary parts) (*SCG*, III, chap. 112, no. 3). In an orchestra, for instance, the musicians are most properly called parts but the stage crew might be called parts in an extended or secondary way. Most properly, only possessing parts share in the good; they possess the good together with the other members. Merely producing parts do not possess the good but only produce it. The stage crew, for instance, does not actually play symphonic music. At most, they might possess the good of listening to music together, but this shared good is not the same as that of the orchestra, which is to play music together.

Because Ben has rejected his own role as a possessing part, he has become a secondary part. In a way, he is a producing part, for he may be harmed for the sake of a goal beyond his own personal good. In another way, he is something more than a producing part, for he still has the potential to be elevated, to change so that he might once again become a possessing part. Retribution depends upon Ben's rejection of the shared good; the medicinal goal of reform depends upon Ben's potential to once again become a possessing part.

Two Levels of Love

This duality within Ben suggests two levels of love. In the fullest sense, we share the good with those we love. Our acts of love are precisely acts of possessing the good together. This love includes two elements (*ST*, II-II, 27, 2, ad 2). On the one hand, we want the good for the one we love. On the other hand, we are united in the good with the one we love.

We cannot have this most complete love for Ben, because he has separated himself from the shared good. We cannot actually share the human good with Ben, at least as long as he refuses to love his own good as a part—that is, as long as he desires the good of others as useful for his own goals. The fullest sense of love, which includes a union with the beloved, is not possible. An obstacle (Ben's own choice) stands in the way of union; it stands in the way of actually sharing the good.

Still, as long as Ben has the potential to return, to become once again a possessing part, we can have at least the first element of love for him (*ST*, II-II, 25, 6). We can desire to share the good with him. We can hope that he will change, so that we can once again share the good with him. This hope—this love—is realized in the medicinal element of punishment. We want what is really good for him; we want him once again to share in the human good.

Someone might protest against this distinction between two levels of love. After all, the Christian injunction to love our neighbors as ourselves applies even to sinners. This objection, however, confuses two different kinds of love. In our discussion of punishment, we have been concerned with a natural love that we have for all other human beings, a natural love that cannot be realized fully for those who have chosen to separate themselves from the good. In contrast, the Christian injunction concerns a supernatural love of charity, by which we love God above all else. This love for God is also realized in the love for our neighbors. With the Christian love of charity, then, Louisa can still love Ben even though he has separated himself from the community. Her love of charity is first of all a love for God in himself; secondarily, she loves God insofar as his good can be realized in Ben. Even when directed to a sinner, then, Louisa's supernatural love retains the full notion of love. It is fully the love of God.

Let us descend from this theological digression and return to philosophy and the natural law. Suppose that Ben does repent. Now we can once again share the good with him. Surprisingly, the very act of punishing him might be an act of sharing the good with him. If he leaves himself alienated, if he continues to reject the shared good, then it cannot be an act of true sharing; it can be only something that might prepare the way for sharing the good. But if he repents, then the punishment can be an act of sharing the good. His good, as shared, demands that he be restored to his place as a part. The punishment achieves this restoration.

At this point, Aquinas prefers not to call it punishment. In the strictest sense, punishment is only for those who remain alienated from the shared good. For those who have repented, Aquinas prefers the word satisfaction (*ST*, I-II, 87, 6–7). Even after he has repented, Ben must make satisfaction. Just as Sebastian, when he is repentant, wishes to make up for his selfish deed, so Ben, when he is repentant, wishes to make up for his offense against Louisa. He wants to take his proper place. He wants to be subjected, as a part, to the community.

In satisfaction, the harm done to Ben is not most properly harm; on the contrary, it may be described as healing or restorative. Suppose that doctors perform a hysterectomy (removal of the uterus) upon Brenda because she has cancer of the uterus. In a way, the surgery is a kind of harm, because it removes one of Brenda's organs. Most properly, however, the surgery is not harm. It is a kind of benefit for Brenda. Similarly, the harm (of being put in prison) is actually a kind of benefit for Ben (*ST*, I-II, 87, 7). Of course, if Ben sufficiently reforms his ways, we might lessen the punishment (or satisfaction). In that case, he is making himself, on his own, into a part that is subjected to the whole.

One more possibility remains. Perhaps Ben refuses to repent. Additionally, he is so hardened a criminal that he has no realistic possibility of repentance. He has irreparably separated himself from the shared good. He no longer has even the potential to share in the good.

Two things follow. First, the possibility of love is entirely snuffed out. We can no longer even hope to share the good with Ben. Second, the medicinal element (seeking the reform of Ben) no longer makes any sense. In relation to Ben, punishment can only be retributive (although in relation to others, it might be a deterrent).

Fortunately, Aquinas thinks this miserable state is never completely reached in the present life. Ben might become very close to this state, but as long as free will remains, the possibility of reform remains. According to Aquinas's theology, evildoers become irredeemable only in the next life; in hell, they become confirmed in evil (*QDV*, 24, 11). For these individuals, we can have no charitable love (*ST*, II-II, 25, 11). We cannot want what is impossible. We cannot want to share the good with them. As long as Ben is alive, however, we can still will the good for him. We can punish him, hoping that he will be restored to the shared good.

Punishment as an Act of the State

Punishment conforms to both of the clarifications (of the precept against harming) suggested at the beginning of this chapter. Punishment is not directed to the innocent but only to the guilty. In addition, punishment cannot be carried out by a private individual but only by the proper authorities of the community (*ST*, II-II, 64, 3).

This latter restriction can be seen by way of contrast with Clare's punitive actions against Sebastian, such as her refusal to talk with him. Clare is refusing to share the good (or an aspect of it) with Sebastian. She has her own part of the shared good, which she can then give to others. She decides that she will no longer give the good of conversation to Sebastian.

This punitive action falls short of punishment because Clare does not take Sebastian's good from him. She just refrains from giving him her own good. For Clare as a private individual, this punitive action may be acceptable. It concerns her own personal good, over which she legitimately has immediate control.

Suppose that Clare goes a step further. In her anger, she takes Sebastian's jacket from him. Now she not only refuses to share the good with him but also takes his good from him. Now she steps beyond her own personal good and into Sebastian's part of the shared good. Within the shared good, Clare is given authority or sovereignty over her own good but not over the good of Sebastian, whose particular part within the shared good falls under his own jurisdiction.

The whole community, however, can sometimes give direction to Sebastian's good. His good is part of the overall shared good. Sometimes the community (or its representatives) can direct the manner in which he should share his good with the community. They might demand (in the form of traffic laws) that his acts of driving should conform to patterns laid down by the community. They might demand (in the form of taxation) that a certain portion of his possessions be used for community projects. We will look at Aquinas's account of private property later (in chapter 24). For the moment, it suffices to mention that property, as far as Aquinas is concerned, must always be used for the sake of the shared good (*ST*, II-II, 66, 2). For this reason (and others), the community can make demands upon Sebastian in his use of property; it can, for instance, take a portion in the form of taxation.

The power of the community to direct Sebastian is limited. Most dramatically, it is limited by the boundary of harm. Since Sebastian is innocent (or has not been judged guilty in court), he cannot be harmed, even by the community (*ST*, II-II, 64, 2). He remains a subject of the shared good. By harming him, we would be directing him to a good alien from himself. Whatever the nature of this alien good, it is not the shared good, which should belong to Sebastian as well as to others. In other words, not only is Clare as a private citizen prohibited from harming Sebastian; so also is the state.

In Ben's case, however, this limitation no longer holds. He himself has rejected the shared good and his part within it. He has ceased to be a possessing part and has become a secondary part. The community, which in general can give direction to his good, can now give direction to his harm. It—and it alone—can direct Ben and his harm to the restoration of the proper order. Louisa herself cannot do so, even though she has been offended against.

Suicide

The prohibition against harm arising from a private citizen is comprehensive. An individual cannot even harm him or herself (*ST*, II-II, 65, 1). For this reason, suicide is against the natural law (*ST*, II-II, 64, 5). If Mark is depressed and no longer wants to go on living, it does not follow that he can kill himself. He cannot determine his own guilt, and even if he has been found guilty, he himself cannot direct his own harm to the restoration of the shared good.

Suppose that Mark has painful terminal cancer and wants to end his suffering by suicide. He decides that his life is no longer worth living. The pain outweighs the joy. Even in this case, the natural law prohibits his suicide. Recall that Mark does not live his life for himself, or at least not for himself alone. He is a member of the shared good. He should seek his good as belonging to others. He should seek to use even his suffering for the benefit of others.

Of course, he can take pain medication and other measures to reduce his suffering, and these measures can, in most cases, eliminate mere physical suffering. They do not eliminate, however, a deeper suffering of the soul. They do not eliminate a sense of isolation, a sense of emptiness, or a sense of humiliating dependence upon others. These sufferings—and not bodily sufferings—are typically what drive people to suicide.

In the individualistic world we have created in our modern age, we each pursue our own personal fulfillment. Other people are important to us to the degree that they contribute to this fulfillment. Otherwise, they only get in the way. Those who are disabled, no longer useful, or unpleasant are often deemed a waste of our time.

When we ourselves become one of these useless eaters (a term that Hitler used for these individuals), when we become an unnecessary consumer of resources, an annoyance and bother to others, then it seems we have no more reason to live. Indeed, some thinkers are now promoting the idea that we, in this condition, have a duty to kill ourselves (Hardwig 1997). After all, we have become a drain upon others, who have better things to do with their lives than waste them upon us. We should not selfishly cling to life. Such, at any rate, is the argument of these thinkers, who have the audacity to label as selfish those who wish to go on living when they have become "unnecessary consumers of resources." This label only increases the burden imposed by the emptiness of our individualistic world.

In reality, this ode to the virtues of suicide comes from a world that finds other people a burden (Ackerman 2000). Even children become nothing more than a burden, an obstacle to our personal fulfillment and aggrandizement, a nuisance in the way of our careers. They can be disposed of like a worn-out T-shirt, at least if they are still in the womb.

In another world, in a world of the shared good, those who suffer from cancer or other disabling conditions and those who are helpless and needy might not feel abandoned or alone and unwanted. They might find, in others, the comfort they need. They might find, in others, a meaning and purpose to their lives.

When suicide is trumpeted as an easy solution, however, then abandonment is likely the long-term consequence. Why should we bother helping those who are suffering when the suffering can be resolved through suicide?

We will all suffer in this life. Not all suffering, however, is a curse to be avoided. Sometimes, it is a source of growth. Sometimes, it becomes the pathway by which we can help others. We are not meant to be alone. We are meant to live our lives for others. Our good must be their good. One consequence of the shared good is that we should not harm even ourselves. We must continue to seek our own good, because our good belongs to others.

The prohibition against harming oneself must be slightly qualified. We do have the authority to do minor reparable harms to ourselves. We can donate blood, for instance, which does minor temporary harm to ourselves. We are given care over our own good, not to the point where we can define our good or to the point of defining ourselves out of the shared good. Rather, we have care to order minor harms to the shared good. Indeed, in some manner, the harm is for our own good. By donating blood, we do a minor physical harm for the sake of a greater spiritual good of helping others (*ST*, II-II, 26, 5). Likewise, by permitting the minor harm of incisions for surgery, we gain a greater bodily good for ourselves.

The prohibition against harm—by the private individual—is indeed comprehensive. We cannot harm others, and we cannot harm ourselves. No wonder, then, that the precept against harm states that we should, "do harm to *no one*."

The harm that is allowed (in punishment) is severely restricted. It can be carried out only by proper authorities; these authorities must follow proper procedures, such as the use of fair criminal trials; and finally, after guilt has been determined, the punishment cannot be a mere utility, in which the guilty person becomes a useful cog for the rest of us. Instead, the punishment must be to restore the proper order and to benefit the guilty person.

chapter 14

War

Unjust war is to be abhorred; but woe to the nation that does not make ready to hold its own in time of need against all who would harm it! And woe thrice over to the nation in which the average man loses the fighting edge, loses the power to serve as a soldier if the day of need should arise!

—Theodore Roosevelt, Speech at the University of Berlin, May 12, 1910

He will win who knows when to fight and when not to fight.

—Sun Tzu, *The Art of War*

Punishment is not the only instance in which Aquinas allows harm. Harm is also allowed in a just war and in self-defense (*ST*, II-II, 40, 1; *ST*, II-II, 64, 7). Like punishments, these two cases are justified only by clarifying the precept against harm. "Do harm to no one" means (1) that we must never do harm as a private citizen and (2) that we must do harm to no innocent person.

The application of these clarified precepts to the case of war is not as obvious as in the case of punishment. Just wars easily conform with the first clarification: they may be carried out only by the proper authorities. The second clarification, however, is more problematic. Many enemy soldiers act in good faith, even though their country might be acting unjustly. On account of propaganda, they may be unaware of any injustice done by their country. Just wars, then, seem to be opposed to the rule "do harm to no innocent person."

Self-defense easily conforms with the second clarification. In most cases of self-defense, the attacker is likely guilty, or at least is choosing to act unjustly. Self-defense, however, does not seem to meet the first clarification. It is not carried out by a representative of the state but by a private citizen. Self-defense, then, seems to be opposed to the rule "as a private citizen, do harm to no one."

These two cases, together with punishment, pose another difficulty. If the natural law allows harming in punishment, in just wars, and in self-defense, then perhaps it will also allow Traci to harm Louis. Perhaps we might describe the hostage situation as a kind of miniature war, or perhaps we might say that Traci is acting in defense of the hostages.

In the end, Aquinas does not condone the act of killing Louis. It cannot be justified after the manner of harming in war or in self-defense. Just as suicide is not permitted, so also Traci is not permitted to harm Louis. In order to better understand the limitations that apply to Traci, we must first understand why harm is allowed in just wars and in self-defense.

Just and Unjust Wars

A great many wars in human history have not been justified. War is often the tool of the powerful to gain more power at the expense of the lives of the poor and exploited. Such wars, even when declared by the proper authorities, do not justify harm to others. Harming in war is justified only when the war itself is justified.

It is not difficult to see that some wars might well be justified. Defensive wars are the clearest cases. If out of greed for power, one country attacks another country, then this latter country is certainly justified in defending itself through military means. When the tanks of Hitler's

Germany rolled through Poland in 1939, for instance, the Polish people were justified in taking up arms in their defense. Other causes besides national defense might also justify certain wars. Suppose the leaders of a country engage in gross injustices against its own citizens. A second country might be justified in going to war to stop these injustices.

The conditions of a just war are fairly stringent (*ST*, II-II, 40, 1):

(1) The war must be declared by the proper authorities, and it must be carried out by the proper representatives—that is, by those (such as soldiers) who have been designated for military operations.

(2) The war must have a just cause. In other words, it should not be carried out for unworthy purposes, such as increased power for the country or the leader. Rather, it must be carried out, as with the examples suggested above, for the sake of justice.

(3) The war must be carried out in a just manner. The most important aspect of this condition, for our purposes, is the restriction on who may be harmed. Innocent civilians in the enemy population may not be harmed, even in a just war.

(4) Peaceful ways of resolving the issue (that seem reasonable) must be tried first.

(5) There must be a reasonable chance of success.

(6) The just cause must be worth all the suffering that will result from the war.

We do not need to examine all these conditions. The sixth condition will be of some interest in chapter 16, but in this chapter we are interested only in the first and third conditions. The first condition requires no further discussion, since it clearly lines up with the idea that private citizens should not harm others.

Combatants and Noncombatants

Only the third condition remains to be discussed. It protects the innocent from harm, even in warfare. The armies carrying out a just war must not kill indiscriminately. In order to uphold this restriction, a distinction is made between innocent civilians and combatants. In a just war, the latter may be harmed but not the former. Bombs should be used, for instance, to target military sites and military personnel. They should not be used to destroy cities and kill the noncombatants living in them.

Soldiers are clear examples of combatants. Healthcare personnel, who are tending to the sick and injured, are clear examples of noncombatants. They are noncombatants even if they are healing injured soldiers who might later return to battle. Their medical acts, while potentially helping the war effort, are not themselves acts of war.

Sometimes the line between combatants and noncombatants is not so clear-cut. For instance, what about the personnel who work in an explosives factory? Unlike soldiers, they are not engaging in acts of killing. On the other hand, they are directly making weapons to be used for the war. Consequently, such individuals are often classified as combatants. Generally, we might define combatants as those who are engaged in the war effort. Admittedly, this definition does not resolve all difficulties, but it provides a standard from which to work.

Innocence and Guilt

Another worry—for the precept "do harm to no one"—is that even the combatants might be innocent. The average soldier under an unjust leader often believes, as a result of propaganda, that their country's cause is just. They themselves may be ignorant of the injustice of their leader. When Hitler unjustly attacked Poland, for instance, many of the German soldiers would have come to believe in the justice of the cause. Or again, many who work in munitions factories are simply trying to make a living to support their families. Unaware of the injustice of the cause, they cannot be blamed for any wrongdoing.

The resolution of this concern depends upon a distinction between performing a wrong action and being to blame for this wrongdoing (*ST*, I-II, 21, 2–3). Sometimes, the distinction is clear enough. Suppose, for instance, that Don is a postal worker who delivers a bomb to Anna, resulting in her death. Delivering deadly bombs is certainly an atrocious action. Nevertheless, Don is not to blame for this action, since he had no idea that the package contained a bomb.

The disconnect between the performance of a wrong action and the blame for it arises on account of ignorance. Don was ignorant that he was delivering a bomb, so he is not to blame for the action. Soldiers within an army might also be ignorant of the evil they do. Don is ignorant that the action he performs is in any way harmful. The soldiers cannot claim such ignorance. Nevertheless, they might have another kind of ignorance. They might be ignorant that the harmful actions they perform are unjustified. They might innocently believe that they are carrying out a just war.

As we have seen, the harm of punishment is justified, in part, because the wrongdoer has been judged guilty in a fair trial. No such trial is given to the individual soldiers. In what way, then, is the harm in a just war restricted to those who are guilty?

Ideally, a fair trial would be given to all. Realistically, no such trial can be given. The needs of the situation demand action. The attacking soldiers must be fought off. No time can be taken for a trial, and the soldiers would not submit to a trial.

While the individual soldiers cannot be properly judged, the nation as a whole can be. Indeed, in a justified war, this judgment upon the nation has been reached to the degree that the circumstances permit. In other words, before war is declared, it has been determined (as part of the second condition) that the enemy nation is engaged in unjust actions. Ignorance might absolve particular individuals (such as certain soldiers) of personal guilt. Nevertheless, they are carrying out the unjust actions of their country. In this sense, at least, they are guilty, even if ignorance might remove some or all of their personal blame.

We should not imagine, however, that in every case the individual soldiers are blameless. Often, they have a sense that their cause is unjust; they have a sense that they should not be cooperating in this evil action. Some individual soldiers, no doubt, are blameless. Nevertheless, the harm done to them is justified because they are engaging in the wrongful actions of carrying out an unjust war.

chapter 15

Self-Defense

The world is in greater peril from those who tolerate or encourage evil than from those who actually commit it.

—Albert Einstein, Tribute to Pablo Casals

In some ways, self-defense is like a just war. Suppose that Scott is attacking Barb, who is forced to defend herself. She takes a gun and shoots Scott, thereby killing him. Barb has done harm to Scott; furthermore, Scott has not been judged guilty through a fair trial. Nevertheless, he may be presumed guilty. He was clearly engaging in an unjust action. The circumstances, however, prevented a fair trial. Barb was forced to act immediately, based upon Scott's patently unjust action. As with the just war, Barb seems justified in setting aside any concern over whether Scott might perhaps be acting blamelessly on account of ignorance.

In self-defense, then, the worry over doing harm to the innocent is addressed in much the same way as in a just war. Unlike a just war, however, the act of self-defense seems to oppose the other restriction upon harm: it is carried out by a private individual. Barb is not a police officer or some other representative of the community. She is only a private individual, and yet she seems justified in harming Scott.

Killing (or otherwise harming) in self-defense will prove to be a more complicated case of harm than any we have so far discussed. In this chapter, we will restrict our considerations to a simpler account, one more in line with the justifications of punishment and just wars. In the next chapter, we will include some instances of self-defense under another justification of harm, one that will avoid the worries of both innocence and private citizenship.

Public Authorities and Private Citizens

Since Barb acts as a private citizen, it seems that she harms Scott unjustly. She violates the precept, "As a private citizen, do harm to no one." Intuitively, however, we think that Barb should not be concerned about her status as a private citizen. She should act in her own defense, even if she must harm Scott. This intuition makes sense when we observe two points.

First, we must recognize that the community (through the government) designates certain individuals as officials that can harm in certain emergency situations. In Pat's hostage situation, for instance, police officers or members of a SWAT team might be justified in killing Pat, although he has not undergone a fair trial. As with a just war, the emergency situation demands action without a trial.

The second point requires an understanding of human law, which we will discuss later in greater detail. For the moment, we need to note merely that most human laws hold for the most part and not in every situation. In some circumstances, they have exceptions (*ST*, I-II, 96, 6). Suppose, for instance, that Jody is in urgent need of medical care. Kevin is driving her to the emergency room at 2 a.m., when little traffic occupies the road. He comes to a red light. It is reasonable for him, in the situation, to drive through the red light (while looking carefully for any cars on the road). The law that he must stop at a red light holds for the most part, but it has exceptions in unusual circumstances.

Sometimes, we can go to an authority and ask for an exception. Someone might go to a judge, for instance, and ask for an exception to some general law. In emergency situations, however, Aquinas says that we cannot have recourse to the proper authority. We must make the exception by ourselves. Kevin is clearly in this situation. He cannot go to a police officer and ask whether, in this case, he can drive through the red light. He has no extra time but must get to the hospital as soon as possible.

The designation of some individuals as officials that can harm in certain situations has its source in human laws. Reasonably, then, this designation has exceptions. Sometimes, individuals who have not been designated as officials (such as Barb) can nevertheless act as officials. Barb does not have time to go to the authorities to ask for designation as a public official. She is like Kevin who, in running the red light in order to get to the emergency room, must make an exception on his own account without going to an authority.

Ownership of property provides a closer parallel than traffic laws to the case of self-defense. Consider the following situation.

> *Raft Rescue*: Beatrice is in the lake unable to swim. Joe hears her terrified screams but is himself unable to swim. Fortunately, he sees a nearby raft, which he uses to save Beatrice. The boat belongs to Cora, whom Joe does not know.

Ownership is designated by human laws. The boat belongs to Cora on account of certain laws concerning buying, selling, and so forth. Should we say, then, that Joe has committed a wrongful act—the act of stealing a raft—in order to save Beatrice? Not according to Aquinas (*ST*, II-II, 66, 7). In emergencies, says Aquinas, the legal ownership no longer holds. Instead, the raft belongs to everyone in need of it, which includes Joe. Once the need has passed, of course, he must restore the boat to Cora.

The parallel with Barb is clear. Joe is not legally designated the owner of the raft, but in the emergency situation, the raft becomes his for use. Similarly, Barb is not legally designated as an official that can use force, but in the emergency situation she becomes such an official.

In some legal jurisdictions, the authority of a private citizen to harm is quite explicit. In other words, the law—under certain constrained circumstances—makes individuals who are otherwise private citizens into individuals with the authority to harm. The so-called castle doctrine, for instance, authorizes the owner of a home to use harmful defensive action. Furthermore, in some jurisdictions, common law gives the authority to use reasonable force (or violence) in self-defense.

Even if the law does not explicitly give Barb authority, she might reasonably act as Joe does with regard to the boat. In an emergency, public authority is given to those who need it.

In this manner, harming in self-defense becomes acceptable. Barb is not acting as a private individual but as a public authority. Furthermore, she is harming someone presumed guilty on account of his guilty behavior. When properly understood, she is not violating the precept "do harm to no one."

Harming the Innocent

After seeing these justifications of harm in the case of punishment, just war, and self-defense, perhaps you are beginning to wonder whether harm might be justified whenever some greater good might be achieved. Perhaps Traci can kill Louis in order to save the hostages after all. Perhaps her case is one more instance of justified harm.

Harming others, we have seen, is not justified in terms of the greater good. It is justified only toward people who have cut themselves off from the shared good. They have chosen to reject the shared good, or at least they have, with their actions, attacked the shared good. Either guilt must be determined through a fair trial or presumed guilt must be revealed in behavior (such as attacking) in situations in which a fair trial is unrealistic. Only under these conditions may harm be done.

These conditions might reasonably be applied to Pat. If Traci has an opportunity to kill Pat, then she may. These conditions do not apply to Louis, however. He is not engaging in any unjust action. Consequently, Traci cannot kill Louis. Killing the innocent is never justified, whatever good results one hopes to achieve.

chapter 16

Consequences

> Human beings are masters of their own actions by way of reason and will. Therefore, those actions are properly called human which proceed from a deliberate will.
>
> —Thomas Aquinas, *Summa theologiae*, I-II, 1, 1

Have we settled the question of what Traci should do? It would seem so. She should not kill Louis for two reasons. First, he is innocent; second, she is a private citizen rather than a public authority. Traci fails the two standards required for harm to be morally acceptable: the person harmed must in some manner be guilty and the person doing the harming must in some manner be a public official.

Despite this seemingly straightforward answer, some questions still remain. After all, some cases of morally acceptable harm do not seem to meet the two conditions. Consider the following situation.

Collateral Damage: Dan is fighting in the cause of a just war. The enemy armies are advancing and are approaching a key bridge that crosses a wide river. Dan is ordered to fly his plane and bomb the bridge in order to prevent

> the advance of the army. If he does not succeed, the enemy armies will cause untold death and misery. As Dan is flying low in order to drop his bombs accurately upon the bridge, he notices a young girl walking upon the bridge. If he destroys the bridge, she will almost certainly die. Dan drops the bombs. The bridge is destroyed, and the girl dies.

Dan's action seems morally acceptable, yet the action does not meet the first condition; the girl he kills is clearly innocent. Still, if Dan does not destroy the bridge, the enemy army will likely kill many more innocent girls.

Consider another familiar case.

> *Runaway Trolley*: A trolley is heading down the tracks, but it cannot be stopped. Trapped upon the track are five individuals who will be killed when the trolley runs into them. By pulling a lever, however, Kay has the opportunity to divert the trolley down another track. On this other track, only one individual (Mike) is trapped. Kay diverts the trolley. The trolley runs into Mike and kills him.

In some way, Kay has harmed Mike, who was in no danger before Kay intervened. Nevertheless, Kay's action seems acceptable, despite meeting neither of the two conditions: Mike is in no way guilty, and Kay is only a private individual.

The Distinction between an Action and Its Consequences

The actions in both *Collateral Damage* and *Runaway Trolley* are seemingly justified based upon consequentialist reasoning; the agent, in each case, appears to bring about a greater good. If such reasoning is acceptable in these two cases, then why not in others? Why not apply this reasoning to Traci's case? In short, why not suppose that Traci's action of killing Louis is justified because it brings about the greater good, saving 20 lives at the cost of only one?

As we have seen, consequentialist reasoning runs afoul of the distinction between doing evil and failing to do good. By killing Louis, Traci does evil. In contrast, by refusing to kill Louis, she does no evil; she merely foresees the evil that Pat will do. Similarly (in *Limited Linda*), by choosing to save Norbert from drowning, Linda does no evil to Chris, although she foresees that he will drown with no one to help him.

Unfortunately, Dan does not seem to have recourse to this distinction. Dan himself harms the innocent girl. Evidently, we should conclude that Dan does evil and that his action is morally unacceptable. Instead, we conclude the opposite: bombing the bridge is morally acceptable, although Dan also kills the girl. Kay is in a similar situation (although less clearly). By diverting the trolley, she positively does harm to Mike. Nevertheless, her action is morally good.

In these cases, another distinction is at work. Or rather, the same distinction is at work, but the need for clarification requires a new manner of speaking. We will now speak of the difference between an action and its consequences (*ST*, I-II, 7, 3). Dan performs the action of destroying a bridge; the death of the girl is a consequence of his action. Similarly, Kay performs an action of diverting the trolley away from the five people; Mike's subsequent death is a consequence of her action.

This distinction is clear in the case of *Limited Linda*. Linda performs the action of saving Norbert from drowning; the subsequent death of Chris might be described as a consequence of her action. Even in the case of *Garrulous Gary*, the death of Libby may be described as a consequence of Gary's action (talking with David). In other words, the distinction between an action and its consequences has already been at work in our analysis of the difference between doing evil and failing to do good.

Unfortunately, in the case of *Collateral Damage*, it is far from clear where we should draw the line between action and consequence. Where does Dan's action end and where do its consequences begin? We naturally say that Dan kills the little girl. Why describe her death, then, as a consequence rather than as part of his action? A similar ambiguity plagues *Runaway Trolley*. We might describe Kay's action as killing Mike. Why suppose, then, that Mike's death is merely a consequence of her action?

Outside the context of morals, we readily distinguish between an action and its consequences. Dan takes medication for his illness, for instance, and he recognizes that it will make him drowsy and give him a headache. These are consequences—or side effects—of his action.

Once again, however, the divide between an action and its consequences is not always clear. We can say, for instance, that Dan made himself drowsy. This manner of speaking, it seems, places the effect of sleepiness within the action itself rather than outside the action (in the domain of consequence). Which is correct? Does Dan perform an act of taking healing medicine with the consequence that he gets drowsy? Or does Dan perform an act of making himself drowsy? Where exactly does Dan's action end, and where do its consequences begin?

Drawing the line between an action and its consequences is critical for natural law theory (*ST*, I-II, 7, 4). In *Collateral Damage*, for instance, the divide between an action and its consequences determines whether Dan violates the precept to "do harm to no one." If the death of the girl is only a consequence, then Dan's action (of destroying the bridge) does not fall under the precept. On the other hand, if Dan kills the girl, then his action does indeed fall under the precept "do harm to no one."

The importance of identifying actions—of determining precisely what an agent does—should be no surprise. After all, law is a directive of human action. We must know what an action is, then, before we can know how it is directed.

The Importance of Plans

The divide between action and consequences seems clearer in another case.

> *Cacophonous Kenny*: Kenny is pounding nails as he builds a shed. As he pounds, he makes a loud noise, which frightens off a flock of nearby crows. He also wakes his neighbor Jean, whose day is ruined on account of the racket.

What exactly is Kenny doing? Is he pounding nails with the consequence that he frightens some crows? Or is he simply frightening some crows? Is he building a shed with the consequence that he wakes his neighbor? Or is he performing the act of waking his neighbor? And so on.

Suppose that Joyce drops by as Kenny is working, and she asks him what he is doing. He answers that he is building a shed. She replies, "Oh, I thought you were scaring off some crows."

Kenny would be forced to reply that he is indeed scaring off some crows. Still, the scaring of crows, he might protest, is not what he is up to. He is properly building a shed, and it just happens that, as a consequence, he also scares off some crows.

To emphasize the point, let us slightly modify the scenario.

> *Bothersome Birds*: Beth is planning to begin work on her shed at 11 a.m., but now (at 7 a.m.) she notices a large flock of crows in her backyard. She decides to go out and begin pounding (as part of her project of building the shed) in order to scare off the crows.

Scaring the crows is not something that Beth just happens to do as she is going about other business. Rather, scaring off crows is part of her deliberate project. Of course, she is also pounding nails, and she is also building a shed. Unlike Kenny, however, Beth is also setting out to frighten the crows. If Joyce asks Beth what she is doing, she might well reply, "I am scaring off some crows."

The difference between the two cases depends upon the agent's plans (Bratman 1987). Kenny plans to build a shed, but he has no plan to scare off the crows. In contrast, Beth deliberately sets out to scare the crows. The difference in plans leads to a difference in what the agent is most properly doing. Kenny is not most properly frightening crows; Beth is.

The importance of plans is no surprise. Human beings are reasoning beings. Consequently, human actions are most properly rational actions (*ST*, I-II, 1,1). With our reason, however, we make plans. Consequently, what we do—precisely as human beings—is what we plan to do (*ST*, I-II, 1, 3).

Another contrast will drive home the point.

> *Troublesome Twitch*: Kenny has a nervous tic over which he has no control; periodically, his head twitches to the left. As he builds his shed, he at times twitches his head.

When Kenny says that he is building a shed, Joyce replies, "Oh, I thought you were twitching your head." In some way, of course, Kenny is twitching his head. He is not doing it, however, as a rational being who makes choices (*ST*, I-II, 1, 1, ad 3). We might say, instead, that the action *happens* to Kenny. It is not an action rationally chosen, but an event that is beyond Kenny's rational control.

Three Levels of Actions

These three cases (*Cacophonous Kenny*, *Bothersome Birds*, and *Troublesome Twitch*) give us three levels of actions. At the highest level, Beth deliberately scares off the crows. At a slightly lower level, Kenny scares off the crows, but it is not what he plans to do; it is more a consequence of what he plans to do. At the lowest level, Kenny twitches his head, over which he has no rational control.

The question "what is Kenny doing," then, can have different kinds of answers. He is building a shed, he is scaring crows, and he is twitching his head. These three answers do not use the same meaning of "action" or of "doing." Most properly, Kenny is building a shed, for that is what he plans to do as a reasoning person. Secondarily, he is scaring crows, which he foresees as somehow belonging to his plan, although it is not what he sets out to do. Finally, Kenny's "action" refers to what his body happens to do completely independent of any rational input from his plans.

A similar distinction can apply to Dan and his action. What exactly is Dan doing when he drops the bombs? How might he answer the question "What are you doing?" He is likely to reply that he is destroying a bridge. If you point out that he is killing the girl, then he must concede the point. If you point out that he is perspiring, then once again he must concede the point.

These concessions, however, come with a qualification. "Yes, I am perspiring," he might reply, "but that is not a human action that I am performing. It is not something that I in any way plan to do." Similarly, he might reply, "Yes, I am killing a little girl, but that is not what I am most properly doing as a human being. Most properly, I am destroying a bridge, for that is what I plan to do. I foresee that my plan comes with the unfortunate consequence that the girl will die."

A slightly modified scenario, parallel to the case of *Bothersome Birds*, clarifies the point.

> *Vicious Victor*: Victor is in the exact same situation as Dan, but when he sees the girl, he is thrilled because he likes killing children. He goes out of his way to make sure that the girl will die.

Both Dan and Victor kill the girl, but they do not seem to be on an equal plane (pun intended). Victor sets out to kill the girl; Dan does not. Victor is like Beth, who sets out to scare the crows. Dan is like Kenny, who does not plan to scare the crows. Most properly, Victor is killing a little girl. In contrast, Dan is most properly destroying a bridge; secondarily, he is killing a little girl, which he foresees as something belonging to his plan, although it is not what he sets out to do. In an even lesser sense, Dan is perspiring, as a kind of action that happens completely independent of any rational input from his plans.

Means and Ends

As reasoning beings, we most properly do what we plan to do. The most obvious part of any plan is the goal we hope to achieve (*ST*, I-II, 12, 2). Kenny aims to build a shed; Dan hopes to stop the oncoming army; Victor also hopes to stop the army, but in addition he aims to kill the girl. This aspect of our plans is unproblematic. It generates no dispute over the identification of rational action.

Another aspect of our plans, however, has given rise to disputes. Our plans include not only the goals we seek but also the means we choose to achieve these goals (*ST*, I-II, 12, 2). Dan's plan, for instance, includes not only the goal of stopping the army but also the means of destroying the bridge. Dan aims to stop the army by way of destroying the bridge. Few people dispute that our plans include the means as well as the end or goal; rather, the dispute concerns the manner of identifying and characterizing the means.

Consider Kay as she pulls the lever. What is her plan? She aims to save the five people (her goal) by way of diverting the train down another track (her means). But is that all? Does she plan to kill Mike? Clearly, killing Mike is not one of her goals, but is it a means that she chooses?

The answer to this question cannot be brushed aside by claiming that we have already identified her means (diverting the train). This reasoning will not do, for we typically choose multiple means to achieve our goals. Kay, for instance, chooses the means of diverting the train, but she diverts the train by means of pulling the lever. A more complete description of her plan, then, would be as follows: she saves the five by way of diverting the train by way of pulling the lever. Does something similar apply to killing Mike? Is this action one of the means she chooses in order to save the five?

It does not seem to be. The death of Mike is like frightening the crows for Kenny. Kenny recognizes that he will scare off the crows, but this result is neither a goal nor a means of building the shed. Similarly, the death of Mike is neither a goal for Kay nor any means toward this goal.

Two Directions of Causality

The direction of causality is important for the plan of action. For Dan, taking medicine causes health, which is his goal. On the other hand, neither getting drowsy nor getting a headache causes Dan to get healthy. Similarly, for Kenny, pounding causes the shed to be built; the frightening of the crows does not cause the shed to be built. For Dan, the destruction of the bridge causes the army to stop; the death of the girl does not. For Kay, diverting the train causes the five to be saved; the death of Mike does not.

The second item in each of these pairs does not cause the goal to come about; rather, the means adopted causes these results to happen. Taking the medicine causes drowsiness; pounding causes the frightening of the crows; the destruction of the bridge causes the death of the girl; the diversion of the train causes the death of Mike.

Within a plan, the means we choose are precisely those things that cause the goal to come about (*ST*, I-II, 14, 5). Kenny chooses the means of pounding nails because this action brings about the goal of building the shed. Dan chooses the means of destroying the bridge because this action brings about the goal of stopping the army.

Indeed, as we are forming plans, we begin with the goal and then look for possible causes to achieve the goal (*ST*, I-II, 14, 5). Dan begins with the goal of stopping the army, and then he looks for causes. Destroying the bridge is one possibility. After settling upon this means, he then looks for causes by which he might destroy the bridge. He can achieve this new (more proximate) goal by dropping bombs upon the bridge. Such is our reasoning when forming plans. We are always looking for causes, which serve as the means to achieve the goal.

Kenny would never reason in the following manner: I must pound nails, and I know that scaring off crows causes the pounding of nails; therefore, I must choose to scare off the crows as a means to cause the pounding. Kenny cannot reason in this manner (at least if he is truly rational) because scaring crows does not cause nails to be pounded; rather, the pounding of nails causes crows to be frightened. The frightening of crows is attached to the pounding not because it causes the pounding but because the pounding causes the frightening.

The Importance of Consequences in Our Plans

When forming plans, we search for the causes to achieve our goals, but we also consider the consequences of the means chosen (*ST*, I-II, 20, 5). Suppose that Bob has the goal of getting in better shape. He recognizes that a regular exercise program is a cause of getting in shape. Then he considers possible exercise programs, such as swimming or jogging. So far, he is looking for the causes that will bring about his goal. But next, he switches gears. He looks at the consequences of these possible means. Jogging, for instance, can have bad consequences for his knees, which are already a little weak. The program of swimming also has consequences. The available times to swim are limited, so that if he chooses to swim, he will be unable to make his weekly meeting with his good friend.

These consequences add important considerations to his deliberations. Essentially, he is trying to evaluate each of his possible means to determine which means is best. The consequences are critical elements of this evaluation.

For the same reason, Kenny might be concerned with the consequences of his action of building a shed by way of pounding. It has the consequence of frightening crows, which may not bother him that much (if he does not care for crows). At the same time, it has the consequence of waking and irritating his neighbor Jean. This consequence might lead him to change his plans, so that he begins building the shed a couple hours later.

Similarly, Dan evaluates the means of destroying the bridge by looking at the consequences. In his mind, many consequences are insignificant. For instance, he will make a loud noise and a bright flash. The consequence of killing the girl, on the other hand, might lead him to reevaluate his plans. Perhaps upon reconsideration, he will go forward with his plan; nevertheless, the consequence of killing the girl is not irrelevant to his deliberations.

The Need for Further Clarification

In this chapter, the divide between action and consequence has been clarified. We do what we plan to do. Our plans include both the goal and the means chosen to achieve the goal. The means are those things that cause the goal (and, in particular, those causes upon which we settle as the way to achieve the goal). The consequences do not cause the goal; rather, they are caused by the means chosen (and sometimes even by the goal itself).

As we proceed, this explanation of the distinction between an action and its consequences will need clarification. Confusion will arise. After all, consequences can also be described as actions. Dan's action, for instance, can be legitimately described as killing a girl. When we see an action described in terms of its consequences, we might become confused over the boundary between the action and its consequences. Potential confusions will be considered in the next two chapters.

chapter 17

Four Errors

> The least initial deviation from the truth is multiplied later a thousandfold.
>
> —Aristotle, *On the Heavens*

The distinction between an action and its consequences can be clarified by considering various erroneous classifications (Bennett 1995). Four common errors cast doubt upon the precise nature of the means chosen. For convenience, we will call these errors (1) lumping together, (2) dropping options, (3) turning a blind eye, and (4) slicing thin.

Lumping Together

As you might expect, the error of lumping together conjoins actions and consequences. The two lose their distinction. Consequences, because they can be described as actions, are deemed identical with the actions that cause them.

This lumping arises on account of three features that actions and consequences share. First (as we have already seen), both actions and consequences involve causality. Second (as we have also seen), both actions and their consequences are important in our deliberations. Bob, for instance, considers both the action of jogging (as a means to getting in shape) and the consequence of damage to his knees. Third, at least sometimes both the action and its consequences can have a certain necessity within a plan. Given the situation, Kenny will necessarily scare off the crows—if he wants to build the shed. For Kenny's goal, then, both the pounding and the frightening of crows are necessary. Similarly, Dan does need to kill the girl on the bridge, if he is going to destroy the bridge. For his goal of stopping the army, then, both the destruction of the bridge and the killing of the girl are necessary.

None of these similarities should distract us from the real difference between actions and their consequences. Both actions and consequences involve causality, but their causality (as we have seen) involves two different directions. On the one hand, the means (which are the actions) *cause* the goal. On the other hand, the consequences *are caused* by the means. In Kenny's case, for instance, pounding *causes* the shed to be built (his goal); in contrast, the frightening of the crows *is caused* by the pounding (his chosen means).

Similarly, both actions and consequences are important in our deliberations, but they are important in different ways. The action of jogging is important to Bob because it causes the goal he hopes to achieve. The consequence of damaged knees is important not because it causes the goal of getting in shape. Rather, it is important because it undermines other goals that Bob has. Similarly, pounding is important to Kenny because it causes the shed to be built; the consequence of waking Jean is important because it undermines his goal of having good relations with his neighbor.

Finally, both actions and consequences can (sometimes) be necessary for the goal, but once again they are necessary in different ways. Actions are (sometimes) necessary in order to cause the goal. Consequences are (sometimes) necessary because they go along with the actions. Destroying the bridge might be necessary (in some situations) as a cause to achieve the goal of stopping the army. In contrast, the killing of the girl is not necessary as a cause of the goal; rather, it necessarily goes along with the action of destroying the bridge.

This first error (of lumping together) turns some consequences into actions. The remaining three errors will do the opposite. They will eliminate some actions, typically turning them into consequences of some sort or other. The three are different because of the manner in which they eliminate actions (thereby turning them into consequences). The second error (dropping options) makes the false assumption that for something to count as a means, it must be necessary for achieving the goal. We have seen (just now) that sometimes the means are necessary; more often, however, the means are optional. The third error (turning a blind eye) ignores some causes that fit within a plan. Dropping options provides a general principle (that the means must be necessary) in order to eliminate some means. The error of turning a blind eye has no principle. It simply overlooks some causes, thereby turning them into consequences. Finally, the fourth error (slicing thin) eliminates some descriptions of actions, relegating them to consequences, because these descriptions do not provide the initial motivating force for choosing an action.

Dropping Options

The second error (of dropping options) ignores certain means—classifying them as consequences instead—because they are optional. The best way to understand this error is to see it in action (pun intended). One philosopher bases his reasoning upon an example like the following (Bennett 1995):

> *Terrorizing Tom*: Like Dan, Tom wants to end the war. He hopes to achieve this goal, however, by massacring innocent civilians and to thereby demoralize the enemy, who will then surrender.

When Tom bombs a civilian area, he is killing innocent human beings, which action opposes the precept "do harm to no (innocent) person." Tom can sidestep this precept, however, if the killing of the civilians is only a consequence of his action. Most properly (the argument goes)

Tom performs the action of terrorizing the population; the killing of civilians is only a consequence.

The argument in support of dropping "killing" from Tom's action continues by examining the manner in which Tom forms his plan. He begins with the goal of ending the war. He recognizes that terrorizing the enemy is one way to end the war. He then looks for a cause to terrorize the enemy, and he recognizes that if he can make many civilians appear dead, then he will terrorize the enemy. All that he needs is the appearance of death. Even if the civilians are not actually dead, the enemy will be so terrorized and demoralized that they will surrender. Killing the civilians—according to this reasoning—is not necessary to achieve Tom's goal. The only thing Tom needs of necessity is the appearance of death.

This argument is based upon a mistaken supposition. It supposes that the means are always necessary. Therefore, what is not necessary (or what is optional) is not a means. In Tom's case, the death of the civilians is not necessary; only the appearance of death is necessary. Consequently, the death of the civilians is not a means and should be described as a consequence of Tom's action.

Is it really the case that the means are always necessary? Clearly not. Kenny can build his shed by various means. On the one hand, he might pound nails; on the other hand, he might choose to build his shed entirely with screws. For the goal of building the shed, then, the means of pounding nails is optional (rather than necessary). It does not thereby cease being a means. Pounding nails is clearly the means that Kenny has settled upon to achieve his goal. The means are not only those things that are necessary for the goal; they are also those things we settle upon in order to achieve the goal.

Perhaps what Tom needs (what is necessary) is simply that the civilians appear dead. Nevertheless, he has chosen to make them appear dead by way of actually making them dead. Just as Kenny's choice settles upon the optional means of pounding nails, so Tom, by his choice, settles upon the means of killing, despite the lack of necessity.

You probably noticed that the argument in support of dropping options makes another mistake. For Tom, killing the civilians is optional (as opposed to necessary) only in the realm of conjecture. We can imagine (in our conjectures) that killing the civilians is optional and that only the appearance of death is necessary. In the realm of reality, however, killing the civilians is necessary. Tom has no other way available to him by which he can make the civilians appear dead. If he had some other option, then we could truly say that killing the civilians is optional. Imagine, for instance, that he could spray the civilians with a gas that puts them in a deep hibernation and makes them appear dead. As it is, however, no other possibilities are available besides killing the civilians. If he wants his goal, the choice to kill is not optional. In short, the error of dropping options often confuses reality with mere conjectural supposition.

Turning a Blind Eye

Fortunately, the error of dropping options is not that common among ordinary people, who are seduced into it only by the specious arguments of philosophers. The third error (turning a blind eye), however, is more widespread. Those who fall into this error are blind to certain means within a plan. They notice some means but overlook others. They then classify what they overlook as consequences.

This oversight commonly arises among the group we have called the revisionists, who often turn a blind eye in the following case:

> *Deadly Defense*: Scott is attacking Barb, trying to kill her. Barb, however, has a gun, which she uses upon Scott, who dies.

Barb's goal is to defend herself and save her life. What are the means that she chooses? Obviously, firing a gun at Scott is one of the means she chooses. But is that all? Having identified the means of firing the gun, the revisionists suppose the matter is settled. Most importantly, the harm done to Scott is not (as far as they are concerned) among the means that Barb chooses. Barb does not plan to harm Scott, they claim, but only to fire the gun at him. As a result, the harm is classified as a consequence of her action.

When identifying the means, the revisionists have a blind spot. They have simply overlooked the means of harming, which is indeed part of Barb's plan. The harm to Scott does in fact belong to Barb's plan as a means by which she achieves her goal of defending herself.

This point becomes clear if we suppose that Barb has a gun that harms no one (perhaps it can fire only blanks). Furthermore, both she and Scott are fully aware that it harms no one. When she is being attacked by Scott, she considers the possible causes by which she might save herself. She might consider the following four options: fleeing, beating Scott over the head with a baseball bat, spraying mace upon Scott, and using her impotent gun.

But wait a minute! How seriously can she consider using the gun? It simply will not work. An ordinary gun might protect Barb in a couple of ways. It might injure Scott, thereby stopping his attack. Alternately, it might frighten Scott away (because he is worried that she might harm him with subsequent shots). Neither of these possibilities works with Barb's gun. Her impotent gun does not injure anyone, nor will it frighten Scott, who is aware that her gun is harmless.

This scenario suggests that when Barb does consider firing an ordinary (harmful) gun, she does so precisely as a means to harm Scott. Her reasoning might be fleshed out more completely using the following logic. In order to save herself, she can either escape (by fleeing) or injure Scott. She can injure Scott by using a variety of means: a baseball bat, a gun, or mace. She settles upon the gun as the most effective means.

Recall that a complete plan includes all the means. Dan plans to stop the army by way of destroying the bridge by way of bombing the bridge. Similarly, Barb plans to save her life by way of injuring Scott by way of firing a gun at him. We cannot skip over the middle step (of injuring) and simply say that Barb plans to save her life by way of firing a gun. This last means (of firing a gun) is precisely a means to injure; only by way of injury is it a means to save her life. Firing a harmless gun does not cause her goal.

Of course, Barb need not aim to kill Scott. She might hope that Scott lives to see another day. She must aim to injure him so that he is incapacitated, but such injury need not always be deadly. The natural law precept under consideration, however, does not say "kill no one." Rather, it says "do harm to no one." Perhaps Barb does not plan to kill Scott, but she definitely plans to injure him. The injury is not simply a consequence of her action.

As far as Aquinas is concerned, some instances of killing in self-defense do involve death as a consequence (*ST*, II-II, 64, 7). Of course, he was not (in the 13th century) thinking of defending oneself with a gun. He probably had in mind hand-to-hand fighting, or some such thing. Consider the following case:

> *Protective Push*: Scott is attacking Barb, trying to kill her. As he reaches for her throat, she forcefully pushes him away. He bumps his head upon a wall and dies of a concussion.

Scott's death is not a means to Barb's defense. Not even his injury is a means. As she searches for a cause to stop the attack, she settles only upon the means of thrusting Scott off of her. Scott's death—even if Barb foresees it—is only a consequence of her action. In this case, Barb can defend herself without taking on the role of a public official, for she does not (most properly speaking) injure Scott.

Slicing Thin

The task of trying to identify the means (as opposed to the consequences) is prone to one final confusion, which we will call "slicing thin." As we have seen, we often describe actions in terms of their consequences. Dan's action of bombing the bridge can be described as killing the girl. The first error (lumping together) arises because of the facility with which we describe actions in terms of their consequences. If we can describe Dan's action as killing the girl, then it seems that the death of the girl must not be a consequence; rather, it must be an action of its own. The error of lumping together combines what should be separated. The error of slicing thin makes the opposite mistake. It separates what should be combined.

Consider the following case:

Murdered Mammal: Bruce (rather than Pat) is holding 20 hostages, threatening to kill them unless Paula goes to the zoo and kills the first mammal she sees. Unfortunately, the first mammal she sees is the zookeeper. Paula shoots the zookeeper.

In the error of slicing thin, Paula might argue that she really did not plan to kill a human being. She planned only to kill a mammal. The only thing she needed to achieve her goal was the act of killing a mammal, not the act of killing a human being. Therefore, killing a human being was just a consequence of her act of killing a mammal.

Surely, Paula is confused. Her action can indeed be described in multiple ways. It can be described as killing a mammal, and it can also be described as killing a human being. These descriptions, however, should not be separated into an action and its consequence. Rather, they should be lumped together as belonging to one and the same action.

Consider another example.

Ruthless Rachel: Rachel plans to kill Sarah, who is the Prime Minister. Sarah also happens to be the sister of Sam, who is a good friend of Rachel. Sam confronts Rachel, protesting that she plans to kill his sister. Rachel responds that she plans no such thing. She merely plans to kill the Prime Minister. Killing Sam's sister is only a consequence of the act of killing the Prime Minister.

Like Paula, Rachel is confused. Her action can be described either as killing the Prime Minister or as killing Sam's sister, but the two should not be separated as action and consequence. They are simply two different ways of looking at the exact same action.

Consider a third example:

Kleptomaniac Kim: Kim takes Mark's car. When he accuses her of theft, she responds that she planned only to take a car; the act of taking Mark's car was just a consequence of taking a car. In no way, then, did she plan to take a car that belonged to someone else (in other words, she did not plan an act of theft); she planned only to take a car.

Like Paula, Kim has separated what should be lumped together. Kenny legitimately separates his act of pounding nails from the frightening of the crows. The pounding does indeed cause the frightening, which is a separate event from his act of pounding. In contrast, Kim cannot separate her act of taking a car from her act of taking Mark's car. The two are not separate events, one of which causes the other. Rather, they are one and the same thing.

Consider a final example:

> *Tottering Table*: Eric cuts off a leg of Brenda's table. When she complains that he has broken or damaged her table, he responds that he has only cut off the leg; the damage was just a consequence of his action.

Brenda might well respond that there are not two things, the loss of a leg and damage to the table. The damage to the table is not like the death of the girl on the bridge. In Dan's case, the event of the destroyed bridge causes another distinct event, the death of the girl. In Eric's case, the loss of the leg is not one event that causes another distinct event (the damage to the table); rather, the loss of the leg is the exact same thing as the damage to the table, although this one reality is described in two different ways. In this case, then, the two should not be separated; they should be lumped together.

The error under consideration is called "slicing thin" because new descriptions can be sliced off from the action even when we have only a single action. By continually slicing off descriptions, the remaining actions are very thin. They include only a minimal description, outside of which everything counts as a consequence.

The cases above seem clear enough, but they lead to a perplexity. How do we know when to separate and when to lump together? In Dan's case, a single action may be described as destroying a bridge and as killing a girl. These two descriptions, however, are separated into action and consequence. In Paula's case (*Murdered Mammal*), a single action may be described as killing a mammal and as killing a human being. These two descriptions should not be separated; instead, they should be lumped together. How do we sort out the different cases? How do we distinguish cases like Dan's from cases like Paula's?

The multiplication of examples is meant to tease out our intuitions that the two sets of cases are indeed distinct from one another. On the one hand, Kenny's act of pounding is separate from the frightening of crows. On the other hand, Eric's act of cutting off the leg of the table is not separate from damaging the table.

Unfortunately, after we have teased out our intuitions, a perplexity remains. What underlies our intuitions? How exactly do we separate the two sets of cases?

Distinct Changes and Distinct Subjects

When we act, says Aquinas, we bring about a change in a subject (*ST*, I-II, 7, 3, ad 3; *ST*, I-II, 18, 2, ad 2). When Brett heats water, for instance, he brings about the change of increased temperature in the subject of water. The complete description of the action includes both of these: both the change and the subject. We might say simply that Brett is heating; more precisely, he is heating water.

The unity of the action depends upon the unity of the change and the unity of the subject. Paula's action, for instance, has only one change (death) and one subject (the zookeeper). In contrast, Dan's action has multiple changes in multiple subjects. On the one hand, he has the change of destruction in the subject of the bridge. On the other hand, he has the change of death in the subject of the girl. Paula's case, then, has only one action, while Dan's case has multiple actions: he brings about multiple changes in multiple subjects.

Of course, Paula's single action can be described in multiple ways. After all, both the change she brings about (death) and the subject (the zookeeper) can themselves be described in different ways. The zookeeper, for instance, can be described as a mammal or as a human being. Consequently, Paula's action can be described as killing a mammal or as killing a human being. Despite the different descriptions of the subject, the mammal is not distinct from the human being. Similarly, despite the different descriptions of Paula's action, her action of killing a mammal is not distinct from her action of killing a human being. In contrast, the bridge that Dan destroys is in fact distinct from the girl that dies.

Similar reasoning applies to any redescription of the change that Paula brings about. The death might be described as the cessation of bodily functions. Or it might be described as that which will satisfy Bruce's demands. None of these redescriptions changes the reality. Only one change takes place and it occurs in only one subject, but it is described in relation to different features of the world. Based upon the different descriptions of the change, we might describe Paula's action as killing or as meeting the demands of Bruce. Nevertheless, these two actions are not distinct.

The subject of the change is more prone to redescription than is the change itself. The subject typically has many aspects or attributes. Sarah, for instance, is both the Prime Minister and Sam's sister. Consequently, Rachel's action can be described as killing the Prime Minister or as killing Sam's sister. Despite the multiple descriptions, we have only one change (death) and one subject of the change (Sarah).

Similarly, a car has many attributes. It is red, large, belongs to Mark, has four wheels, and so on. Kim's action (in *Kleptomaniac Kim*) might be described as taking something that is red, taking something that is large, taking something that belongs to Mark, taking something that has four wheels, and so on. Despite these multiple descriptions, there is only one change (transferring ownership or use to herself) and one subject of the change (the car, however described).

Redescriptions of the change introduced are less flexible but still possible. The loss of the leg on a table can also be described as damage to the table. One and the same reality is considered in different ways. First, it is considered just by itself. Second, it is considered insofar as it relates to the function of the table.

As we have seen, the good is that which completes some movement to an endpoint. Being sharp is good for a knife, for instance, because it partially completes the movement of the knife to cutting (the function of the knife). What is bad (including damage) also involves a relation to function: what is bad undermines the function. The damage to the table, then, is not something distinct from the loss of the leg. It is simply the loss of the leg considered in relation to the function of the table.

In all these actions, then, the agent introduces a change into a subject.

The change can be redescribed, and the subject can be redescribed. Consequently, the action itself can be redescribed. Through all the redescriptions, however, we have only one change and one subject.

The same cannot be said for Dan. He introduces the change of destruction into the bridge. Consequently, the girl dies. Dan does indeed introduce death into the girl, so we can redescribe his action as killing the girl. This redescription, however, does not concern one and the same subject with one and the same change. The girl is a distinct subject from the bridge, and death is a distinct change from destruction (if only because the subject itself is different). Since an action most essentially introduces a change into a subject, then in this case we have two separate actions (one of which can be the consequence of another); we have two separate changes in two separate subjects.

The Unity of Actions

The separation of these actions leads to a puzzle. Previously, we said that Dan's single action can be described in two ways, either as destroying a bridge or (in terms of its further consequence) as killing a girl. Now it seems we are saying the opposite. We do not have a single action with multiple descriptions. Rather, we have multiple actions. Which is it? Do we have multiple actions or one action with multiple descriptions?

Surprisingly, the answer is "both/and." We have both a single action with multiple descriptions and multiple actions. This seeming contradiction arises because actions have two sources of unity. On the one hand (as we have already seen), they are unified through a single change in a single subject. On the other hand, they are unified through a single origin. Dan's diverse actions (destroying a bridge and killing a girl) have a single origin. They both arise from Dan, and they both arise from one and the same behavior (dropping bombs).

Actions have multiple sources of unity on account of their nature. As Aristotle notes, an action involves an agent giving rise to some change in some subject (*Phys*, bk. 3, chap. 3; *In Ph*, 306). Kenny's action of pounding, for instance, involves Kenny (the agent) giving rise to a change of place in the nail (entering the wood). Kenny's action, then, has two sources of unity. He himself, as the origin of the action, provides one source. The change in the subject provides the other. These two sources of unity derive naturally from the very definition of an action as an agent giving rise to a change in a subject.

On the one hand, an action can involve a single change in a single subject. Paula's action, for instance, has one change (death) in one subject (the zookeeper). Diverse descriptions (the effect that Bruce wants, a mammal, a human being, and so on) do not eliminate the unity of the change and of the subject. Nor do they change the unity of the action.

On the other hand, an action can involve a single agent with a single originating impetus. The action of pounding, for instance, is one and the same with the action of waking Kenny's neighbor Jean. These both arise from Kenny and from the single impetus of moving his arm while holding a hammer. In this case, these two actions are one action, but they also remain two distinct actions. They involve different changes in different subjects. The action of pounding involves the change of place in a nail. The action of waking involves a change of sleep state in Jean. The multiple descriptions of Kenny's single action, then, identify a diversity of actions within the one action.

In no way, however, does Paula's action have a numerical diversity. It is numerically one in both ways. On the one hand, it has a single change in a single subject. On the other hand, it arises from a single origin (from Paula pulling the trigger). Consequently, the action of killing a mammal differs from the action of killing a human being only in description and not in reality.

In Kenny's case, we have numerically distinct actions united through a single origin. One of these actions, then, can cause another. The act of pounding, for instance, can cause the act of frightening the crows. In Paula's case, we do not have two actions, one of which can cause the other; we have only a single action with multiple descriptions. The action of killing a mammal does not cause the action of killing a human being, for these two are not in fact distinct.

Furthermore, when we have a numerical diversity (in Kenny's case),

Table 17-1. Four common errors

Name	Error	Example
Lumping together	Joins actions and consequences	Bob jogs and does damage to his knees; the damage is not counted as a consequence.
Dropping options	Counts unnecessary (or optional) means as consequences	Tom makes the civilians appear to be dead, but actually killing them is only a consequence of his action.
Turning a blind eye	Overlooks certain means	Barb shoots Scott in self-defense, but the harm done to Scott is counted as a consequence.
Slicing thin	Classifies certain descriptions of actions as consequences	When Paula kills the zookeeper, she kills a mammal, but killing a human being is a consequence.

then the agent can relate to the two different actions in diverse ways. Kenny tries to pound, but he does not try to frighten crows. In contrast, when we have an action that is one in number (as in Paula's case), then the agent relates to only one action, despite the multiple descriptions. Paula tries to kill a mammal, but in so doing she tries to kill a human being.

The perplexing assortment of different actions, then, can be readily distinguished based upon the very notion of what an action is. Sometimes, multiple descriptions can be separated into a proper action and a consequence. At other times, multiple descriptions must be lumped together. Why? Because of what an action is. Sometimes, the agent introduces distinct changes into distinct subjects. These cases have multiple actions, one of which might happen to be a consequence. At other times, the agent introduces one change into one subject, but both the change and the subject can be redescribed. In these latter cases, one and the same action can have multiple descriptions, but no consequences can be separated out from the action itself.

You may find that this material is far from easy. If so, you might be comforted by the following thought. In your initial intuitions, you may have already grasped the essential points. If your intuitions tell you that Paula performs a single action that cannot be pulled apart into action and consequence, then you may be recognizing (without fully realizing it) that she is bringing about a single change in a single subject. If your intuitions tell you that Dan performs an action of destroying a bridge with the consequence that a girl dies, then you may be recognizing (without fully realizing it) that he is bringing about multiple changes in multiple subjects. Furthermore, you might be recognizing that some of these changes (such as the destruction of the bridge) can cause others (such as the death of the girl), resulting in what we have called consequences of an action.

chapter 18

Two Test Cases

If a mother can kill her own child, what will prevent us from killing ourselves, or one another?

—Mother Teresa of Calcutta, Speech for Nobel Prize, December 10, 1979

Practical wisdom concerns not only universals but particulars, which become familiar from experience.

—Aristotle, *Nicomachean Ethics*

This chapter examines two test cases, the craniotomy case and the grenade case, by which we can apply what we have learned. We will see how to separate actions and consequences, how to keep lumped together what should be lumped together, and how people like the revisionists might go wrong in analyzing these cases. Readers should be cautioned that some of the details of the first case may be disturbing.

The Craniotomy Case

> *Craniotomy*: A pregnant woman is in labor with a complication called cephalopelvic disproportion, which means that she has a small pelvis and her baby has a large head. His head is so large that it cannot fit through her pelvis. As such, he can never be delivered naturally. Labor will continue indefinitely until the woman dies of exhaustion; typically, the baby dies with her. Standard treatment today involves delivery by C-section, which saves both the mother and her baby. Before C-sections were safe, however, another procedure was sometimes used. This procedure is often called a craniotomy. (Technically, it should be called a destructive craniotomy, in order to distinguish it from a therapeutic cutting of the cranium. For convenience, we will follow convention and refer to it simply as a craniotomy.) In this procedure, the doctor crushes the baby's skull (which is the largest part of a baby's body) so that the baby can be delivered. Then the labor is ended and the mother is saved. Obviously, the baby, who has suffered fatal injuries to his head, is not saved.

What exactly does the doctor do? His action can be described in multiple ways. He crushes the skull of the baby; he harms the baby; he kills the baby; he reduces the size of the baby's head; he saves the mother; and so on. Do some of these descriptions reflect the doctor's proper action and others reflect the consequences of his action? Or do all these redescriptions involve one and the same change in one and the same subject?

Can the craniotomy be placed alongside Dan's action, in which he destroys the bridge with a consequence that the girl dies? Or must the craniotomy be placed alongside Paula's action, in which the action of killing a human being is the exact same action as killing a mammal? Does the doctor perform one action—perhaps reducing the size of the baby's head—and consequently harm the baby as a side effect? Or does the doctor harm the baby, properly speaking, in order to save the mother? We must pay careful attention when answering these questions.

The Argument of the Revisionists

The revisionists place the doctor squarely within Dan's camp. We will divide their argument into four steps (Boyle 1977; Tollefsen 2006).

Step 1. According to the revisionists, the doctor most properly reduces the size of the baby's head; he harms the baby only as a consequence. The revisionists begin (appropriately) by noting the plan of the doctor. He begins with the goal of saving the mother. This goal can be achieved by ending the labor. The labor can be ended by getting the baby out. The baby can be removed if his head is smaller. Therefore, what the doctor must do in order to achieve his goal is to reduce the size of the baby's head.

Step 2. When he reduces the size of the head by performing the craniotomy, the baby will die, and this death is a serious harm to the baby. Nevertheless, the death does not cause the head to be smaller; rather, because the head is made smaller, the harm of death follows. In this respect, the death of the baby is like the death of the little girl on the bridge. Her death does not cause the destruction of the bridge (but vice versa); likewise, the death of the baby does not cause the head to be smaller (but vice versa). The injury of death, then, is not a means because it is not a cause of the goal.

Step 3. The action of crushing the skull has two effects. On the one hand, it causes injury to the baby. On the other hand, it reduces the size of the baby's head. Which of these effects does the doctor hope to achieve by crushing the skull? He does not aim to injure the baby. Rather, he aims only to reduce the size of the baby's head. It follows that he most properly reduces the size of the head and injures the baby only as a consequence.

Step 4. Besides, the crushing of the skull is not really necessary within his plans. Sometimes, the baby can be removed simply by compressing the head (with forceps). Because the baby's skull has soft spots (fontanels), this compression can sufficiently reduce the size of the head, so that the baby can be delivered. In these cases, the baby is uninjured, or at least injured only slightly. The doctor, then, need not plan to crush the baby's skull. He plans simply to compress the skull and thereby reduce the size of the head.

What are we to make of this account? Let us consider it step-by-step.

Step 1

The revisionists first trace the doctor's deliberations from the goal of saving the woman back to the means of reducing the size of the head. At this point, however, they have committed the error of turning a blind eye. They have overlooked a needed means. How is the doctor going to reduce the size of the head? He will do so by crushing the skull. A full account of his deliberations, then, must include the crushing among the means he chooses.

Indeed, the most complete account includes even more details, which we have not mentioned above. Before crushing the skull, the doctor must scoop out the brains of the baby. This gruesome procedure is needed in order to reduce the internal pressure within the skull.

By ending the doctor's deliberations with "narrowing the head," the revisionists have overlooked two important steps. The head is narrowed by way of crushing, and the skull is crushed by way of removing the baby's brains.

Step 2

They continue with this error in the next step. The injury of death, they say, results from reducing the size of the head while performing the craniotomy. We are left with the impression that performing the craniotomy is simply reducing the size of the head. In fact, it is an act of crushing the skull in order to reduce the size of the head.

Despite this oversight, they do (in step 2) seem to make a valid point. The doctor does bring about multiple changes: the crushing of the skull and the death of the baby. These two are not one and the same change, although they are closely related. This diversity of changes seems to place the doctor in the same camp as Dan. Dan brings about multiple changes (destruction and death) in multiple subjects (the bridge and the girl); consequently, his actions can be pulled apart. The destruction of the bridge is one action; the killing of the girl is a consequence.

In the doctor's case, the diversity is not quite as great. It does not involve two subjects but only one. The doctor, then, seems to be midway between Dan and Paula. Dan brings about two separate effects (destruction and death) in two separate subjects (the bridge and the girl). Paula brings about a single effect (death) in a single subject (the zookeeper). The doctor is like Dan in one way and like Paula in another. He does not have two separate subjects. Both the crushed skull and the death are changes that take place within the baby. In this respect, he is like Paula. On the other hand, he does have two separate effects. The crushed skull is not the same change as death. In this respect, he is like Dan.

His action, then, can indeed be pulled apart, even if not so dramatically as in the case of Dan. On the one hand, he crushes the baby's skull; on the other hand, he kills the baby. This conclusion may seem to settle the matter. The doctor reduces the size of the baby's head with the consequence that the baby dies.

Despite these valid points, the revisionists ultimately slip into the error of slicing thin. They do so by making another oversight. Just as they focused our attention upon reducing the size of the head (and overlooked the crushing of the skull) so they have focused our attention upon the harm of death. While this harm is the greatest suffered by the baby, it is not the only harm that the doctor inflicts upon the baby. He also causes massive blood loss; he also causes a crushed skull, which is itself an injury. This last injury should be the focus of our attention.

Examining a similar case might prove helpful.

> *Samurai Sebastian*: Sebastian is a samurai warrior who has a new sword. It is standard practice among samurai to test a new sword upon an unsuspecting traveler upon the road. A good sword must make a cut from the shoulder down to the opposite hip, clean through the person. As Sebastian waits by the side of the road, Clare approaches. He leaps out and cuts her in half, from shoulder to the opposite hip. Clare dies.

Sebastian insists that he has not killed Clare, at least not properly speaking. Rather, her death is merely a consequence of his action. Most properly, he has cut her in half from shoulder to hip. This change is distinct from the change of death. Although both changes have only a single subject (Clare), they remain distinct. Consequently, these two actions (cutting Clare in half and killing Clare) can be pulled apart.

As odd as it may sound, this analysis is correct. The two changes are not identical. Rather, the cutting in half causes the death, which may in fact occur a couple of seconds later.

Has Sebastian escaped the precept "do harm to no one"? Can he claim that he harms Clare only as a consequence? Not quite. Death is not the only harm he inflicts upon her. She also suffers massive blood loss. More importantly, she is cut in half, which is itself an injury.

This last injury makes Sebastian like Paula rather than like Dan. Paula brings about a single change (death) that can be described in various ways. It can be described simply as death, but it might also be described as "cessation of life" or as "that which satisfies the demands of Bruce." These new descriptions do not give us a new change. Similarly, Sebastian brings about a single effect (cutting in half) that can be described in various ways. It can be described simply as "cutting in half," but it can also be described as injury. These two descriptions do not give us a new change. Being cut in half is itself a kind of injury (a pretty serious one). It is not the same as the harm of death, but it itself is an injury.

When Eric cuts off the leg of the table, the loss of the leg can be described in various ways. It can be described simply as the loss of a leg, but it can also be described as damage to the table. These two descriptions do not identify two separate changes or two separate effects. Rather, they identify only one effect, but this one effect may be considered in different ways, either in itself or in relation to the function of the table, in which case it is described as damage. Eric, then, does not perform two separate actions. He does not cut off the leg and then also damage the table. He does one thing, which may be described both as cutting off the leg and as damaging the table.

Similarly, Sebastian does not do two separate things to Clare. He does not cut Clare in half and then also injure her. He does one thing. He cuts her in half, which is also to injure. Subsequently, of course, other injuries follow (such as loss of blood), and perhaps some of these injuries—and ultimately death—can be described as consequences, but these injuries should not distract us. Sebastian has not avoided the precept "do harm to no one." He has done a very serious harm to Clare (being cut in half), and this harm cannot be separated as a consequence of his action. He plans to cut her in half in order to test his sword. He also plans to injure her in order to test his sword. These two cannot be separated.

The parallel with the craniotomy is clear. A crushed skull and injury are not two separate changes. Rather, a crushed skull is itself a kind of injury (and a serious one, at that). The crushed skull is described as an injury when considered in relation to the function of an intact body; a crushed skull does not fulfill the function of a skull. Considering the crushed skull in a new light—as an injury—does not generate a separate change. It merely redescribes one and the same change. These two descriptions (crushing the skull and injuring the baby) cannot be pulled apart but must be lumped together. Just as Paula kills a human being in order to save the lives of the hostages, so the doctor injures the baby in order to save the life of the mother.

The same point can be made, perhaps with even greater force, for another injury inflicted by the doctor: the injury of removing the brain matter. Certainly, having one's brain matter removed causes a variety of injuries. More importantly, however, the removal of the brain matter is itself an injury. The action of "removing the brain," then, cannot be pulled apart from the action of "injuring the baby." These two must be lumped together.

The revisionists have distracted our attention in several ways. First, they have focused our attention upon reducing the size of the head and distracted us away from the crushing of the skull. Second, they have focused our attention upon the death of the baby and distracted our attention away from the injury of a crushed skull, which itself is a lethal injury. Aquinas says that if we inflict a lethal injury (even if the death itself is strictly speaking outside of our plan), then we may be guilty of murder (*ST*, II-II, 64, 8).

Step 3

We are getting ahead of ourselves, however. We have not yet finished sorting through the arguments of the revisionists. Their next step seems to imply that the above reasoning is irrelevant. Even if a crushed skull is identical with injury, it does not matter. What matters, when looking at actions, is what the agent hopes to achieve. The doctor does not hope to achieve injury to the baby. He hopes to achieve only a smaller size for the head. Therefore, his action may be described as reducing the size of the baby's head with the consequence that the baby is injured.

We should be suspicious of this new focus upon what the doctor hopes to achieve. Potentially, it can justify any action we want. When Paula kills the zookeeper, she hopes to achieve the death of a mammal. She does not hope to achieve the death of a human being. Similarly, when Tom kills his wife Brenda, he really hopes to eliminate the policyholder of a life insurance policy of which he is the beneficiary; he does not really want to kill Brenda (or so he tells himself). With enough imagination, "what we really hope to achieve" can scrub away any evil description of our actions.

The doctor definitely does want this act of crushing the baby's skull. It is the means by which he ends the labor and saves the mother. Furthermore, injuring the baby is not a consequence of crushing the skull; rather, the two descriptions identify one and the same action. In the end, then, the doctor definitely does want to injure the baby. It is the means by which he ends the labor and saves the mother. He hopes to achieve the injury of a crushed skull as a means to save the mother.

Paula wants to kill a mammal, but there is no such thing as an abstract action of killing a mammal. Every action of killing a mammal is an action of killing some particular mammal. In this case, it is an action of killing a human being. Paula does not want an abstract action of killing a mammal, for no such thing exists. She wants a concrete action of killing a concrete mammal. As it is, she wants this concrete action of killing a human being. Similarly, the doctor does not want an abstract action of crushing a skull. He wants a real concrete action of crushing a skull, and this action is nothing other than injuring a baby.

Step 4

The final step falls into the error of dropping options. The revisionists claim that crushing the skull is not necessary: it is optional. Sometimes it suffices for the doctor to momentarily compress the skull with forceps. This reasoning follows the pattern of *Terrorizing Tom*. According to the error of dropping options, he does not need to aim at killing the civilians. He only needs to aim at making them appear dead long enough to demoralize the enemy into a surrender.

This conclusion is erroneous, as we saw, because the means chosen need not be necessary (they can be optional). Kenny chooses the means of pounding nails, although he might have chosen to use screws instead. Furthermore, the option (of not killing the civilians) is only conjectural. In reality, killing the civilians is the only means Tom has available to make them appear dead.

Similar defects can be found in the reasoning of the revisionists. Sometimes, it is true, a doctor can deliver the baby simply by compressing the skull (without crushing it). A doctor who is performing a craniotomy, however, has opted to crush the skull rather than compress it (just as Kenny has opted to use nails rather than screws). This decision cannot be doubted. After all, by the time he crushes the skull, the doctor has already removed the brains (which, as noted above, is a necessary preliminary to crushing the skull). He has no reason to choose the option of compressing the skull (as opposed to crushing the skull) on a baby whose brains are already missing.

Furthermore, as with Tom, the option of compressing the skull is only conjectural. In some instances, compressing the skull does suffice for delivering the baby, but by the time the doctor performs a craniotomy, he has already tried this option and it has failed. At this point, then, the possibility of compressing the skull is only conjectural. In reality, only crushing the skull will suffice.

The Grenade Case

We will close these considerations by examining another case often misunderstood by the revisionists.

> *Daring Damsel*: A grenade is thrown in the midst of six people. Payton leaps upon the grenade, preventing its shrapnel from reaching the other five. Payton dies.

What does Payton do? Most particularly, does Payton kill herself properly speaking? Or, on the other hand, does Payton stop the grenade with the consequence that she dies? Her action can be described in multiple ways, such as blocking the shrapnel or as killing herself. Can these descriptions be separated into action and consequence? Or must these descriptions be lumped together, like Paula's actions of killing a mammal and killing a human being?

An examination of the case reveals that the two actions can be pulled apart. Most properly, Payton does not kill herself; rather she interposes an obstacle in the way of a projectile (namely, the shrapnel coming out from the grenade). She then foresees the consequent harm upon herself. The point might be clearer in another parallel case.

> *Blocking Bureau*: A grenade is thrown in the midst of six people. Jody quickly pushes a large bureau of drawers over the grenade. Although the grenade explodes, the movement of its shrapnel is blocked by the bureau of drawers. No one is harmed, but the chest of drawers is damaged.

Jody realizes that she must stop the shrapnel from reaching the people. She then recognizes that placing an obstacle in the way of the shrapnel will bring about her goal of protecting the people. In her quick search for an obstacle, she spies the chest and pushes it over the grenade. The cause that Jody needs, in this case, is for the chest to act upon the shrapnel. The chest must stop the shrapnel from reaching the people. As it is, the shrapnel also acts upon the chest, damaging it. This other change, however, is not the cause that Jody needs. Shrapnel acting upon the chest does not protect the people; rather, the chest acting upon the shrapnel protects them.

In an action, an agent introduces some change into some subject. Jody aims to change the shrapnel, stopping its movement. She does not aim at the equal and opposite reaction, in which the shrapnel acts upon the chest. She does aim to change the bureau, but the change she aims to achieve, in this case, is a change of place (it must be placed over the grenade). She does not aim at the change of damage.

In the craniotomy case, a crushed skull is not, in fact, distinct from a kind of harm to the baby. The same reality is described in different ways. In *Blocking Bureau*, the stopping of the shrapnel (by the chest) is not the same change as damage to the chest (done by the shrapnel). Although these two are intertwined (since every action has an equal and opposite reaction), they are not simply two descriptions of the same reality. Rather, they are two distinct changes. Their distinction is revealed most clearly by the distinction in subjects. The stopping of movement (which is the change Jody aims at) is found in the shrapnel; the change of damage is found in the chest.

This analysis is easily carried over to the original case, in which Payton jumps upon the grenade. She aims to stop the shrapnel by way of her own body rather than by way of a chest of drawers. She does not aim at any damage to her own body. Rather, she recognizes that by acting upon the shrapnel, the shrapnel will also act upon her. The harm that results is distinct from the stopping of the movement of the shrapnel.

When Payton jumps upon the grenade, then, the harm to herself is a consequence. Just as the harm to the girl is not a means by which Dan destroys the bridge, so the harm to herself is not a means by which Payton stops the shrapnel. Dan chooses a means (destroying the bridge) that causes other effects, including harm to the girl. Likewise, Payton chooses a means (using her body to act upon the shrapnel) that causes other effects, including harm to herself.

Payton does not properly harm herself. She does not commit suicide in order to save the five. Rather, she puts herself in harm's way for the sake of stopping the shrapnel. Since the harm is a consequence, her action does not fall directly under the precept "do harm to no one."

chapter 19

Consequent Harm

> From the neglect of a real duty, she became the slave of a false one.
>
> —George MacDonald, *Mary Marston*

Why does this lengthy discussion of actions matter? Why should we care what the doctor really does? Why should we care whether he crushes the skull or injures the baby (or both)? In either event, he does what he needs to do in order to save the mother. In either event, it seems, he achieves a needed good; indeed, he seems to achieve a greater good.

We are trying to understand the natural law precept "do harm to no one." We have seen that this precept, properly understood, is narrower than it first appears. It means "do not harm the innocent"; or it means "as a private citizen, do harm to no one." These added restrictions allow for a few precisely defined cases in which harming other human beings is morally acceptable. They allow for punishment, for instance, or they allow for harming in a just war, both of which can be carried out only by the proper authorities.

We are now investigating another possibility. Perhaps some harm is permissible even to the innocent, and perhaps some harm is permissible even by a private citizen (Cavanaugh 2006). These possibilities depend upon another addition that might be applied to the precept. Perhaps it should read as follows: "do harm—properly speaking—to no one." The addition of "properly speaking" allows for another kind of harm. When Dan bombs the bridge, he also harms the little girl. As we have seen, however, this harm can be described as a consequence of his action. Most properly, Dan does not harm the girl, so his action (which is an act of destroying a bridge) is not directly prohibited by the precept.

In the craniotomy case as well, the proper description of the doctor's action might be important. Suppose he is really reducing the size of the head, and the injury is only a consequence. Then his action does not fall directly under the precept. On the other hand, if he most properly injures the baby (as we have argued), then his action is prohibited by the precept.

Even with this new qualification added to the precept, the previous discussion on actions may still seem far removed from—perhaps even irrelevant to—the morality of the situations at hand. All that matters, one might think, is that we bring about the good. The precise nature of our actions is irrelevant. In this chapter and the next, we will see why the precise nature of our actions does indeed have moral significance.

The Precept to Help Those in Need

Since Dan does not harm the girl properly speaking, his action may not oppose the precept "do harm—properly speaking—to no one." It does not follow that his action is morally acceptable. It might run afoul of other precepts of the natural law. Consider the following case:

> *Lumberjack Larry*: Larry is cutting down an unsightly tree in his front yard. As he is making the final cuts that will send the tree falling to the ground, he sees a little girl playing in the path of the tree's likely descent. Larry continues to cut. The tree falls upon the girl, who is seriously injured.

Larry might defend himself by claiming that his action was not harming properly speaking. Properly speaking, it was an act of cutting down a tree, with the consequence of harming the girl. His action, then, does not oppose the precept against harm. While Larry is correct on this particular point, we are unconvinced by his reasoning. Clearly, what he does is wrong, whether or not it precisely opposes the precept against harm.

But what is wrong with Larry's action if it is not against the precept "do harm to no one"? His action opposes another precept, an even more fundamental precept. It is against the precept to love other human beings. This precept, we have seen, applies even in those cases in which the precept "do harm to no one" does not apply. It applies, for instance, in the case of punishment. When the proper authorities harm the guilty, they do so, in part, for the sake of those who are punished. The punishment restores them to their proper place; furthermore, it might help them to reform their ways.

Similarly, even if Larry's action is not properly speaking an action of harm, he is still bound to love the girl. Love demands that Larry modify his action. He must make sure that the girl is out of the way before he makes the final cuts. If he fails to take these precautions, then he is morally to blame for the harm that befalls the girl. From the precept to love others, then, we might deduce a more particular precept: to help those in need. Although the harm to the girl is only a consequence of Larry's action, he still must help the girl, protecting her from the danger of the falling tree.

Our Limited Ability to Help

Can the same be said of Dan? Must he make sure that the girl is out of harm's way before he bombs the bridge? It would seem not. He has no easy way to get the girl out of the way. Furthermore, his action of destroying the bridge will save many lives and it cannot be long-delayed. His action seems justified, and the death of the girl is unfortunate collateral damage that he regretfully accepts.

But what about the precept to love other human beings? What about the precept to help those in need? Dan's harm to the girl, although a consequence of his action, seems opposed to the love he should have for her.

How can he claim to love her—to seek her good—when his action brings about her evil?

As we have seen, Linda (in *Limited Linda*) can love both Chris and Norbert, although she is unable to save both. When she chooses to save Norbert from drowning, she does not give up her love for Chris, who dies as a consequence of her choice. On account of our limitations, we cannot always fulfill every positive precept. These precepts, says Aquinas, hold always but not in every situation. Linda cannot simultaneously help everyone in need: she must choose whom to help now.

Dan is also limited. He has no way by which he can destroy the bridge (thereby stopping the advance of the army) and also save the girl. If some means of saving the girl (without thereby giving up his mission) were easily available to him, then he would be obliged to take it. Let us fancifully suppose, for instance, that he has some mechanism on his plane by which he can transport her away from the bridge. Then he would be required to use this mechanism, just as Larry is required to make sure that the girl is not in the vicinity of the tree.

Seeking the Greater Good

This imaginative scenario still leaves much unexplained. Something more is at play besides the easy ability to protect the girl (either the girl playing or the girl on the bridge). Suppose (unrealistically) that Larry has no way to get the girl out of the way of the falling tree. We would not conclude that he can proceed to cut the tree down. Larry's limitation (of being unable to remove the girl from the situation) does not absolve him of the responsibility of helping the girl in need. He must help the girl by giving up his project of cutting down the tree.

Why is Dan different? Why can he, unlike Larry, go ahead with his project of destroying the bridge despite the harm to the girl? The obvious difference is the importance of the project. Dan's mission is important enough to continue even if it harms the girl. Larry's project is not.

We have seen this sort of reasoning before. Linda's decision not to save Chris (but to save Norbert instead) is acceptable, but Garrulous Gary's decision not to save Libby (but to chatter away with David) is unjustified. The act of saving Norbert is more important (or at least as important) as the act of saving Chris. In contrast, the act of conversing with David is far less important than the act of saving Libby.

This reasoning should not be confused with consequentialist reasoning, which seeks to produce the greatest amount of good for the greatest number of people. Linda is not trying to produce the greatest amount of good. She is trying to do what is most important in her situation; she is trying to share the good most completely. When she evaluates different acts of sharing, she will consider the potential to share the good with more people. She will also consider the potential to share more important goods.

These considerations, however, are not consequentialist considerations. She is not evaluating effects; rather, she is evaluating actions of sharing, actions which do indeed have good effects. The ability to share greater goods, however, is not the only factor in evaluating acts of sharing. As we have seen, Linda's evaluations include a consideration of how close she is to Norbert. He is her brother while Chris is a stranger. Norbert's proximity to Linda produces no greater good, but it is important nevertheless because she is not concerned with producing goods. She is concerned with sharing goods, and she shares the good more completely with those with whom she has a more intimate connection.

Sharing the Good More Profoundly

Unfortunately, when it comes to harms that result from our actions, many natural law theorists have used reasoning indistinguishable from consequentialism. They have argued, for instance, that Dan's action is acceptable because he saves many more lives than he kills. In contrast, Larry produces the small good of beautifying his yard but the greater evil of harm to the girl.

Instead of such consequentialist reasoning, the natural law follows the reasoning of Linda. Dan is ultimately seeking to share the good. He does so by protecting many people from the onslaught of the enemy army. At the same time, Dan cannot (in a single action) share the good with everyone. In particular, he cannot protect the girl from his own action. Or rather, he can protect the girl from his action but only by abandoning his mission.

Dan is now in the same situation as Linda. She has two possible actions of sharing: she may save either Norbert or Chris, but she cannot do both. Similarly, Dan is faced with two possible actions of sharing. By destroying the bridge, he shares the good with the many people who will be saved when the army is checked in its progress. By changing his plans (and thereby not destroying the bridge), he shares the good with the little girl. He protects her from the danger that his own plans introduce. Like Linda, Dan cannot perform both acts of sharing.

Linda does not use consequentialist reasoning. Rather, she considers the best way that she can share the good. In part, she more completely shares the good by producing a greater good, and in this way her reasoning can look like consequentialist reasoning. She also shares the good more completely, however, by sharing with those who are more intimately connected to her. Linda has a part to play within the greater whole. In her part, she (immediately) shares the good with some people but not with others. She shares the good most of all with her closest friends. This intimate sharing is precisely where the human good is most profoundly realized. Ultimately, then, Linda shares the good best by fulfilling her particular role.

Dan is no different from Linda. He must realize the shared human good in his limited acts of sharing, which directly concern some people but not others. For Dan, the number of people that he protects is an important factor, which leaves the impression (to the casual observer) that he is using consequentialist reasoning. In fact, he is concerned with the role that he must play in sharing the good. How does he, with his part to play, most profoundly share the good with others? The number of people with whom he shares the good is important; the significance of the good shared is also important. Like Linda, however, Dan must also consider other factors, such as his own proximity to the people involved.

Removing Unnecessary Dangers from Our Actions

Consequent harms, as we have already mentioned, play a significant role in our deliberations. Kenny's action of building the shed has the consequence of waking and irritating his neighbor Jean. As a result, he reevaluates his plan. He had planned to start building the shed at 7 a.m., but now he delays his starting time until 10 a.m. Kenny modifies his plan of action so that he no longer risks waking Jean.

Similarly, Larry could modify his action of cutting down the tree by first making sure that the girl is not in harm's way. Unfortunately, in the realistic scenario Dan is unable to modify his action in order to protect the girl: if he bombs the bridge, then it will (almost certainly) have the consequence of killing the girl. Dan does have another option, however. He cannot modify his action, but he could modify his overall plan. He could decide not to bomb the bridge at all in order to protect the girl. We have suggested, however, that it would be better for him to keep his plan. In this way, he shares the good more completely.

A similar analysis applies to the trolley case. Kay does not properly harm Mike; rather, the harm is a consequence of her action. The death of Mike does not cause the trolley to be diverted; rather, the diversion of the trolley causes Mike to die. Kay, then, has two choices before her. On the one hand, by diverting the train, she can seek to protect the five people trapped on the track. On the other hand, she can seek to protect Mike from her own action (which puts him in danger). She does not settle between the two by adding up net results, as does consequentialism. Rather, she considers her possible acts of sharing the good, and she seeks to share the good as best she can.

In this reasoning, consequent harms do not fall under the negative precept to do no harm. Rather, they fall under the affirmative precept to love others; more particularly, they fall under the precept to help those in need. Surprisingly, in these cases, we must protect others from the consequences of our own plans. Kenny must protect Jean from the consequence of his plan to build the shed at 7 a.m.; Larry must protect the girl from the consequence of his plan to remove the tree from his yard, and

Dan must do what he can to protect the girl on the bridge. Unfortunately, he has few options, at least if he wants to fulfill his role of sharing the good. Similarly, Kay may be limited in what she can do to protect Mike from the consequences of her own plans.

The affirmative precept to help those in need demands that, when possible, we remove from our actions what is harmful to others. Sometimes, as with Dan, these consequent harms can be removed only by abandoning more important acts of love. These cases are like that of *Limited Linda*, who chooses not to help someone because she prefers a more important act of sharing the good.

A Corollary

When we perform an acceptable action, such as destroying a bridge in order to stop a menacing army, we are responsible to take sufficient care to remove from our action anything that is harmful or destructive. We are to blame for the consequent harm when we do not take sufficient care (*ST*, II-II, 64, 8). Since Larry does not take sufficient care to remove the harm that follows upon his act of cutting down the tree, he is to blame for the consequent harm to the child. In contrast, when we do take sufficient care, then we are not to blame for the consequent harm. Dan does take sufficient care to remove what harm he can from his action, but in the situation he cannot (while protecting his country) remove all the harm from his action. He is not to blame for the harm that befalls the girl. We still might say that Dan is "responsible" for the harm; after all, he caused it. Nevertheless, he is not to *blame*, for he can provide a sound justification for his responsibility.

The principle that we must take sufficient care to remove harm from our action has an interesting corollary: when we perform an evil action, we are to blame for all the evil that foreseeably follows (*ST*, I-II, 73, 8). Dan performs a good action (protecting his country from the oncoming army), which has negative consequences. Someone else might perform an evil action that has further negative consequences. Consider the following situation:

Poisonous Patti: Patti puts poison in Jim's bottle of wine in hopes of killing him. Jim, however, shares his bottle of wine with Ariel, who also dies as a result of Patti's action.

Patti does not aim to harm Ariel. The death of Ariel, then, is a consequence of her action. Following the guidelines given above, Patti should try to remove from her action any danger to Ariel. She might change her plan, for instance, by poisoning only Jim's glass of wine, rather than his whole bottle of wine. Then she would be less likely to poison anyone else. This change of plan, of course, does not make Patti's action into a good action, for she still aims to kill Jim. Nevertheless, it might be less of an evil action.

The corollary under consideration blocks this kind of reasoning that parallels Dan's reasoning. Dan concludes that he has done all that he can reasonably do to remove the danger attached to his action. Consequently, he is not to blame for the death of the girl. Patti might try a similar defense. She has done all that she reasonably can to remove unnecessary dangers from her action. She might reason, for instance, that if she chooses to poison Jim's glass (instead of his bottle), then she will put herself at unnecessary risk of getting caught.

This reasoning will not do, because Patti's action (unlike Dan's) is an evil action. Dan claims that he cannot remove the danger from his good action. Patti claims that she cannot remove the extra danger from her evil action. She does not consider, however, that she might remove the action itself. Dan does not remove the action of destroying the bridge because it is a noble act of sharing the good. Patti has no similar reason for retaining her plan to murder Jim. While Dan foresees the harm to the girl, Patti did not foresee the harm to Ariel. Nevertheless, the harm was *foreseeable*. From dangerous actions such as poisoning, we foresee the possibility of much unintended harm. Consequently, Patti is to blame for any foreseeable harm from her action; she should have avoided this possible harm by removing the action itself.

We will close our extended treatment of harming others in the next chapter, where we will consider evil actions of harming (rather than good actions that have consequent harm).

chapter 20

Doing Harm

Fiat justitia, ruat caelum ("Let justice be done though the heavens may fall.")

—Ancient Latin adage

At all times, treat humanity as an end and not only as a means.

—Immanuel Kant, *Groundwork of the Metaphysics of Morals*

According to the natural law, cases of consequent harm are profoundly different from cases of harming properly speaking, which fall under the precept "do harm to no one." Dan's case, for instance, is profoundly different from Traci's case. If she kills Louis, Traci does not perform an act of protecting the hostages with the consequence of harming Louis. She reasons back from the goal of saving the hostages and looks for possible causes. Given Pat's demand, the act of killing Louis is a cause by which she can save the hostages.

Avoiding Confusing Descriptions

She should not fall into the confusions of the revisionists. She should not, for instance, overlook the causes necessary to make a means effective. In self-defense, Barb does not simply fire the gun to stop the attack. Rather, she stops the attack by way of harming Scott, which she achieves by way of firing a gun. Similarly, in the act of killing Louis, Traci does not merely fire a gun in order to save the hostages; she does not merely foresee that Louis will die as a consequence of her act of firing the gun. Rather, she saves the hostages by way of killing Louis, which she achieves by way of firing a gun. Killing Louis is necessary because that is precisely the condition that Pat has laid down.

Nor should she suppose that every description of her action can be sliced off; she must recognize that some descriptions must be lumped together. Paula kills a human being, although what she "really wants" is merely to kill a mammal. Similarly, Traci kills a human being, although what she "really wants" is merely "to meet the demands of Pat." In these cases, the diverse descriptions do not provide us with an action separate from its consequences. Paula does not perform an action of killing a mammal with the consequence that a human being dies. Rather, she performs an action of killing a mammal, which is also an action of killing a human being. Similarly, Traci does not perform an action of meeting Pat's demands with the consequence of Louis's death. Rather, she performs an action of meeting the demands of Pat that is also an action of killing a human being.

If Traci is honest, she must recognize that she plans to kill one human being in order to save other human beings. The harm to Louis is not merely a consequence of her action. Her action is essentially an act of harming Louis. It falls directly under the precept "do harm to no one."

Unfortunately, we lack convenient words to express the difference between Dan killing the little girl (as a consequence of his action of bombing the bridge) and Traci killing Louis (as a means to save the hostages). Both of these cases involve harmful actions. As we have seen, however, Dan does not most properly harm the girl; in contrast, Traci does most properly harm Louis. Besides speaking of proper actions, we can adopt a verbal convention to distinguish these two sorts of cases. Cases like Dan's may be described as doing an action with consequent harm. Cases like Traci's may be described as doing harm. The category of "harmful actions," then, is divided into two kinds: actions with consequent harm and actions of doing harm. This latter kind involves harm not just as a consequence; the very action itself is directed toward harm. Most properly, then, the agent is engaged in an act of harming.

Love of Others within the Shared Good

Why does the essence of Traci's action matter? Is she not doing much the same thing as Dan? In his efforts to save many lives, he harms the girl. Similarly, in her effort to save the hostages, Traci harms Louis. Why should it matter that Dan most properly destroys a bridge and harms the girl only as a consequence? Why should it matter that Traci most properly harms Louis? The upshot is much the same. The goal of each is much the same.

In order to answer these questions, we must keep our eye on the shared good. We must not get distracted by a sum total of goods, which is a sham substitute of the shared good. What Traci wants—or at least what she should want—is to share her good with those around her. She wants to share the good with the hostages, saving them if she can. At the same time, she desires to share the good with Louis. In both cases, she does not desire a sum total of goods; she does not desire merely effects produced by her actions. Rather, she desires to possess the good with others. She desires to make her own good to be also the good of others and the good of others to be also her own good.

Traci desires not just the existence of certain goods. She also loves certain people. She does not desire only that goods exist; she desires goods *for the sake of* those she loves. She wants those she loves to have the good. Every good is the good of some subject, even as being sharp is the good of a knife. Traci wants the good precisely for some subject.

Traci's desires extend beyond her own limited self. She is not the only subject for whom she wants the good. Rather, she wants the good together with others. She does not want the good as solitary, as belonging only to herself. She wants her own good to be more than just her own. She sees herself not as solitary but as united with others. She wants the good, then, not for a solitary subject but for a united subject. She wants to have the good for herself and Louis as united; she wants the good for herself and the hostages as united.

She loves these people as possessing parts of the good, not as merely producing parts. She even loves Pat, who has separated himself from the shared good. She loves him to the degree that she hopes that he will change, so that he can then share in the good. She recognizes, however, that he has made himself into a secondary part, into a kind of producing part. If she were an official of the community, she might choose to kill him (if she were able), and thereby direct him productively toward the shared good.

In no way, however, should she kill Louis, who remains a possessing part of the shared good. He has not rejected the shared good. He has not turned himself into a secondary part. Even if Traci were a representative of the community, then, she would still not be permitted to kill Louis.

Using Others As a Means

Why does the difference between doing harm—harming properly speaking—and consequent harm matter? The little girl that Dan kills is also a possessing part; she has not made herself into a secondary part merely by wandering upon the bridge. Why, then, may Dan harm the girl but Traci may not harm Louis?

We must look at what Traci aims to achieve in the act of killing Louis. As we have seen, in every action we seek to introduce some change in some subject. Traci (if she chooses to kill Louis) seeks to introduce the change of death into Louis. What good does Traci see in this change? It is not the good of Louis. Rather, she sees Louis's death as usefully good for a good that is alien to Louis's own good. His death is useful because it will modify Pat's behavior, so that he sets the hostages free. This useful good is alien to Louis's own good because it is his harm.

Dan is different. He does not aim to introduce a useful good into the girl. Indeed, we have seen that he does not aim to introduce any change into the girl. Rather, he hopes to introduce a change (destruction) into the bridge, and he foresees that this action will have the consequence of changing the girl. Dan, then, is not using the girl as a means to stop the army. In contrast, Traci is using Louis as a means to save the hostages.

Treating as an End

This observation may lead you to think of the philosopher Immanuel Kant, who said that we should always treat others as an end and not merely as a means. For many, even for those who have never heard of Immanuel Kant, this dictum rings true. Indeed, Aquinas himself suggests that we should not be using other human beings as a means (*SCG*, III, chap. 112, no. 1; *ST*, I, 96, 4; *ST*, II-II, 64, 2, ad 3).

Aquinas, however, does not say that we should treat others as an end. If Traci loves Louis as someone united with herself, as someone with whom she shares the good, she does not love him as an end. He is still a member of the community, and she loves him by his role within the community; she loves him as a possessing *part*, not as a possessing *end*. She loves him as ordered beyond himself. He is not an independent subject nor an independent good. He and Traci (and others as well) are jointly the subject of a shared good. His good is not an independent end. Rather, his good is also Traci's good, and Traci's good is also his good.

Aquinas could adopt Kant's terminology, as long as "treating someone as an end" means that we love him or her as a possessing part. This meaning of "end," however, does not seem to be what Kant had in mind, nor does Aquinas generally speak in this manner, although he does say that human beings are to be desired for their own sake (*SCG*, III, chap. 112, no. 3).

According to the natural law, Dan's action is acceptable, and Linda's action of saving Norbert rather than Chris is also acceptable. In both cases, the person who dies does not seem to be an end. Dan prefers to protect others (from the army) rather than to protect the girl (from the consequences of his own action). The girl, then, is only one part of his good, and in the situation, she seems to be a lesser part. She has a lower place—within his action—than do the many that he hopes to save. Similarly, Chris is not a final stopping point (an end) for Linda. He is part, and only part, of the subject of her shared good. Indeed, Chris seems to be a lesser part than Norbert.

On the other hand, neither is Norbert an end. He is only part of the end. The complete end includes Linda, Norbert, and Chris (as well as others). Linda does not seek simply Norbert's private good as an end; rather, she seeks a shared good, a good that is "ours," a good that belongs to "us" as united. Because Linda is limited, she can act to achieve only part of this good. She pursues "our" good as it is realized most especially in Norbert. In Linda's action, then, Chris has not been excluded. Linda is seeking the shared good that belongs to Chris as well as to Norbert. The good that is realized in Norbert is not only Norbert's good; it also belongs to Chris.

Similarly, Dan is limited in his pursuit of the shared good. He cannot achieve it all. By bombing the bridge, he shares the good most especially with those who will be protected from the army. By refusing to bomb the bridge, he shares the good most especially with the girl. No single individual is an end of his action. He seeks a shared good that belongs to all. By pursuing the good that is realized most especially in those that will be protected from the army, he does not exclude the girl. This good is her good as well. The girl, like Chris, is treated as a part, as a possessing part of a good that Dan seeks to share with others.

When Evil Becomes Our Good

Neither the girl nor Chris, then, is treated as an end. On the other hand, neither is treated—as is Louis—as a means to some alien good. If Traci chooses to kill Louis, then his evil has become her good. His death is, for her, a productive good. In contrast, Chris's death never becomes Linda's good. Rather, his life remains good for her, but because of her limitations, she cannot actively pursue it.

By making Louis's evil into her good, Traci excludes Louis from the shared good. He is not a possessing part. His good, which should belong not only to himself but also to Traci, has become a kind of evil, for it excludes the good that Traci really wants: it excludes the productive good by which she can save the hostages. When seeking the shared good, Traci should say, "Your good is also my good." If she chooses to kill Louis, then Traci says, "Your evil is my good." Louis ultimately becomes a producing part of the good that Traci seeks. Through his death, Louis produces the good that Traci really wants. In contrast, Chris's death produces no good for Linda. His death remains a loss for Linda, not a good.

The importance of our actions—properly speaking—is linked to the good we pursue and the subject for whom we pursue the good. What we do most properly is what we pursue as an end or as a means. Our actions, then, reveal what is our good—both what we consider good to achieve in itself (the end) and what we consider good as useful (the means). Traci, who most properly harms Louis, pursues his death as a useful good. She uses him for an alien good. She excludes him from the shared good. She loves his evil as her good. In contrast, Dan does not harm the girl properly speaking but recognizes that consequent harm will befall her. Dan does not pursue the death of the girl as any kind of good, useful or otherwise. For him, her death is not a good; it is a loss, an absence of the complete shared good that he desires.

In the craniotomy case, does the doctor merely narrow the size of the baby's head or does he—properly speaking—harm the baby? More to the point, does he merely crush the baby's skull or does he harm the baby? The revisionists think that these two descriptions can be separated. In fact, crushing a skull is harm. By crushing the skull, the doctor treats the baby as a means, as a productive part by which to save the life of the mother. The baby's evil becomes the doctor's good. The crushed skull is usefully good to the doctor. Using the baby—which amounts to the evil of the baby—becomes part of the doctor's good. Fortunately, by way of C-sections, this whole tragedy can be avoided. The baby and the mother can both be saved.

Do Harm to No One

We have spent a long time (chapters 11 through 20) on the precept "do harm to no one." For two good reasons, this precept deserves the extended treatment given to it. First, modern understandings of this precept are often muddled. Consequentialism furnishes the greatest befuddlement. It loses sight of the shared good and concocts a sum total of goods, which belongs to no one. The difference between harming and failing to do good disappears entirely. Sharing the good through our actions becomes irrelevant. Only producing results matters.

Confusion arises as well from the very complexity of the precept itself. "Do harm to no one" requires three clarifications. First, we must never harm the innocent. Second, we must never harm (even the guilty) when acting as a private individual. Third, we must never harm most properly (as opposed to harming as a consequence of our actions).

This third clarification implies that we may sometimes harm not in our very actions but in the consequences of our actions. This (sometimes) acceptable harm was explained in the last chapter. We are enjoined, with a positive precept, to remove from our actions that which is harmful to others. Sometimes, however, it is acceptable to leave these harmful aspects in place. In other words, consequent harm does not fall under the negative precept "do harm to no one." Rather, it falls under the positive precept to help those in need. A complete understanding of the negative precept "do harm to no one," then, has required an understanding of the positive precept to love others.

For another reason, the precept "do harm to no one" deserves the extended attention we have devoted to it. This precept is one of the most fundamental of the natural law. It applies to all human beings, excepting the state-sanctioned harm that can be done to the guilty in punishment. Furthermore, it guards a principal aspect of the shared good.

The shared good is possessed together through acts of sharing. We must seek our good as belonging not only to ourselves but also as belonging to others. Consequently, we must give our personal good to others. Because we are limited, we share the good immediately (in our actions) only with a limited number of people and in a limited number of actions. In short, we cannot do all good. We can, however, avoid all evil. We can avoid the harm that tears asunder the fabric of the human community. We can, thereby, protect the good we possess together with others.

The importance of the precept "do harm to no one" is linked to the importance of justice, which is one of the most central goods for our shared human completion. Justice demands that we do good to others and avoid harming others (*ST*, II-II, 79, 1). By doing good to others, we share the good with them. By harming others, we exclude them from the shared good. For the shared human good, justice is foundational, while injustice is ruinous.

As we proceed to consider other aspects of the shared good, we must never lose sight of the importance of justice; we must never forget the devastation inflicted by injustice.

Before we proceed, you may wish to know that Traci decided not to kill Louis. A SWAT team, however, was able to save the lives of the 20 and apprehend Pat, who was justly punished.

part III

Society

chapter 21

Authority

The man who rules efficiently must have obeyed others in the past, and the man who obeys dutifully appears fit at a later time to be a ruler.

—Cicero, *On Laws*

All power is inherent in the people; that they may exercise it by themselves; that it is their right and duty.

—Thomas Jefferson, Letter to Justice William Johnson (1823)

Authority directs the actions of the members within a group (Simon 1962). It arises in communities that require coordinated activity (*DR*, bk. 1, chap. 1, 3–4). The orchestra, for instance, needs some kind of authority, such as a conductor, to determine tempo, volume, and so on.

Different Kinds of Authorities

Sometimes the authority can be democratic in the fullest sense: every member agrees to the course of action. Imagine, for instance, that Bob and Carol are planning a trip together. They need an authority to coordinate their activity, but the authority is simply the two of them getting together and working out the details. Similarly, a smaller musical group than an orchestra, such as a quartet, might have no single leader; they might work out together the details of playing.

Sometimes the authority can be democratic to a lesser extent; then the authority is more properly called representative. The members agree upon some official or officials who will direct the activity. Bob and Carol, for instance, might simply agree that it is best for Carol to work out the details of the trip all by herself. Likewise, in many countries in the world today, we elect representatives to make decisions about how to coordinate the activity of the nation. Some of these representatives make laws; others make particular policies; still others enforce the laws; and so on.

For other groups, the authority is not democratic or representative at all. The authority is determined without the input of the members. The conductor of the orchestra, for instance, might be hired by those who fund the orchestra. Similarly, in many countries throughout human history, the supreme authority was determined by hereditary, such as with a king.

Sometimes, even these authorities can be considered democratic in a very minimal sense. To the degree that the individuals consent to be members of the community, they also consent to the authority that has been placed over the community. They do not choose the authority, but they agree to be under the authority. In many situations, of course, they have feeble alternatives. A peasant in a monarchy, for instance, may have the alternative of submitting to the authority or living in prison.

Limitations of Authority

Authorities direct and coordinate activity, but they do not direct every single detail of the activity. We call some authorities micromanagers because they are so obsessed with the details, but even they must leave some determination up to the members of the group. Carol might micromanage the trip, but she will not tell Bob exactly where to place his feet as he walks down the sidewalk. She will leave at least that detail up to him. A sergeant who orders a private to mop the floor must still leave the particular details—of each stroke of the mop, for instance—up to the private.

Sometimes quite a bit of discretion is left to the person given the command. A general might command a major to capture a certain fort, but he leaves all the details up to the major. The major does not choose the fort to be captured, but he does choose where to position his troops, what parts of the fort to target, and so on. The major himself will direct his lieutenants toward certain goals but will leave the details up to them. He might, for instance, direct one lieutenant to attack the south wall, but the lieutenant himself will choose the movement of his troops. And of course, even the privates will be making some decisions themselves. They will fire their guns at certain enemy troops without waiting to be told by their commander.

Authorities are unable to direct every detail in part because they have limited knowledge. The general knows that this fort must be captured, but perhaps he is not on the scene, so he does not know much about what is needed for the attack. The major, who is on the scene, knows these details, but even his knowledge is limited. He cannot know everything that is happening during the battle. Consequently, he must leave some decisions up to others who do know the details of the particular situation (such as what is happening on the south wall).

Because authorities have limited knowledge, the directions they provide do not go into every nitty-gritty detail; rather, the directions are somewhat generic. The command of the general, for instance, is quite generic: it simply directs the major to capture the fort without saying exactly how.

Policies

Some commands are generic in yet another way. Not only do they omit the details; they also cover a whole class of actions. They do not direct to one single action, like attacking this fort, but to every instance of a certain kind of action, or at least to most instances. The major, for instance, might give the following command to his troops: "when crossing an open field, run in a zigzag fashion." This command is generic in the first way, since it does not tell the troops every step they must take, but it is also generic in the second way. It is not telling a single soldier about a single crossing of a field. Rather, it is telling every soldier about every crossing of an open field. Commands that are generic in the second way might be called policies. It is the major's policy that anyone crossing an open field should run in a zigzag fashion.

Human laws are almost always policies. They give direction for a whole class of actions (*ST*, I-II, 96, 6). The law to drive on the right side of the road, for instance, does not just direct one person on one particular trip. Rather, it directs every act of driving (or nearly every act of driving) by every driver (in a particular jurisdiction). This law, of course, is also generic in the first sense. It does not tell drivers every detail of what they must do on every trip.

Although policies are given in the universal, as if they cover every instance under a class, they typically do not cover every single instance within the class; rather, they cover *almost* every instance. Suppose, for example, that Joyce is driving on the right side of the road, but then she comes across a section in which the right side of the road is flooded but the left side is open; furthermore, currently the left side of the road has no oncoming traffic. Joyce reasonably judges that the law does not command her to drive through the flooded section, so she drives on the left side of the road to get past the flooded section.

Has Joyce broken the law? It seems that she has. After all, it tells her to drive on the right side of the road, but she has chosen to drive on the left side. On the other hand, maybe she has not broken the law. After all, the law could not reasonably have been written as a command to drive through a flooded street. Perhaps she could have followed the strict letter of the law by backtracking and taking an alternate route. But suppose she is driving on a lonely country road (with few alternate routes) and that she must get to her destination soon. What is she to do?

The Letter of the Law and the Spirit of the Law

According to Aquinas, this question concerns the difference between the letter of the law and the spirit of the law (*ST*, I-II, 96, 6). The letter of the law is the explicit policy or command written (or spoken). The spirit of the law, says Aquinas, is what the lawmaker aims to achieve in making the law. The letter of the law, for instance, commands drivers to drive on the right side of the road. The spirit of the law, on the other hand, aims at safe driving. By making sure that everyone drives on the right side of the road, collisions will be minimized. In Joyce's situation, however, driving on the right side of the road is not safe, while driving on the left side is safe. In this case, then, the letter of the law and the spirit of the law conflict with one another.

Unfortunately, lawmakers are never fully able to express, in words, what they hope to achieve (which is the spirit of the law). This disconnect is inevitable because the world in which we live is a messy place. The lawmakers try to achieve some goal by way of coordinating human actions. They try to achieve safe driving, for instance, by coordinating the actions of drivers so that they always drive on the same side of the road. Because the world is a messy place, however, circumstances will arise in which this particular coordination does not achieve the goal. The world has too many interacting causes for one solution to work in every situation. Perhaps the solution will work in most situations, but it will inevitably fail at least in a few situations (*ST*, I-II, 96, 6).

The lawmakers cannot possibly hope to discover all these situations. Some situations they may indeed foresee, and they might include these situations in the written law. On the other hand, they might not. After all, including only a single exception might make for an extremely lengthy law.

Imagine the following exception to the law concerning driving on the right side of the road: "drivers may drive on the left side of the road in the following situation: (1) when they come across a flooded section of the right side of the road and (2) when the left side of the road has no oncoming traffic and (3) when they have no easy alternative. Even after all that, the lawmakers may not have described the situation accurately enough. Imagine writing exceptions not only for this possible situation but for all other possible situations in which the law might fail. The law would be very lengthy indeed. Even so, some exceptions would have been missed, for the lawmakers simply cannot discover every single exception.

It is wiser, then, to state the law simply and to leave the determination of exceptions to individual cases. Just as the general allows the major to determine the details of his attack upon the fort, so some laws—in their spirit—allow individuals to make determinations of those instances that do not fall under the law. To be clear, these determinations are unusual; they are not often needed. In most instances, the law should be followed without question. Furthermore, some laws are more stringent than others in their application. Some laws, for instance, may designate recourse to proper authorities for determining exceptions. Only in cases of urgency should the law be set aside apart from the proper authorities.

Sometimes, commands that are generic only in the first way can have exceptions based upon information not available to the one giving the command. In World War II, for instance Major Richard Winters was told to take his troops across an open field in order to attack the enemy. Major Winters, being on the spot, had much more information than did the authorities who gave him the command. He recognized that the troops carrying out this maneuver would be killed without gaining any benefit; furthermore, the enemy was going to be defeated anyway. He did not send his troops across the field. He reasoned based upon the spirit of the command rather than upon the letter of the command.

Communities of Utility

Lack of information is not the only reason for issuing generic commands (for which the person carrying out the command makes some determinations of his or her own). The second reason is more central to the shared good, but it is also more difficult to understand. It depends upon the nature of the shared good. Consequently, this second reason will not apply to some communities, which lack a true shared good.

Consider a band of thieves intent on robbing a bank. Suppose all the members care only for themselves. They want their portion of the money, and they have no regard for anyone else in the group. Still, the robbers need some authority to coordinate their activity, or they will never succeed.

In this community of utility, each member sees the others solely as useful. If Michele is given the task of driving the getaway car and Kyle is given the task of cracking the safe, then Michele views Kyle as useful for opening the safe and Kyle views Michele as useful for getting away. Each is given a task by Larry, who is the gang leader, but each views the tasks of the others as merely useful for gaining the desired money. Similarly, they view the authoritative role of Larry (of assigning tasks to others) as merely useful; if they did not have an authority to coordinate their activities, they would not succeed.

The gang members want a shared utility, which is a kind of good, but they do not want to possess the good together. They want the utility of robbing the bank, which can be done only together with others. No inherent good is shared. Only a useful good. Consequently, their community is rightly called a community of utility.

Communities with a Shared Good

As we have seen, not every community is a community of pure utility. Sometimes the members want to possess the inherent good together. Suppose our orchestra members really want to play together. They want the activity of playing symphonic music as a united good. In that case, the members are not merely useful to one another, and the task that each is given is not merely useful.

Clare, for instance, is given the task of playing the cello. Sebastian, who sings in the chorus (the orchestra is playing Beethoven's Ninth Symphony), does not view Clare as merely useful. Her activity is part of "our" activity, which is the good that he wants. Her activity does not merely produce a good in which he takes a part. He wants Clare to act because he wants to act with her. He wants to play music with her.

Clare is a possessing member of the good, not a producing member. Her activity is an act of possessing the good. Clare and her activity go together: they cannot be separated. Sebastian does not want only the activity of Clare. Nor does he want Clare herself apart from the activity. He wants the two together. He wants Clare playing the cello.

Although the members are not merely useful to one another, they still need an authority. Their actions must be coordinated to form a united activity. Louis the conductor achieves this coordination. Like the other members, Louis is not merely useful. The very coordination of the diverse actions (which he achieves) is itself part of the united activity.

The Good of Independence

The role of authority differs slightly between a community of utility, like the gang, and a community with a true shared good. In both, the authority provides direction that does not fill in every detail of what is to be done. Larry, for instance, might direct Michele to take a certain escape route, but he is not going to tell her exactly when to put her foot on the gas, on the brake, and so on. As an authority, Larry is limited; he is simply unable to provide all these details.

In the case of the shared good, however, this reason is not the only one for a limited authority. Even apart from his or her own limitations, the authority figure wants the members to contribute their own actions. Those actions are part of the shared good the authority seeks; they are not mere utilities. Clare's action of playing the cello is part of what Louis wants when he provides direction. Ultimately, then, he wants her to have her own input, so that the action can be truly hers (*ST*, I, 65, 2).

The same cannot be said for Larry and Michele. Larry would lose nothing by providing—if he were able—all the details of what Michele needed to do. After all, her action is only useful. The benefits of her action are entirely in what it produces. No benefit derives from the action being hers.

The difference between the two examples can be expressed in terms of independence. Both Louis and Larry want the others in the group to have some independence, but Larry wants the independence only because he is, by himself, inadequate to the task. Louis is also inadequate, but in addition he wants to share the good. He wants Clare to have her good as part of the overall good of the whole. Her independence is itself part of his good.

Louis, then, has a reason that Larry lacks for giving generic commands: he wants the members of the orchestra to contribute their part. Correspondingly, Clare has a reason beyond utility—a reason that Michele lacks—for following the direction of authority. She wants a united activity, an activity that is not only her own. She wants her activity precisely insofar as it is coordinated with the others. It receives this coordination, however, through the direction of Louis. Clare wants to follow Louis, then, so that her action can not only be her own action but also so that it can belong to the whole. By following the lead of Louis, then, Clare allows her good to become the good of others.

In contrast, Michele asks only what is in it for herself. Larry's commands are useful so that she can achieve her own good. If he gives a command that lacks this utility, then she has no reason to follow it. Suppose, for instance, that the police arrive on the scene before Kyle can crack the safe. Larry orders everyone to evacuate, so that Michele can drive them away. Michele, however, calculates that the longer she waits for the other gang members to get in the car, the less likely it is that she herself will escape. If she drives off without waiting, then she gains her freedom. If she waits, then she gains no money and possibly ends up in prison. Larry's command, then, seems to have little utility for her, so she drives off without the others.

Limitations on Authority

All human authority is limited. As we have just suggested, authority based upon utility is limited by the utility itself. Authority within a truly shared good, however, has other sources of limitation. Aquinas says that it has two sources of limitation, what might be called the limitation from above and the limitation from below (*ST*, II-II, 104, 5). The limitation from above is fairly straightforward. An authority is always limited by higher authorities. The authority of a military major does not extend to the point of making decisions that contradict a general.

The examples given above might suggest otherwise. Sometimes, it seems, a subordinate can oppose the order of a higher superior (as Major Winters did). These examples, however, concerned the spirit of the command rather than the letter of the command. Furthermore, to some extent these examples relate to the other limitation on authority, the limitation from below. This limitation depends upon the aspect of the shared good just noted: the various parts, including the subordinate parts, each have something to contribute. Their activity is valuable in itself, and not just for the sake of some utility. Some decisions, then, should be left to the subordinate, and an authority that tries to micromanage is extending beyond the scope of his or her authority.

Aquinas, who is focusing upon the individual as an individual, gives two examples: the immediate care of one's own body and the union of marriage. His examples, however, need not be taken as exhaustive. For one thing, he is focusing upon commands given to an individual as an individual. The limitation from below, however, does not merely concern what can be commanded to an individual; it also concerns what can be commanded by a higher authority to a lower authority.

According to this idea, an authority has a certain scope. Obviously, for instance, a military authority has domain only over military decisions and not over private decisions, such as marriage. But even within the domain of military decisions, the authority is limited by the contributions that must come from below. The military may be a bad example, since it is often concerned almost exclusively with utility. An army is more concerned with the outcome of victory than it is with a shared activity. Outside the context of an actual war, however, the military might operate more like a community with a shared good (rather than just a shared utility). Then the contributions from below become more important.

Later thinkers have used what is called "the principle of subsidiarity" (Behr 2019). According to this principle, not everything should be managed at the highest level; rather, lower levels must be left to provide their appropriate contributions. The national government, for instance, should not manage everything; rather, lower intermediary governments—such as state, county, provincial, or city governments—should manage those affairs proper to these lower levels. Decisions should not all be made at higher levels. We should leave at lower levels what can be managed at a lower level. Otherwise, we trample upon the shared good, which depends upon each part contributing its own activity and not merely its own utility.

Both limitations on authority will be important for the natural law. The natural law is itself a higher authority that places limitations upon human authorities (*ST*, I-II, 96, 4). Human beings have no authority to command evil actions, actions that oppose the higher authority of the natural law. No human authority, for instance, can command Traci to perform the evil action of killing Louis. She should follow the higher authority of the natural law, which prohibits this action. Natural law also sets limits that come from below. An authority, for instance, should not place unequal burdens upon his or her subjects (*ST*, I-II, 96, 4).

Roles within a Community

For both the community of utility and the community with a shared good, the authority gives the members particular roles to fill within the whole. Sometimes the role can be quite small. The sergeant who orders the private to mop the floor gives the private the role of mopping this floor at this moment. The role is not for mopping in general but only for mopping this floor at this time. On account of the authority, this very small role has been given to the private. He fulfills his part within the whole by following the directives of the authority. By disobeying the order, he rejects his part within the whole; he rejects his order to the shared good.

For policies (such as traffic laws), the authority does not so much give the role as define the role; it sets the parameters for the role. The law to drive on the right side of the road, for instance, does not give someone the role of driving. Rather, given that somebody is driving, the law lays out the manner in which this activity can fit within the whole. Drivers who want their activity to be ordered to the good of the whole must follow this parameter. Drivers who disobey the law desire to drive for the sake of some other good besides the shared good of the group. They set aside the shared good for the sake of some other good.

Natural laws, we will see, are no different in this regard. They often define the roles by which we realize our human good. They show us the way to attain the human good as shared.

chapter 22

Political Society: Utility

Mere anarchy is loosed upon the world,
The blood-dimmed tide is loosed, and everywhere
The ceremony of innocence is drowned;
The best lack all conviction, while the worst
Are full of passionate intensity.

—William Butler Yeats, "The Second Coming"

In this war of every man against every man, . . . the notions of right and wrong, justice and injustice, have no place. There is . . . continual fear and danger of violent death, and the life of man is solitary, poor, nasty, brutish, and short.

—Thomas Hobbes, *Leviathan*

The prevalent modern conception of the political community (which we will call, for convenience, "the modern vision") differs dramatically from the classical vision in which natural law finds its home. In the modern vision, the political community is like the gang of robbers discussed in the last chapter; in the classical vision, the political community is like the orchestra.

The modern vision is epitomized by the quote of Thomas Hobbes at the head of this chapter. By nature, he claims, human beings are not social; rather, they are pitted against one another in a war of every man against every man. No morality—no right or wrong, no justice or injustice—can adjudicate this war, and as a consequence human life is "solitary, poor, nasty, brutish, and short." Only the utility of avoiding such a miserable fate propels us to unite with others into political society.

Self-Sacrifice

In the modern vision, people join together in a community on account of some useful advantage (Hobbes 1994). Michele calculates that she can get a portion of the bank's money if she joins with others in robbing the bank; similarly, citizens within the political community calculate that they can get certain benefits through the community. They can get better food, better clothing, better shelter, and so on. In addition, they can have better security, both from the surrounding environment and from other human beings. Just as Michele follows the directives of Larry only insofar as they are useful for her own benefit, so the citizens (in this modern vision) follow the directives of society only insofar as the directives prove useful for the citizen's private interests.

Despite Larry's command, Michele is unwilling to wait for the others unless it is to her advantage. Similarly, citizens will be unwilling to follow the commands of society if those commands prove disadvantageous. Most dramatically, citizens will refuse self-sacrifice.

Suppose, for instance, that Max's country is being attacked, and now he is asked to serve in the military. Max has no reason (within the modern vision) for risking his life, except insofar as it might redound to his own advantage. Maybe he gets paid (as being part of the military) or maybe he calculates that his chances of survival on his own are insignificant. In no way, however, does he think that his act of sacrificing his life—if it should come—is good for him.

Plausibly, his calculations might go in the other direction. He might decide that the possibility of self-sacrifice is simply not worth the possible utility. He might calculate as follows: if I serve in the military, I have a high chance of dying. On the other hand, if I disobey orders and turn and run, then I have a good chance of surviving. Since my country is only useful to me, I have no good reason for defending it. In the current situation, my country has outlived its utility.

In the classical vision, the political community does have (as with the modern vision) a mutual advantage of utility, but it has something more. The citizens want more than utility. They want to unite with others in possessing the good. They want to achieve a united activity, an activity of the whole. Members of the community, then, can take pleasure in the accomplishments of their united community. We perform (the citizens might say) greater deeds together than we could ever do by ourselves.

Consequently, the risk of self-sacrifice has more to it than personal utility. The very act of sacrificing is itself a good (*ST*, II-II, 123, 7). Suppose that Vince is asked to sacrifice his life in order to defend his country. If he reasons like Max, then he will conclude that he should abandon his post. The sacrifice is not good for him, since it has no utility for his personal good. But if Vince pursues a shared good, then he will recognize that his good is realized in others. By abandoning them, he abandons his own good. The very act of self-sacrifice is an act of achieving the good with others. Through this action of self-sacrifice, Vince's good belongs to others.

Unions of Deprivation and Unions of Transcendence

This last example requires clarification, for the political community, even with the classical vision of a shared good, is not exactly like the orchestra. We have already noted the difference in passing: to some degree—even to a great degree—the political community forms on account of mutual utility. Within the political community, for instance, some members will take on the role of farming—that is, of producing food. Other members will be construction workers, and so on. Through these specializations of tasks, each member benefits, for there is more food to go around, better buildings to be had, and so on. The union is useful for achieving goods that the individual members lack, or for achieving better goods.

Imagine we were all like Robinson Crusoe, living on our own. We might get by (or we might not), but our lives would be materially (and socially) worse off. Our food might not be as abundant, or it might not have the same quality. The same might be said for our shelter and clothing. Defending ourselves against an enemy would be more challenging, perhaps impossible, without the aid of others.

Consider a group, such as an orchestra, that has no similar goal of utility. The members of this particular orchestra simply want to play music together. They are not getting paid, nor are they getting any side benefit. No member of the orchestra gains any utility by joining with the others. What each member gains is the united activity of playing together. This activity, however, is not a useful means for producing a good that the members otherwise lack. Rather, the united activity is the very good desired. It is the goal to be achieved, not a useful tool for producing other goods.

Robinson Crusoe and the orchestra members reflect two different ways in which individuals might be insufficient or inadequate. Robinson Crusoe is unable to achieve even his own individual good, or at least to achieve it well. Babies provide clear examples of this first insufficiency. They cannot get the food they need, the clothing they need, the shelter they need, and so on. On their own, babies do not achieve even their own personal good.

The orchestra members exhibit another kind of inadequacy. Let us suppose that each member is a virtuoso on his or her particular instrument. The members lack nothing for their own particular good. Nevertheless, they cannot, by themselves, play symphonic music. As a cello player, for instance, Clare might have all the skill that can be hoped for in a cellist. Unlike the baby, she needs no help to attain her individual good of playing the cello. Nevertheless, by herself she cannot play symphonic music. She has her complete individual good, but she is still inadequate. The full completion of a cellist—perhaps achieved without any assistance—is itself inadequate; it must be filled in by others.

With regard to our individual good, we are all in some measure like babies. We do not produce our own food, we do not make our own clothes, and we do not build our own houses. We are not independent Robinson Crusoes. Even if we were, we would still lack some aspects of our own personal fulfillment. Like babies, we need others because we are unable, on our own, to achieve our individual completion.

Our imagined virtuoso musicians are unlike babies (with regard to the good of music). Clare does not unite with the other members of the orchestra so that they can produce, in her, some personal musical good that she lacks. She lacks nothing of her individual good. Rather, she unites with others because her own good, complete in herself, is inadequate. She unites to possess a good that is more than her own good. She unites with others so that, together, she and they can possess the good of playing symphonic music.

For the sake of convenience and clarity, it would be nice to have some brief terms that capture this difference between Clare and the baby. Unfortunately, adequate terms are not easy to find. We will have to settle upon some tolerable terms. Let us say, then, that Clare has an inadequacy of transcendence; she must transcend beyond her own activity to form a more complete united activity with others. In contrast, babies have an inadequacy of deprivation; without others, they are deprived even of their own personal good.

These two kinds of inadequacies give rise to two kinds of unions between individuals, what might be called a union of deprivation and a union of transcendence. The gang members have a union of deprivation. They cannot, by themselves, produce the individual good (of money) that they desire, so they unite with others to overcome this inadequacy. The orchestra of virtuosos has a union of transcendence. They do not need the other members in order to overcome a deprivation in their individual good. Rather, they need the other members to transcend beyond their individual good to the good of playing symphonic music.

Political Society as a Union of Deprivation

What kind of union is found within political society? As we have already suggested, political society helps to alleviate many of our inadequacies of deprivation. We are all like babies to some extent. We unite with others in order that they might help us to produce our own personal good. Through being a member of political society, we get food, clothing, shelter, and many other benefits that we cannot produce on our own. No one will deny, then, that political society is a union of deprivation.

We have emphasized what might be called the bodily needs of babies, such as the needs for food, clothing, and shelter. But babies clearly have other needs as well. They cannot form their minds on their own. In other words, they must be educated. Babies simply cannot teach themselves. The myth of Romulus and Remus being raised by wolves is indeed a myth. This need for education does not disappear as infants grow. Young children must be educated; high school students must be educated; college students must be educated. Even so-called "self-taught" individuals rely upon books or other media, in which they are still learning from others.

Besides these mental or intellectual needs, babies also have emotional needs. On their own, they cannot form the proper emotional dispositions. They must be trained, for instance, to restrain their desires. Otherwise, they become "spoiled brats." The inability to control their own wants, to endure any frustration of their desires, and to pursue long-term goals makes such individuals very unpleasant to be around. These inabilities also make them unable to care for themselves. Emotional immaturity in children, then, is a deprivation of their own private good.

Many individuals, of course, remain like babies for life. Despite their bodily maturity, they never achieve mental or emotional maturity. This failure is sometimes a result of poor upbringing, what might be called a "bad environment." At other times, the individual is to blame. He consistently chooses his own gratification, thereby neglecting his emotional development and refusing to advance his mental capacities. Often, of course, the failure is a combination of environment and personal choice.

For the moment, we are simply trying to emphasize that human beings must unite with others. Only then can they fill in the inadequacies of their personal goods. Some of these inadequacies concern bodily goods; others concern mental goods. The latter inadequacies are more profound, and they more profoundly need the assistance of others. Consequently, political society—as a union of deprivation—most of all concerns the fulfillment of our mental goods.

Self-Sufficiency

Because of our various deprivations, we form diverse societies. We are deprived of physical goods, so we form economic societies. We lack intellectual proficiency, so we form educational societies. Even the basic unit of the family is one such society. We lack immortality, so we form a society to pass on our nature. The family also meets basic economic and educational needs, although it still leaves these needs unmet at higher levels.

The family is also essential for the most significant human deprivation, the lack of emotional maturity and moral virtue. Without a favorable family environment, in which the parents lovingly guide their children toward virtue, the possibility of attaining virtue becomes remote. Even a good family, however, does not always successfully pass on virtue.

This inadequacy of the family, thinks Aquinas, is the chief motivation for political society properly speaking. Because we lack moral virtue, we must coordinate our activities in order to produce moral virtue. For this reason, we coordinate our family lives in discipline and love. Society picks up where the family leaves off. In particular, thinks Aquinas, society steps in for those unruly individuals who cannot be restrained by the family (*ST*, I-II, 95, 1). Society provides a discipline of its own. It provides the discipline of law and the discipline of state-sanctioned punishment.

Political society, says Aristotle, is a self-sufficient society (*Pol*, bk. 3, chap. 1; *ST*, II-II, 50, 1). In economic matters and in educational matters, society certainly supplies much-needed benefits. In these domains, however, it is not entirely self-sufficient. Economically, one society trades with another, acquiring materials and products that they themselves do not produce. Intellectually, one society learns from another. Individual societies, then, are not fully self-sufficient in these domains.

The self-sufficiency of political society is in the domain of discipline. The purpose of society is to coordinate our activities toward virtue; its purpose is to provide the needed discipline of law—with the sanction of punishment to enforce it—in order to form and shape individuals in virtue, or at the very least to restrain them from vice. A society without the discipline of law, then, is no political society at all.

Just because political society is self-sufficient, it does not follow that it always achieves its goal. On the contrary, the record of human history is a record of failure. Despite laws against murder, there have been innumerable murders. Despite laws against theft, there have been innumerable thefts. Despite laws against rape, there have been innumerable rapes. The list goes on. Nevertheless, we can say—in favor of political society and its laws—that without these laws, the record would be even worse. Political society has often placed restraints upon the treachery of the human heart (*ST*, II-II, 123, 5, ad 3).

chapter 23

Political Society: Transcendence

> Without justice, what else is the state but a great band of robbers?
>
> —Augustine, *City of God*

> Modern civilization is a worn-out vesture: it is not a question of sewing on patches here and there, but of a total and substantial reformation, a trans-valuation of its cultural principles.
>
> —Jacques Maritain, *True Humanism*

Does political society involve anything beyond a useful union of deprivation? Does it also involve a union of transcendence? The modern and the classical visions provide different answers to this question.

Political Society and the Union of Transcendence

In the modern vision, political society has only utility; it does not have transcendence. We unite with others solely on account of deprivations. The political union is useful—and only useful—to achieve our own personal goods. Like the gang of thieves, the members unite to overcome their inadequacies for attaining private goods. Through union with others, we can get what we are unable to produce on our own.

In the classical vision, political society does indeed have utility, but it has something more; it also involves a union of transcendence, in which even the complete individual must transcend beyond his or her own private good in order to attain a good together with others (*ST*, I-II, 95, 1; *ST*, I-II, 96, 2, ad 2; *ST*, I-II, 100, 9, ad 2; *DR*, bk. 1, chap. 15, 106). Even if we have completely attained our own individual good (through the assistance of society), we are still inadequate. The personal good that we have achieved is itself inadequate. Just as the members of the orchestra must unite for the sake of a transcendent achievement, so the members of society must unite their personal goods with others in order to attain a good that can be had only together with others. When all our bodily needs have been met, and even when we have amply achieved our mental capacities, we are still inadequate. We have achieved only a part. Like the orchestra members, we must act together with others, so that we can then achieve a good that transcends our particular and limited accomplishments (*ST*, II-II, 58, 6).

Imagine that Payton has achieved maturity in all areas. She is physically able to care for herself, she has realized a high level of education, and she is emotionally mature. Payton has achieved what Aquinas would call virtue, both moral and intellectual. She has attained her own private fulfillment.

Despite her achievements, Payton does not fully realize the promise found in her rational nature. There remains so much more to learn, so much more to know. In short, Payton still has the inadequacy of transcendence. She must unite with other virtuous individuals in order that together they might know the wonderful world in which they live. They must form an orchestra that plays together. This union of transcendence, found in the classical vision, far surpasses any union of utility.

The first realization of this union of transcendence is not on a grand scale. It is not found in Payton uniting with all other human beings, for instance. Rather, it is found at the local level; it is found in the friendships that Payton forms. She unites with others at a personal level, engaging in coordinated activities. These activities can be as simple as reading a book together, watching a movie together, or playing a game together. These simple unions, which we so much cherish with our friends, are unions not of utility but of transcendence.

Of course, we also find our friends useful. They are the first ones we turn to when we need help. But even then, their assistance is more than a mere utility; it is more than merely productive. Apart from any good produced, friends are united in their very activity. They are acting together to achieve their united good.

The Transformation of Utility into Transcendence

The classical vision, then, includes more than a union of utility; it includes a union of transcendence. This union of transcendence transforms the union of utility. The utility is no longer *only* a utility. The productive actions of others are no longer *only* useful. They become part of the transcendent music of the shared human good. They are no longer good only on account of what they produce, for they have become good in themselves. Indeed, our acts of helping one another become more important than the goods they produce. Let us examine this transformation.

Imagine an orchestra whose members do not yet know how to play their parts. As a cellist, for instance, Clare must first learn how to play the cello; as a vocalist, Sebastian must learn how to sing; and so on. This orchestra has another unusual feature. The members do not learn how to play from outside instructors. Rather, they discover that they need one another's help in acquiring the needed skills. In short, they must train one another.

Our imaginary orchestra has both kinds of inadequacy. It has the inadequacy of transcendence because the members (once they learn their needed skills) must coordinate their activity into a united activity. It has the inadequacy of deprivation because the members lack what they need to contribute their own parts; their individual skills must be produced through united activity.

Consequently, the members need two kinds of coordination. On account of the inadequacy of transcendence, they must coordinate their acts of playing music into a united action. On account of the inadequacy of deprivation, they must coordinate their activities to bring about the needed skills. The first coordination does not aim at producing something; rather, it aims at a united activity. The second coordination aims at a product; it aims at the skill in each member. Even in this case, however, the product is not the main concern. United activity is still the chief good.

This last point becomes evident when we consider the starting point of the union. The goal that first unites the band of thieves is a product, for each member wants the acquisition of money for him or herself. This goal, of course, will be the last thing that they actually achieve (*ST*, I-II, 14, 5, ad 2). Nevertheless, it is the starting point in their desires. It is the first goal that the members set. Given this goal, they then recognize that they can achieve this product only through united activity. The united activity, then, is a useful means to their goal.

In contrast, the orchestra members begin (in their desires) with united activity. They begin with the desire to play music together. Then they come to recognize that playing together requires certain products. Since each lacks the needed skill, the members must first produce the skill in one another. Just as the band of thieves must coordinate their activity in order to produce the money, so must this imaginary orchestra coordinate their activities in order to produce the skill of the individual members.

On account of their different starting points, however, the coordination of the orchestra differs from the coordination of the band of thieves. For the thieves, the coordination is only useful in order to produce the desired result. For the orchestra, the coordination is indeed useful to produce the individual skills. Because of the starting point, however, the coordination is more than merely useful (*ST*, II-II, 47, 12). The orchestra members begin with the desire to unite with one another in the coordinated activity of playing symphonic music. They now discover the need for a different coordinated activity, the activity of helping one another attain musical skill. This new united activity is one more way in which the members can unite in their pursuit of the good. It is one more way in which they can possess the good together. In other words, their productive activity has been transformed—on account of the initial desire for union—into an activity of sharing the good (and not merely of producing the good).

The starting point makes all the difference. From the beginning, the members are aiming at a shared good, not a useful good. From the beginning, the members have a union of transcendence. When they coordinate their productive activities, they do so as a united whole that seeks "our" good. They do not form a mere union of utility, like the thieves, because they are already united in transcendence.

The Inversion of Consequentialism

This transformation inverts the consequentialist perspective according to which the human good is found in results or products. Actions (in the consequentialist view) are for the sake of their products. What ultimately matters is not our actions but how much good our actions produce. In Linda's act of saving Norbert, for instance, all that really matters is the result (that Norbert's life is saved). Linda's action of saving is secondary; it is good only insofar as it produces this result. For consequentialism, the gift is more important than the giving. Indeed, the act of giving is important only as useful for the sake of the gift. Acts of giving goods are merely acts of producing goods.

The consequentialist good—the greatest good of the greatest number—is a product. Any consequentialist community, then, resembles a band of thieves. Michele views her fellow thieves and their actions as merely useful, as productive of her portion of the money. Similarly, within a consequentialist community, the members are merely useful. As a member of a consequentialist community, for instance, Eric helps to produce a good (the sum total of goods) that is not his own. He is like a pen that is useful for writing, and his productive actions are like the act of writing, which is useful for the written words.

We might well be suspicious of this vision. A world filled with good results but empty of acts of giving is a barren world. If we have lots of good things—lots of good results—but we have nobody who wishes to give us anything, then we live in solitude. In contrast, if we have few things but we have a friend who cares enough to give, then our life is rich.

Indeed, we feel enriched by the act of giving even when it fails. Suppose that Bruce plans to give Joyce a book that she has long desired. Before he physically gives it to her, however, the book falls in a puddle of water and is ruined. Although Joyce does not actually receive the book, she has something much greater. She has Bruce, and she has the cherished act of giving.

If Joyce chooses to bemoan the loss of the result—the loss of the thing—then she passes up a greater good. She forgoes the good of Bruce with his act of giving. A consequentialist focus upon results leaves her life empty when it could be rich with the friendship of Bruce.

The consequentialist account, it seems, makes Bruce and his act of giving like a pen and its act of writing. The pen is merely useful in order to write, and the act of writing is merely useful in order to produce written words. Similarly, Bruce (in the consequentialist vision) is useful in order to produce acts of giving, and the acts of giving are useful merely to produce the gifts (or the good things).

Our acts of giving, however, do not need to be only useful, as consequentialism would have it. The act of giving can be an act of sharing the good, an action more important than the gift itself. This transformation from a useful action into a cherished act of possessing the good together depends upon the starting point. We must begin (as the orchestra imagined earlier) with a transcendent union. We must begin not by desiring products. Rather, we must begin by desiring to act together. In this manner, Bruce's act of giving becomes part of the very goal Joyce hopes to achieve. Just as the good of the orchestra can be separated neither from

Clare nor from her playing, so the shared human good can be separated neither from Bruce nor from his acts of giving.

Insofar as modern political theory adopts a consequentialist approach, society begins with the union of utility. It begins with the band of thieves, with self-interested individuals who find coordinated activity useful for producing good results. It never gets beyond this utility. It ends where it begins.

Within the classical vision, society also ends where it begins, but it does not begin with the union of utility. Rather, it begins with a transcendent union. It begins with individuals who want to possess the good by acting together. Even their acts of producing the good become coordinated actions of possessing the good together.

Political Society Aims at Virtue Rather than Utility

The need for political society arises from inadequacies of deprivation. Suppose that every individual within society were perfect as individuals; suppose their only inadequacy were an inadequacy of transcendence. Then they would indeed unite to coordinate their actions. The society they form, however, would not quite be a political society as we know it. It would be, we might say, a society of angels.

For political society, we must distinguish between its immediate goals and its ultimate goals. The immediate focus of political society is the useful tools needed to remedy our deprivation of virtue. Laws and the punishments that go with them ultimately aim at forming virtue in human beings (*ST*, I-II, 95, 1; *ST*, I-II, 96, 2, ad 2; *ST*, I-II, 100, 9, ad 2). The ultimate goal of political society is transcendent. It aims at realizing virtue in human beings (*In Pol*, bk. 1, lect. 1, 31; *DR*, bk. 1, chap. 15, 106). It aims at a shared good that goes beyond the needs of deprivation.

Unfortunately, some political regimes have actually encouraged vice rather than virtue. In recent history, we can think of the regime of Nazi Germany or the many communist regimes, most especially the USSR under Joseph Stalin. Even these regimes have attempted to maintain some semblance of justice among parts of the population. They have encouraged murder and pillage among their cronies, and they have unjustly imprisoned innocent people. At the same time, however, they have selectively upheld laws against murder, theft, and so on. On account of these regimes, society is overall worse off, but even these regimes are not unjust in everything they do. The force of law is so effective that it still provides some benefits even in the ravages of tyranny. It is sometimes said that tyranny is preferable to anarchy.

In general, modern regimes have lost sight of the goal of political society and law. They do not aim to encourage virtue. Rather, they aim to achieve a host of other useful goals, many of which should indeed be a part of any society, such as good roads. Even the best of these regimes, however, still follow the model of a band of thieves. In the pursuit of useful goods, these regimes often neglect virtue and the moral law.

They also overstep their bounds, accomplishing their goals by coercive measures that disregard the role an individual must play in achieving the shared good. In a transcendent union such as the orchestra, the activity of the members is essential. The good is precisely the united activity of the members. In the classical model, then, the free activity of individuals must always be respected. Virtue cannot be forced; it must be chosen. The coercive sanction of punishment does not *make* people virtuous: it only lays the groundwork for virtue. It constrains external behavior in order to avoid grave injustices, but it cannot force people to share their good with others. It can only encourage.

Ultimately, what is desired, in this model, is that the members should contribute their part. The members can never be treated as solely useful. Where the modern regime will be inclined to coercion in order to achieve some useful good, the regime that follows the natural law will hesitate. It will approach any useful coercion with caution. Individuals must not be trampled upon—in the name of some useful good—so that they no longer contribute their own action. This contribution, of each member providing his or her own acts of sharing the good, is the very goal that has given rise to the union of peoples in society.

The modern focus upon useful benefits tends to concentrate the mind upon what might be called worldly or bodily goods—goods such as wealth, power, and pleasure. These goods ultimately leave the human spirit dissatisfied, for it is made for greater things. The dissatisfaction leads to frustration, and the frustration leads to obsessive and compulsive behavior, a desire to get more and more of what satisfies less and less. On account of this downward spiral, the freedom often touted within modern systems leads to an ever-increasing bondage of the will to passions. This bondage, in its turn, leads to a willingness to subject oneself to those who can provide the satisfaction that has now come to be craved. The final upshot of this focus upon worldly goods, as Plato noted long ago, is a slavery not only to the passions but also to those who hold the strings of power (*Rep*, bk. 9). The logical conclusion of (typical) modern political theory is tyranny.

Friendship: The Goal of Political Society

According to the classical vision, we form political society within the framework of a transcendent shared human good, but the immediate and initial goal of our political union aims to meet an inadequacy of deprivation. Every human being is born deprived of virtue, both moral and intellectual. Every human being needs help to achieve virtue. This help is found at the local level, in our friends and family, but many human beings need further guidance. They need the guidance of law, which is provided by society. Of course, our political societies also supply for other needs, such as bodily and educational needs. Their primary purpose, however, is to aid in the formation of virtue.

Virtue itself, we have seen, includes a further union of transcendence. Having attained virtue, Payton must unite with other virtuous individuals, coordinating her activities with theirs so that together they can know the world around them and love the good. This last coordination is found in acts of friendship, which typically require no authority beyond the agreement of the friends. Virtuous individuals do not need laws to tell them how to be friends (*ST*, I-II, 96, 5).

The goal for which political society is instituted is the virtue of its members. This virtue itself, however, finds its meaning in yet a further goal; it is fulfilled only in virtuous friendship. The ultimate purpose of political society, then, is friendship (*ST*, I-II, 99, 2). With their laws, human societies hope to provide the environment in which friendship can flourish. Such, at any rate, is the classical vision, the vision that Thomas Aquinas found compelling.

When friendship is lost, when society becomes a collection of self-interested individuals, then the ground is laid for totalitarian tyranny. Our interpersonal connections—both with our intimate friends and relations and with our associates at a more local level (promoted by the principle of subsidiarity, mentioned previously)—are like the interwoven fibers of a plank of wood, which, when bound together, form a structure of incredible strength. When these fibers are worn away or shattered, we are left with sawdust, isolated individuals adrift without meaning, filled with insecurity and anxiety. In their solitude—sometimes in their defiant solitude—these segregated individuals crave union with others, so that their (sometimes vaunted) independence tends to servile submission. The sawdust can now be glued together into particleboard, a mass of individuals bereft of intimate contacts, ready to be formed and shaped into a glutinous whole, subservient so that they might at least belong.

The choice between the modern vision and the classical vision is momentous. The stakes are high. The worth of friendship cannot be overestimated. As we will see, the bonds within small communities—especially the community of the family—furnish the union of true sovereignty.

chapter 24

Human Laws

A community without law is but a shell.

—John F. Kennedy, Address to the United Nations, September 15, 1961

Wherever law ends, tyranny begins.

—John Locke, *Second Treatise on Government*

All human law, says Aquinas, derives from the natural law (*ST*, I-II, 95, 2). Laws against murder, for instance, derive from the precept (discussed previously) that we should not harm others. We begin with the natural law "do harm to no one"; we then recognize that death—or the bringing about of death—is a certain kind of harm. We conclude that we should not kill. When this conclusion is reached by the proper authorities and promulgated to the members of society, then it is a human law.

Two Manners of Derivation

Human laws are derived from natural laws in two ways (*ST*, I-II, 95, 2). First, sometimes we deduce a human law from a natural law. The example above fits this pattern. Second, sometimes we fill in needed details for a rather general natural law. We might begin with the natural law precept that wrongdoing should be punished. We recognize that car theft is a certain kind of wrongdoing; therefore, it should be punished. So far, we have followed the pattern of deduction. But then we must decide exactly what kind of punishment we will give. Should we give a fine? Should we give a prison sentence? If a prison sentence, should it be three years, five years, or some other length?

Filling in these details, says Aquinas, is not a matter of simple deduction. Rather, he compares it to an architect who begins with the general idea of a house but then fills in the details of a floorplan. From the general idea of the house, we might be able to deduce that we should have bedrooms, bathrooms, a kitchen area, and some family living space, but we will never be able to deduce that the master bedroom should be on the right or that the bathroom should be at the end of this hallway. Nevertheless, these details must be filled in, or we would never build the house. Similarly, the details of punishment must be filled in, or we would never punish. Human law fills this gap.

The law against killing might also be viewed as filling a gap. The natural law is general, simply directing us against harm; it does not fill in the details of particular kinds of harm. The law against murder fills in such a detail. We should not harm, says the natural law; more particularly, says the human law, we should not murder.

Nevertheless, Aquinas thinks this case is different. The kind of reasoning is not the same. Beginning with general knowledge, deduction adds some specific detail, and then it reaches a more particular conclusion. We might begin, for instance, with the general knowledge that mammals have lungs; we add the detail that whales are mammals; finally, we conclude that whales have lungs. Since whales look like fish, we may have thought that they have gills, but our deduction has provided the correct details. Similarly, we begin with the idea that we should not harm; we add the detail that killing is a kind of harm; we conclude that we should not kill.

Such reasoning will never fill in the details concerning the construction of the house. Neither will it fill in the details of punishment. Another kind of reasoning is needed. For these derivations, we use means/end reasoning.

Suppose, for instance, that Bob wants to get in shape. He recognizes that he should exercise, but he still must fill in the details. What kind of exercise? For how long? At what times? He considers a variety of options. He might run, he might swim, he might do aerobics, and so on. No deduction will lead him to settle upon one rather than another. Rather, he considers the pros and cons of each and ends up settling on one. He must still decide what time of the week to exercise and for how long. Once again, he considers various pros and cons. Bob is engaging in means/end reasoning.

We use the same sort of reasoning in settling upon a certain kind of punishment. We consider the options, we look at the pros and cons, and we make a determination. Typically, the determination involves no necessity. Bob might settle upon a half hour of aerobics five times a week, but no necessity leads him to this conclusion. Similarly, we might settle upon three years in prison for car theft, but we could have reached a different conclusion instead. In contrast, when we know that we should not harm and we know that murder is a certain kind of harm, then we necessarily reach the conclusion that we should not murder.

Only in rare cases does means/end reasoning reach necessity. For a house, for instance, we might reach the necessary conclusion that we need some kind of entryway—that is, some way to get in and out of the house. No necessity, however, determines the precise features of this entryway. Similarly, we might conclude with necessity that car theft should have some kind of punishment, but no necessity will ever lead us to the precise details of this punishment.

The Law of Nations

Some human laws differ from society to society. Other human laws are the same in all societies, or at least they should be the same according to Aquinas. Traffic laws clearly differ between societies. Furthermore, the determination of punishments (such as three years in prison for car theft) also differs between societies. In contrast, all societies have laws against murder.

This difference arises, in part, from the two different manners in which human laws are derived from natural laws. Laws against murder are conclusions deduced from the natural law. As such, they should be found in all human laws. In contrast, traffic laws are determinations arising from means/end reasoning. As such, they can (and will) differ from society to society.

Based upon this distinction, Aquinas divides human law into the law of nations and civil law (*ST*, I-II, 95, 4). In the modern context, these terms are misleading. For the "law of nations," we might think of certain agreed-upon rules about how nations should interact with one another. Laws about how to deal with prisoners of war, for instance, might be part of the law of nations. By "civil law," we mean laws that regulate contracts and private interactions. With this meaning, civil law is not opposed to the law of nations; rather, it is opposed to criminal law.

With his distinction, Aquinas has something else in mind. The law of nations includes the laws found in all nations because they follow as conclusions from the natural law. In contrast, civil law includes the laws unique to each society; it includes the determinations that each society makes for itself.

The law of nations is more complicated than Aquinas's simple division suggests. Aquinas says, for instance, that human laws that are reached by way of deductions from the natural law are still part of the natural law (*ST*, I-II, 94, 4). In other words, these laws are both natural laws and human laws. As human laws (but not as natural laws), they belong to the law of nations rather than to the civil law. Consider the example given by Aquinas: according to the natural law, we should do harm to no one; by way of deduction, we conclude that we should not kill; finally, we make a human law to this effect. The law against killing, however, is not only a human law; it also belongs to the natural law.

In contrast, the law stipulating that car thieves should be punished with three years in prison is only a human law. This human law arises from a natural law, and it ultimately derives its force—that by which it obliges us to act— from the natural law, but it is not part of the natural law.

The division between the law of nations and civil law is a division of human laws. Human laws against murder belong to the law of nations. The corresponding natural law against murder is not a human law, although it has the same content as some human laws. Consequently, it does not fit within this division between the law of nations and the civil law.

The law of nations has another complicating factor. It seems to include some laws that do not belong, strictly speaking, to the natural law. When considering what is naturally right, Aquinas makes a division between what follows absolutely from nature and what follows based only upon some proportion of one thing to another (*ST*, II-II, 57, 3). What follows absolutely is natural to both human beings and other animals, such as sexual relations between male and female. What follows by a proportion is natural only to human beings. Aquinas gives the example of private property. Human beings have the right of private property, but squirrels do not.

What exactly does Aquinas mean when he distinguishes between what follows absolutely and what follows by some proportion? The answer to this question is far from clear. Plausibly, the two manners of derivation are once again at work. What follows absolutely follows by a kind of deduction. What follows by proportion involves some means/end reasoning, which is why it belongs to human beings, who can recognize the causal relations by which a means relates to an end. The case of natural rights to which Aquinas refers, however, must include only those rare cases in which the means are necessary, as an entryway is necessary for a house. As we will see, Aquinas seems to conceive of private property in just this way.

Table 24-1. The law of nations and civil law

Kind of law	Ultimate source of its force	Relation to the natural law	As realized in societies	As compared to the natural law
Law of nations	The natural law	• Conclusions of the natural law • Also some necessary determinations	The same in all human societies	Its precepts correspond to precepts of the natural law.
Civil law	The natural law	Determinations of the natural law	Differs from society to society	Its precepts do not correspond to any precepts of the natural law.

The law of nations contains within it both kinds of natural rights: those rights that follow absolutely from nature and those rights that follow based upon some proportion of one thing to another. The law of nations, then, seems to include laws concerning private property. Now we said earlier that the laws that belong to the law of nations can also be found in the natural law. We should expect to find the right of private property and the laws concerning this right, then, within the natural law. As it turns out, however, the institution of private property belongs to the natural law but only by way of some kind of addition (*ST*, II-II, 66, 2, ad 1).

To sum up this rather intricate account, we can say that the law of nations includes those laws common to all nations, such as laws against murder and laws concerning private property. All these laws are also in some way contained within the natural law. Their relation to the natural law, however, is unequal. Those laws that concern a right following absolutely from nature are contained unqualifiedly within the natural law. Those laws that concern a right following upon some proportion of one thing to another are contained within the natural law by some kind of addition.

To add to the confusion, the actual division of property (as opposed to the institution of private property) belongs to the civil law. In other words, the civil law determines that this plot of land belongs to Roy and that plot of land belongs to Pete and so on (*ST*, II-II, 66, 2, ad 1). These determinations are like the determination of the punishment for car theft, which differs from nation to nation and belongs to the civil law.

Private Property

By what kind of reasoning does private property get added to the natural law? It does not seem to be the kind of deductive reasoning used to conclude that killing is wrong. Rather, it seems to involve means/end reasoning.

Aquinas provides three reasons for private property (*ST*, II-II, 66, 2). First, human beings take greater care of those things that belong to themselves alone. Second, human affairs will be much more orderly if everyone is given the responsibility to care for their particular property. If everyone was told to care for property but which property in particular was never stipulated, then confusion would ensue. Third, people will be more satisfied when they have certain possessions clearly marked as their own. Otherwise, they will quarrel over who gets to use a given piece of property. Private property, then, reduces quarreling and leads to a more peaceful society.

All three of these reasons seem to fit within means/end reasoning. Nevertheless, Aquinas reaches the conclusion that private property is *necessary* for human life. Private property, then, does not belong to those variable things, like traffic laws and specific punishments, that differ from society to society. Rather, private property belongs to the law of nations.

The case of private property seems to involve one of those instances in which means/end reasoning reaches a necessary conclusion. Given the purpose of a house, we might conclude with necessity (by means/end reasoning) that it needs an entryway. This conclusion does not arise from the kind of deduction by which we know that whales must have lungs. Rather, it follows because this means is necessary for the goal. Similarly, the institution of private property is a necessary means for the goal of human beings coordinating their activity for the shared good. In contrast, driving on the right side of the road is a means to safe driving, but it is not a necessary means (since everyone might drive on the left side of the road instead). Since private property involves means/end reasoning, it is an addition to the natural law. It is still natural, but it is natural in a secondary way, in a way that is peculiar to human reasoning and not shared with the animals.

Legal Positivism

In our day, many legal theorists do not welcome the idea that human laws derive from the natural law. Indeed, they often reject the very idea of a natural law. Some of them, at any rate, will acknowledge an objective morality, which (as we have seen) is one minimal meaning of natural law. Even so (they insist), human laws are not based upon this objective morality. They advance a view called legal positivism, which claims that the force of human laws does not depend upon morality (Hart 2012).

Legal theorists distinguish between malum prohibitum and malum in se, which may be translated, respectively, "evil because it is prohibited" and "evil in itself." If "evil" is too strong a word for a given situation, then we might translate them as "wrong because it is prohibited" and "wrong in itself." Many traffic laws are malum prohibitum. Whether you drive on the right side or the left side of the road, for instance, is not evil in itself. Driving on the left side, however, becomes evil (or bad), when the law stipulates that you must drive on the right. It is evil (or wrong), then, because it has been prohibited by the law. Murder, on the other hand, is evil in itself. The law also prohibits murder, but the act of murder does not become evil simply because it has been prohibited.

Traffic laws are largely up to the discretion of the lawmakers. They can choose to have people drive on the right side of the road, but they can just as well choose to have people drive on the left side of the road. They can choose to have people stop when the light is red, or they can choose to have people stop when the light is green.

Typically, we do not suppose that lawmakers have the same leeway when making laws concerning murder. They cannot choose to make murder acceptable on Tuesdays and Thursdays but unacceptable on other days. In the case of murder, the lawmakers do not make the action evil by way of their prohibition (it is not malum prohibitum); rather, they recognize that murder is evil (malum in se), and consequently they prohibit it.

We might conclude that legal positivism is true for traffic laws (and for other mala prohibita) but it is not true for murder (and for other mala in se). Aquinas will insist, however, that even traffic laws depend upon the natural law. In contrast, legal positivists will insist that no human laws, even laws against murder, derive their force from morality.

Even traffic laws are determinations of some natural law. We might know by nature, for instance, that we should not put other people in danger unnecessarily. Then we might conclude that we should drive safely; otherwise, we would be putting other people in danger. But how are we to drive safely? Is it safe to drive 70 miles per hour? Is it safe to turn left? Is it safe to take a U-turn? The answers to these questions are a matter of determination. In other words, traffic laws are determinations of the moral conclusion that we should drive safely, which itself depends upon the natural law that we should not put other people in danger.

The Force of Law

This matter of how laws are derived, however, is not the essential dispute between Aquinas and legal positivists. Some legal positivists might concede that every human law is a kind of determination of some moral belief. Nevertheless, they insist that human laws do not derive their force from morality (or from the natural law). They might very well concede, for instance, that laws against murder do arise from moral beliefs. As far as legal positivism is concerned, however, even these laws do not get their force from morality.

The real bone of contention, then, surrounds this notion of the "force" of law. According to Aquinas, the reason we should follow human laws is on account of the natural law (*ST*, I-II, 96, 4). Part of the natural law, in effect, is the idea that we should follow proper human laws. After all, we should follow the natural law, and human laws are derived from the natural law. According to legal positivism, on the other hand, the reason we should follow any law is simply the threat of punishment that comes from the state that has made the law.

The dispute does not simply concern motivation. Aquinas will grant that avoiding punishment does provide one motivation for following the law, and for some people it is the only motivation (*ST*, I-II, 96, 2). Furthermore, legal positivists will grant that some people (because of their particular beliefs) are motivated to follow the law on account of morality.

Ultimately, the dispute concerns obligation, not motivation. Why are we "obliged" to follow the law? Aquinas thinks the obligation is a moral obligation. Legal positivists think that the only kind of obligation is from a cost/benefit analysis based upon a threat of punishment.

An Unjust Law Is No Law

The difference between legal positivism and natural law culminates in an interesting teaching of Aquinas. He maintains that any human law that is not derived from the natural law is unjust, so it does not in fact have the character of a law (*ST*, I-II, 93, 3, ad 2). In Germany, for instance, the Nazis made a law condemning anyone who criticized Hitler and his policies. This law, Aquinas might well claim, was not properly derived from the natural law. Consequently, it was really no law at all. Of course, we might call it a law (as we just did), but it did not have the formal characteristics to make it a true law. As such, Germans had no obligation to follow this law.

In contrast, legal positivists will insist that this German law was truly a law. Indeed, they will insist that Germans were legally obliged to follow this law. After all, the Nazis backed this "law" up with the threat of punishment (capital punishment, at that). Aquinas will acknowledge that Germans might have had motivation to follow this "law," but he will deny any obligation, legal or moral, to follow this "law," for it was no law at all.

These different views derive from the different visions, classical and modern, of political society. In the classical vision, the laws of political society are meant to coordinate our activities in order to achieve the human good. By following the laws, we play our part within the human community, just as Clare plays her part within the orchestra. In the classical vision, we want to take our proper place within society, and human laws define the proper parameters of that place. If we choose to drive a car, then the human traffic laws provide the guidelines of how to keep our driving ordered to the shared good. We are fulfilling our part by following these laws.

In the modern vision, the laws of political society are simply useful rules that help us produce desirable goods. In this view, we follow laws only for the sake of utility, in order to achieve our private goods. One of those goods, of course, might be the avoidance of punishment. We can follow laws, then, in order to avoid punishment, but it makes no sense (in the modern vision) to follow laws in order to take our proper places within society.

For both the classical and the modern vision, human laws have a hypothetical necessity attached to them. In the modern vision, we may use the following hypothetical reasoning: "If you want to avoid punishment, then you ought to follow the law." Such is the hypothetical necessity championed by legal positivism. Of course, the natural law, within the classical vision, also has this hypothetical necessity. In addition, it has another: "If you are going to play your part within the shared good, then you should follow the law." Any law that does not provide a true sharing in the good—that is, any unjust law—cannot fit within this latter hypothetical necessity; as such, it lacks the force of law and has only the force of fear.

chapter 25

Monogamy

> Marriage is more than your love for each other. It has a higher dignity and power, for it is God's holy ordinance, through which he wills to perpetuate the human race till the end of time. In your love you see only your two selves in the world, but in marriage you are a link in the chain of the generations, which God causes to come and to pass away to his glory, and calls into his kingdom.
>
> —Dietrich Bonhoeffer, "A Wedding Sermon from Prison"

In our day, a dramatic shift in outlook has arisen concerning the raising of children. Throughout diverse cultures, past ages have preserved traditional family structures. Certainly, different cultures have seen slight variations in this structure, but the disparity between societies has often been grossly exaggerated. Even the most dramatic difference—between monogamy and polygamy—is negligible in practice, since in polygamist societies most people practice monogamy. All in all, the family structure in different places and in different times has been amazingly monolithic.

Recently, however, all sorts of novelties have been introduced, perhaps in part on account of advances in technology. Many people, for instance, conceive a child by way of in vitro fertilization (IVF). Some are now advocating the use of cloning technology to conceive children.

Natural law has much to say on these issues. According to the natural law, for instance, we should have children not by way of IVF but by the means that nature has provided—that is, by way of sexual relations between a man and a woman. And yes, the natural law affirms that male and female are really biologically different, a difference established by nature for the begetting of children.

Natural law provides a kind of authority that guides our sexual activity. Just as traffic laws define the parameters by which our acts of driving can fit safely within the whole community, so also the natural law—arising from the design of our nature—defines the parameters by which our sexual activity fits suitably within the shared good of the whole human community. While driving, a slight diversion to the left or right—crossing the line—might lead us into a head-on collision. Similarly, by setting aside the sexual standards of the natural law, we risk calamity. We stand over an abyss. A step to the left or to the right may send us plunging into chaos or tyranny.

The Necessity of Monogamy

Monogamy is perhaps the most significant moral implication of the natural design found within our power of reproduction. As noted previously, this norm is nearly universal in human history. Societies have deviated from this norm only in a few exceptions. Even within polygamist societies, the standard of polygamy is an exception. Monogamy is the norm.

Aquinas thinks that we can begin by perceiving the ultimate goal of reproduction and then come to recognize the necessity of monogamy (*ST*, II-II, 154, 2). Reproduction is a movement (within our natural capacities) toward new life, new human life in particular. The goal of reproducing, however, does not stop with the mere existence of new life. We do not aim to produce lots of babies and then leave them to starve. Rather, the goal goes beyond existence. Ultimately, it aims at forming a mature member of the species.

Reproduction, then, must be accompanied by those conditions through which a child can be raised to maturity. Some of those conditions are material. The child must be fed, for instance. Nature has provided the first means in this regard in the form of the mother's milk. We may conclude that the mother is not meant to give birth and then abandon the child; rather, she is meant to give birth and then care for and feed the child.

The standard of monogamy, however, does not arise merely from the physical means needed to achieve bodily maturity. Rather, thinks Aquinas, monogamy arises from spiritual and emotional needs. We seek not only bodily maturity but also—more importantly—maturity of mind and heart. We seek a shared good with our children; we want them to be part of the orchestra, so to speak. We want them to play their part, but in order to play their part they need more than bodies. They need minds and hearts that are mature. They must have minds that can grasp the truth and hearts that can restrain selfish desires, so that they are free to pursue the good as shared with others.

Raising a child in virtue requires devotion. This goal will not be achieved by plopping a child in front of the television, the smart phone, or the computer screen. The child must be raised in discipline, a discipline that requires continual attention. More importantly, children must be raised in love. Children learn to love from those around them, from those closest to them—ultimately from their parents. Where the parents lack love, children themselves become stunted in love. The shared good is lost, and only an isolated good remains.

The devotion of discipline and love is persistent and ongoing. It does not stop at the age of five, nor does it stop at the age of ten. It continues to the point of independence; indeed, it continues even further. The child, now grown to maturity, still needs the example of love.

Both father and mother, then, must remain with their children beyond birth. It does not suffice for them to hand off their children to "society" or to some communal "custodians." They must remain with their children as they grow. They must remain with them, in faithful love, throughout their lives.

Why are both father and mother needed? Because the discipline needed for moral maturity demands the attention of both (*SCG*, III, chap. 122, no. 6). Raising a child—especially raising a child to moral maturity—is not a one-person job. Even the bodily needs of a child are quite demanding and can be met only inadequately by a single person. The mental, emotional, and spiritual needs of a child demand the attention of father and mother even more.

Someone might grant that children need the attention of more than a single person, but they might resist the conclusion that the father and mother should remain with the child. After all, the mother could find assistance from others—from her parents, for example, or from the community at large. Furthermore, sometimes one or both parents die, and then the help of others is certainly needed. In short, the continued presence of mother and father does not seem necessary; at least sometimes, a child can be raised by some substitute, replacing the father and mother with others. Indeed, the institution of adoption provides the legal structures for raising a child outside the context of the biological parents.

Of course, when the natural structure breaks down in some way, through death or financial difficulty or some other unfortunate circumstances, then adoption may provide the best avenue for raising the child to maturity. Apart from these situations, however, the presence of both parents is most fitting for raising children. This conclusion follows from an important psychological fact: we care more for that which is our own. As noted above, Aquinas uses this psychological fact as part of his justification for private property (*ST*, II-II, 66, 2). A material possession will be better cared for by the person who can say it is his or her own. Unlike material possessions, however, a child needs more than physical care. The child needs love.

We love more that which is our own. We love more those who are closer to us (*ST*, II-II, 26, 6). This greater love is no surprise. Parents sense this love from the moment the child is born, and typically even from before the birth of their child. This love calls forth sacrifice. And sacrifice is needed. Being a faithful parent is not the task of a selfish narcissist.

Children must be born in love and raised in love. Nature provides that love—or at least the first step toward it—in the innate love of parents for their children. Monogamy builds upon this love, providing the environment in which the child can be best raised in discipline and love.

Familial Failures

The failures we see in our own families and in families around us sometimes seem alarming. The family does not always provide a nurturing and loving environment. The mother and father, for instance, may not love one another. The child may have been conceived more in lust than in love. The mother and father may not always love their children, sometimes even descending to the depravity of abusing their children.

We make a mistake, however, if we perceive failures of the family and then call for the dissolution of the family. The family, even with all its imperfections, provides the best environment to raise a child. We should not see its failures and then say it has no worth. Rather, we should see its failures and seek to remedy them.

The sociological evidence clearly supports Aquinas's conclusion that the family, with the two biological parents, is the best environment for raising children (Wallerstein, Lewis, and Blakeslee 2002). Despite the many shortcomings of families, children fare best within the intact family. Children raised in single-parent households and children who have suffered the divorce of their parents do not fare as well as those raised in intact families, even when compared with imperfect and marred intact families. Children should find love from both parents, but they find—when the family structure is fractured—a sense of rejection from one or both parents, leading to persistent emotional scars. Consequently, the children face increased incidence of drug abuse, criminal activity, psychological disorders, promiscuity, and many other difficulties.

Of course, the majority of children from broken families are free from most or all of these difficulties. The point is not that children from broken families always have problems; rather, the point is that they are at much greater risk for such problems. If we want to provide the best environment for children, we will keep both parents bound together, ideally united in love.

The many blemishes of the monogamous family, then, should not lead us to dissolve the family but to mend it. And of course, most families are not abusive. Despite their imperfections, the parents love their children and raise them in discipline, even if imperfectly.

Fidelity

According to Aquinas, the ideal of mother and father raising their own children gives rise to another feature of the monogamous family—namely, sexual exclusivity (*SCG*, III, chap. 123). Mother and father should have sexual relations with one another but not with anyone else. If they practice sexual promiscuity, then the children will belong to many parents. The two biological parents will not be together to raise their children, for their children will be scattered.

This last point is particularly critical for the father (*SCG*, III, chap. 123, no. 5; *SCG*, III, chap. 124, no. 2). With natural conception and birth, the mother—even the promiscuous mother—is likely to remain with her own children. The same cannot be said for the father. With the practice of promiscuity, his children will be scattered and likely will have little to no contact with him. Furthermore, among the children of his current mate, he will find some that are not his own. Of course, with modern methods of conception (such as IVF), which take place in a laboratory, even the mother may find that the children are not her own.

Beginning with the goal of reproduction—new life brought to maturity—we see the need for monogamy and sexual exclusivity. Children should be conceived in that environment most conducive for raising them to maturity. The natural law, then, forbids sexual relations outside of marriage. A couple should not have sexual relations unless they have committed to one another in love so that they can properly raise the children who might be conceived. Reproduction is not happenstance. It is by design. Sexual activity is—by design—directed toward conceiving new life. Consequently, the new life should be conceived in the environment in which he or she can be nurtured to maturity.

Aquinas reaches the conclusion of monogamy by means/end reasoning. The goal is a new individual brought to maturity. The means is the raising of the child in discipline, a means requiring long years of attention, attention that can be best met not by a single individual but by a couple. The raising of the child in discipline requires devotion spurred on by natural love, by which we have a greater love for that which is our own. Sexual activity, since it is ordered to this new life, must be kept exclusively within the monogamous relationship.

A Tangle of Emotions

Throughout history, these norms of natural law have posed an immense challenge for many people. Our sexual desires imperiously demand satisfaction. They balk at the restrictions required by monogamy. Not only can sexual pleasure be intense; it is also intimately associated with love, or at least with the sense of being wanted by another. Ironically, the need to feel this love leads to infidelity. It leads to sexual indulgence even though the commitment of love is absent. These problems are aggravated in our day through easy access to sexual imagery and pornography, which propel the sexual desire outside the domain of monogamy.

Most people cannot comprehend the swirl of emotions that surround their sexual desires. They do not recognize, for instance, that their intense need for pleasure may be spurred on by their need to relieve themselves of stress. They do not even recognize their need to be wanted by others. Nor do they recognize their guilt, which arises when they have used others for pleasure. Amid this tangle of mysterious emotions, they pursue sexual gratification all the more desperately.

Precisely this immaturity of selfish gratification is the target that monogamy aims to restrain. The intensity of sexual gratification turns individuals inward on themselves. As they focus more on their own satisfaction, their ability to turn outward toward others becomes diminished. The very act that, by design, is directed outward to new life—that is, the sexual act—becomes the occasion of an ever inward spiral. The shared good is lost sight of, the union with others is set aside, and love is dissolved into dissipation.

In our society, many people think that true fulfillment will be found in sexual gratification. We imagine that a life without sex is a stunted life, and we suppose that everyone has something like a right to sexual gratification in whatever way he or she sees fit. Our ultimate end or purpose (in this vision) seems to be found not in reason but in sex.

We would discern more clearly if we recognized that true fulfillment is found in sexual restraint. Sexual indulgence leads only to disappointment. It leads to solitude and the loss of the ability to love. The natural law provides the parameters—the restraints—by which sexual desires can fit within the good of the whole. Our own good is only a part of that greater good. We must take our place within the whole, the place that nature has given to us. That place, for our sexual desires, is found within monogamy. Our personal good is not found in rebellion against the law within our nature but in submission to it.

The Necessity of Monogamy Revisited

The norms concerning monogamy are something like a determination from a more general plan. Just as we begin with the general plan of a house and then determine where particular rooms will be, so we begin with the general plan to direct ourselves (in the sexual act) toward the shared good of reproduction; we then conclude that we must realize this plan by way of monogamy. This conclusion, which involves means/end reasoning, does not seem to be a deduction, like the conclusion that murder (as a kind of harm) should be avoided.

Despite the means/end reasoning, however, this conclusion is not a variable determination, like the traffic laws that direct us to drive on the right side of the road. Rather, it is like the entryway of a house. Every house must have some entryway. In other words, the means of an entryway is not optional, given the goal of a house or dwelling. Similarly, monogamy is a necessary means toward the goal of sharing the human good.

Within monogamy, we share a good of reason with future generations; outside of monogamy, we set aside the shared good.

Someone might object that monogamy is not, in fact, the necessary means for bringing new life to maturity. After all, one of the parents might die shortly after the child is born. Must we conclude that the child, who lacks the education and rearing derived from the full force of both biological parents, can never attain to moral maturity? Certainly, the child may be at a disadvantage, but it seems overly strong to say that the means of both parents is absolutely necessary.

Aquinas acknowledges that a particular child might be raised well even with one of the parents missing (*QDM*, 15, 2, ad 12). The necessity of monogamy, then, does not concern the actual practice of raising a child. Monogamy is certainly the best environment, but it is not absolutely necessary. Rather, the necessity concerns the order of the parents to the shared good of bringing their child to maturity. If they are to order themselves to this good, then they must be in an exclusive monogamous relationship (*QDM*, 15, 2, ad 12). Without this relationship, the good might sometimes be achieved, but the order to the good will be lacking.

Consider the following case as an analogy.

> *Deadly Disease*: Doctor Teresa is confronted with her patient Sarah, who has a deadly disease. Only one known medication can cure Sarah, but Teresa chooses not to give it to her. Nevertheless, Sarah is healed. Perhaps she consumes the medication through some mysterious source, or perhaps she eats some food that, unknown to the medical community, can be helpful for her condition.

In the situation, two questions of necessity arise. First, what is necessary for Sarah to be healed? Second, what is necessary for Dr. Teresa to order herself to the healing of Sarah? The prescription, although it might be best, is not absolutely necessary for Sarah to be healed, and indeed, she happens to be healed without the prescription. On the other hand, giving the prescription is necessary for Dr. Teresa to order herself to the healing of Sarah. When she chooses not to give the prescription, she fails in her role as a doctor, even though her patient happens to get better (*QDM*, 2, 2).

Similarly, with regard to the shared good of reproduction, we might ask two questions concerning necessity. First, what is necessary for a child to be born and brought to maturity? Second, what is necessary for a couple to order themselves to the shared good of new life brought to maturity?

In answer to the first question, we can say that sexual relations within a monogamous relationship provide the best environment for bringing new life to moral maturity. Nevertheless, a child might be conceived outside of a monogamous relationship. Indeed, a child might be conceived, as with in vitro fertilization, outside of sexual relations. Furthermore, the child who is born outside of a monogamous relationship might come to moral maturity. The monogamous relationship, then, is not absolutely necessary to bring about the result.

Nevertheless, the only way the *couple* can order themselves to the shared good is by way of sexual relations within a monogamous relationship. By any other means—by IVF, by cloning, or by premarital sex, for instance—they fail in their role within the shared good, even if the result happens to come about. The couple is like the pen that wants to write the letter "H" without the crossbar; they choose to direct themselves to some other good besides the shared good.

Of course, people often regret their actions and later order themselves to the shared good. Perhaps the mother, after she has conceived through premarital sex, decides that she must do all that she can to raise her child toward bodily and spiritual maturity. She is now directing herself to the shared good of new life brought to maturity. When she engaged in premarital sex, however, she was not. She was directing herself to some other good, alien to the shared good.

The Importance of Order Rather than Results

The shared good is not found in results; it is found in ordered actions. Bruce shares the good with Joyce by ordering himself to her good through the act of giving her a book. Suppose that Bruce does not give the book; nevertheless, Joyce acquires it through a different avenue. In that case, her acquisition of the book is not a good she shares with Bruce. The two can share goods through actions, such as the act of giving. The result of Joyce acquiring the book is not the same as sharing the good. Neither is the result of a mature child the same as sharing the good.

Imagine that Clare sits down to play the cello and what she plays just happens to fit in with the music being played by a nearby orchestra. The resulting sound is symphonic music, including Clare's part. Nevertheless, Clare does not order herself to play symphonic music. She is not, in fact, playing together with the others. The sounds just happen to coordinate. She is not sharing in the good. Her good does not belong to the others, and their good does not belong to her, for she has not ordered herself to play together with the others. This order requires that she play as a part.

Or consider another analogy:

> *Reckless Rachel*: Rachel drives to the grocery store and breaks 15 traffic laws. She breaks them for no good reason, but simply because she is in a rush. Nevertheless, it happens that Rachel arrives at the grocery store safely, harming neither herself nor anyone else.

Rachel has not ordered herself to the shared good of safe driving, although her driving resulted in no harm. She can order herself to the shared good of safe driving only by submitting herself to the parameters set by the proper authorities.

The natural law sets the parameters for the shared good, including the shared good of future generations. Just as human laws define the role of driving within the community, so the natural law defines the role—the part within the whole—of bringing about new life and leading it to maturity. It defines the manner in which a couple must act as a cause of new life, in order thereby to share the good. They must be male and female united in sexual intercourse; they must be united in an exclusive monogamous relationship. Only by following the natural law can the couple attain the good as a truly human shared good.

Let us return to the question posed earlier: is monogamy necessary for new life to come to moral maturity? As we have seen, it is not necessary for the result of a morally mature individual, but it is necessary for the order to this goal. The natural law is concerned precisely with this order. It directs our actions so that we can take our part in the whole, so that we can unite our actions with others, who are also ordered to the good. It is not concerned, then, with the first kind of necessity, with the necessity of a result. Rather, it is concerned with the necessity of order. In this sense, monogamy is a necessary means.

chapter 26

Sexuality

Any man's death diminishes me,
Because I am involved in mankind.
And therefore never send to know for whom the bell tolls;
It tolls for thee.

—John Donne, "For Whom the Bell Tolls"

Let your desires be governed by reason.

—Cicero, *On Duties*

Mortality is the greatest human limitation. We must all die. Consequently, our attainment of the human good—our realization of the human function of reason—is limited to the span of our lives. We have seen, however, that a broad function together with an individual limitation reveals the need for a shared good. Together with others, we can overcome the limitation of our mortality. Others may outlive us, continuing to attain the human good. In union with them, then, we can attain the good together through time. We live on in our family and friends.

Sharing the Good with Future Generations

This extension through time is limited by the mortality of others, who also must die. The human limitation of mortality, then, demands new life; it demands a new generation of human beings, and then another generation, and another. Ultimately, then, we must share our good with subsequent generations. Through them, our good reaches into the future.

Realistically, of course, we concurrently share the good only with a handful of future generations. Parents, for instance, can share the good with their children, with their grandchildren, perhaps with their great-grandchildren, and rarely with their great-great-grandchildren. Our good, however, extends even beyond these generations. Our good is realized in distant future generations, and the good of past generations is realized in us. Insofar as future generations want the human good, they also want to share the good further into the future. Our own good, then, will continue even after we die.

This continuity can be seen clearly in united projects that span several centuries. Charting the movement of heavenly bodies as they travel through the skies, for instance, cannot be achieved in a single lifetime. Acquiring accurate measurements has been an ongoing project through countless generations. The explanation of these movements, as well, has spanned the centuries. Newton's explanations, for instance, provided a foundation for Einstein's developments two centuries later. On a more parochial level, a family farm might be developed through multiple generations. More importantly, a kind of family wisdom can be passed on and developed over time.

Past ages had a better sense of this connection through time. Families remembered previous generations into the distant past. Stories were passed along from generation to generation. Even without this strong sense of familial connectivity, however, most of us recognize that our good is not limited to our insignificant lifespan. It is realized in individuals who lived before us; it will continue to be realized in those who live after us. Something of our good would be diminished if none came before us.

Their accomplishments are our own, and without these accomplishments, we would have attained less of the human good. Likewise, something of our good would be lost if human beings would cease to be. We desire to be remembered, even after we have died.

Modern Problems with Sexuality

As noted in the previous chapter, a dramatic shift in outlook has arisen concerning the manner in which this generational good is to be achieved. This shift began with the slow but steady waning of monogamy. More recently, novelties have permeated into other domains of sexuality. We have witnessed the widespread acceptance of sexual relations not only outside of marriage but even outside the union of male and female. On account of new technologies, the begetting of children is no longer reserved for sexual relations but is achieved in the laboratory. Even the possibility of cloning is entertained. Finally, the very identity of male and female is being called into question.

The last chapter also noted that the natural law has much to say concerning these novelties. We should have children not by way of cloning, for instance, but by the means that nature has provided—that is, by way of sexual relations between a man and a woman (*ST*, II-II, 154, 11). Again, a male is male by nature and a female is female by nature. The natural law provides something like traffic laws for sexual activity. It defines the parameters by which our sexual activity fits suitably within the shared good of the whole.

In this chapter, we cannot examine all the contemporary novelties concerning sexual activities and reproduction. We can consider only a few of the many issues, through which we will be able to perceive the general structure that natural law provides for our sexual activity. By the nature of the topic, some explicit discussions will be necessary.

Sexual Identity

Someone who is biologically female might feel, psychologically, as if she would be better off as a male. Nevertheless, her body remains physically designed for having children. Furthermore, the physical design is part of her order to the human function or purpose. Every function or capacity, including the power of reproduction, gives us a potential role to play within the human good. With regard to the human good of offspring and future generations, we ourselves do not define the part we must play. We are given a part, and we must discover it.

People who are disturbed about their sexual identity have two options. On the one hand, they might try to conform their body to their psychological inclinations. On the other hand, they might try to conform their psychological perceptions to the physical realities. Friends of these individuals might also take these two approaches. They might help the person transform his or her body, or they might help the person to overcome the psychological turmoil.

Suppose that Louis believes he is the king of France and that everyone should treat him as such. What would be our reaction? We would not be inclined to cater to his whims by bowing in his presence, calling him "Your Highness," or obeying his orders. Rather, we would think it best for him to correct his beliefs. Yet when a female believes that she is male, some suggest that we should comply with her wishes, changing her body if she so desires. But just as with Louis, so also with her. We would serve her better by helping her overcome her psychological turmoil. People can be confused, and we do them no service by encouraging the confusion. Our desires, after all, should reflect the real good that fulfills our real human function.

Some people find sexual pleasure in cannibalism. Armin Meiwes was found guilty of manslaughter after eating his lover Bernd-Jürgen Brandes. Surprisingly, Brandes consented to the act, since he identified as somebody who takes pleasure in being eaten. Should we encourage this "identity," or should we seek to correct it?

The Importance of Design

As we approach these issues, the role of design is difficult to overemphasize. We design cars by considering the goal of transportation and then determining what will be necessary to achieve this goal. We recognize, for instance, the need for a frame, in which passengers can sit, and the need for an engine, which propels the frame. We then come to recognize the need for other details as well. We start with the goal and then seek the design necessary to achieve the goal.

Similarly, the nature of reproduction is not haphazard. It follows upon the overall human function, which is realized in the activity of reason. Just as the goal of transportation requires an engine, so the goal of understanding the world through reason demands various capacities. The function of reason can be fully realized, for instance, only by continuing the species, which requires the power of reproduction (*SCG*, II, chap. 55, no. 13).

The capacity to reproduce follows from our individual mortality, together with the shared nature of the human good. The good of reason cannot be attained by any single individual but must be attained together with others, each of whom contributes his or her small part in the shared good. Because we must all die, however, nature has provided a means—the power to reproduce—in order that the human good might continue even after our deaths. Nature has arranged the details of reproduction by way of the difference between male and female.

This arrangement is not in itself necessary. Some organisms, for instance, reproduce asexually. Nevertheless, this sexual arrangement has been fittingly provided for human beings. It is fitting, for instance, that the good of new life should itself be achieved by way of a united activity. In other words, it is fitting that new life should come to be through the cooperation of male and female. It is also fitting that this united sexual activity should be linked to love. The human good is shared through loving activities, and the shared good of new human life should also be the object of love.

This arrangement is by design, not by happenstance. Human beings are not haphazard collections of capacities. Just as a car has many capacities that are unified by the overall function of transportation, so human beings have many capacities that are all unified by the overall function of reason. Among these many capacities, the ability to reproduce is rather prominent. It is a very definite capacity. It is not, for instance, the capacity to bring about another cat or another dog; rather, it is the ability to bring about another human being. Furthermore, the manner in which this new life comes to be is clearly delineated by nature. A man and a woman come together in sexual relations and conceive a new human being.

New life is a shared good. Consequently, the act of reproducing fittingly involves cooperation. The division between male and female is a reflection of the shared nature of the good of offspring. By nature and by design—and not by blind chance—reproduction is a cooperative activity. The very power of reproduction is itself designed to be cooperative; it is designed with the distinction between male and female. Consequently, this distinction is not arbitrary. It does not depend upon the whim of our particular desires or psychological perceptions. It is rooted in the very design of our rational nature.

The Role We Have to Play

Every function and every nature defines a role, a part to be played within a greater action. The function of a pen, for instance, concerns only a part of a greater action. The pen does not write on its own. Rather, the author writes by way of the pen. The author and the pen together engage in the united action of writing. For the pen, the function of writing concerns only its small contribution to the greater act of writing. The pen contributes only the ink and the distribution of it. The author provides the form and shape of this distribution. Imagine an anthropomorphic pen that fancies itself able to write on its own, achieving the whole act of writing without the author. This pen, failing to perceive the function that has been given to it—its part within the greater action—would be delusional and narcissistic.

Our power of reproduction also defines a role, a part to be played within a greater action. We are like the pen. We contribute only a small part of the act of reproducing. Nature has given individuals a role to play. In an alternate universe, reproduction could happen without our contribution. Apart from any conscious choice, for instance, new offspring might begin growing from our bodies like buds from a plant. Since we are conscious beings, however, it is fitting that we should deliberately contribute our part to the act of reproducing. Just as the pen contributes the distribution of the ink, so also do we contribute to the act of reproducing.

In the voluntary act of sexual intercourse, the male provides the sperm, and the female provides the ovum. The rest is accomplished without their conscious contribution. The sperm unites with the ovum, and new life is conceived. The new life implants in the woman's uterus and continues to grow. The woman's body provides nutrition but not by a conscious act, although she does consciously prepare her body by eating healthy food.

The act of sexual intercourse is a conscious act engaged in by the couple (or it should be). It is the conscious part we have been given to play in the greater action of bringing forth new life. This conscious role of the male and female may be more precisely defined. As we said previously, the male provides the sperm while the female provides the ovum. This description, however, is inadequate. It is compatible, for instance, with the sperm being extracted from the male, the ovum being extracted from the female, and the two being joined in a laboratory. This manner of reproduction, however, is not by natural design. The small part the couple has been given—their conscious part—is the deliberate union in sexual intercourse.

This part—this union—might be described in more detail. Ultimately, the male deposits the sperm into the woman's vagina. He does not, for instance, ejaculate into her mouth or into her anus. This depositing of the sperm in the vagina is a joint activity. The woman and the man do not achieve this small part alone. They work together. The man deposits the sperm only through a united activity with the woman, through a union of bodies. As we saw in the last chapter, this conscious union is also a union of love. Through this union, the couple becomes a part of something much greater.

We have been given a role to play—by the design of nature—within the shared human good of reproduction. We delude ourselves, like the narcissistic pen, if we suppose that we achieve reproduction on our own. Such narcissistic delusion is found in an act of cloning a new human being. In this action, we reject our role—our very small part to play—and set aside the union of bodies and the union of hearts, a union of two individuals committed to one another. We choose to become the entire author of reproduction.

A Defective Good

The design of nature is not something to be tampered with. New reproductive technologies, such as cloning, have momentous consequences for the human good. As we take what looks like a great leap forward (as in the example of cloning), we in fact leave our humanity behind. In some way, we direct ourselves to new life, but ultimately we desire something defective.

The new life itself, of course, need not be defective (although with current technology, clones inevitably are defective). Nevertheless, the *desire* for this new life has something defective. What should the desire look like? The child should be desired insofar as he or she is linked with the shared human good. By the design of human nature, new human life is shared through the power of reproduction engaged in through the mutual activity of man and woman. The act of cloning rejects this order, leaving a defective desire. The good of the clone is cut off from human nature. Consequently, it is cut off (in our desires) from the human good. While bringing a cloned child to term is not possible with current technology, other technologies such as IVF also involve the separation of the child from the shared good. In all such technologies, we are "making" a child rather than sharing the good of new life. The child may indeed share in the human good, but he is not *desired* as such; he is desired as an individual good, as a private accomplishment designed for the makers' own purposes.

When Clare wants to share her good of playing the cello, she desires her action as coordinated with the other musicians, so that they might play together. She desires her action not simply as her own and as arising from herself. Rather, she desires it as belonging to the others; she desires it as part of the action of the group; in short, she desires it as arising from the group, of which she is only a part. Her action arises from the group, however, through Louis the conductor, who is the authority that coordinates her activities with the others.

Similarly, when we desire new human life as part of the shared human good, we desire this new life not simply as arising from ourselves. We desire it as arising together with others who share our human nature. We desire it, then, as arising from our human nature, which is a kind of authority that coordinates our activities into a united activity of attaining the human good.

The point might be conveyed by considering two different attitudes that parents might have toward their children (Jensen 2014). The first can be called true love, and the second can be called overbearing love. In true love, the parents seek to share their good with the child; they want the child to have the good, so that he or she can enjoy it even as they themselves do.

In contrast, overbearing love, if it can be called love, seeks the good of the child for some further purpose. The parents want some ideal perfect child, perhaps to promote their own reputation. Junior will be the best tennis player not so that he can enjoy playing tennis but so that the dad can enjoy the success of his son.

In true love, the good of the child is received by the parents as something in which they themselves can share. In overbearing love, the good of the child is not received but made; it is perceived as the product of the parents. Ultimately, the child is not a possessing part with the parents. Rather, he is a producing part. The child himself is a product, meant to produce an ideal.

In a similar way, a clone is a product. The parents decide ahead of time what their child will be like, and then they fabricate the child in a laboratory. Junior is made to live up to some ideal, perhaps as a kind of replacement of the person cloned. The child, once produced, becomes nothing more than a producing part for the good of the parents. Although the "makers" might desire the child to be in some way "perfect," they ultimately desire him to be defective, for the good they desire in him is cut off from the shared good. They desire him not as a possessing part but only as a producing part.

This rejection of the shared human good follows from the rejection of the natural capacity of reproduction. Just as the good of the pen is realized in fulfilling its function of writing letters, so also the human good is realized in fulfilling the human movement toward the good. By design, this movement reaches out to the good of new life by way of the power of reproduction, which involves the union of male and female. By rejecting this union, we reject the shared good. The cloned child is not someone with whom the "designers" share the human good; rather, the "designers" treat the child as someone—or something—out of which they fabricate a good of their own making. Although cloning brings about an actual human being—an actual person—who shares in the good of human nature, he or she is not loved as someone who shares in this nature.

Ultimately, overbearing love, with its effort to produce the ideal child (rather than lovingly receiving what nature provides), culminates in hatred for the real imperfect child. This hatred is graphically portrayed in the real-life story of Aurora Rodríguez and her daughter Hildegart. Aurora desired to produce the eugenically perfect human being, so she conceived with a chosen mate and then raised her offspring to "perfection." Born in 1914, Hildegart was indeed an astonishing child. She was reading by two, writing by three, and playing the piano by four. By the age of ten, she spoke seven languages. In her teenage years, however, her mother Aurora began to perceive imperfections. Hildegart, for instance, did not hold firmly to Aurora's Marxist beliefs. In 1933, unable to endure the imperfect child she had made, Aurora killed Hildegart with four shots of a revolver.

When we want to produce perfection, we come to hate imperfection. The alternative is to recognize our own limitations. We possess—imperfectly—only a fragment of the human good, and our role is not to produce some perfection. Rather, our role is to be one small member, who shares the good we have with those around us, with other limited and imperfect human beings.

Other Deviations

By aiming at the good of reproduction apart from the union of male and female, cloning, IVF, and certain other reproductive technologies set aside the role that nature has given us within the good of reproduction. These technologies, however, are far from the most common ways in which human beings reject their role in the shared human good of reproduction. Having sex outside of marriage, which steps outside the path laid down by natural law for bringing children to moral maturity, is far more common.

Other deviations from the guidance of nature are also fairly frequent. Because sexual intercourse is linked with intense physical pleasure, we pursue it outside the parameters laid down by nature. Furthermore, sexual intercourse is associated with a deep need to be loved. Consequently, we often yearn for the feeling of love that sexual intercourse can provide, but we are blind to the manner in which disordered sexual desires can destroy our union with others.

While sexual intercourse outside of marriage sets aside the commitment by which we can order ourselves properly to the moral maturity of children, it leaves intact other aspects of the shared good of reproduction. Even in premarital sex, for instance, male and female still unite. The couple still joins in a united activity, culminating in the male ejaculating into the woman's vagina.

Sometimes the desire for pleasure, or the desire to feel wanted, induces individuals to set aside even this union. Masturbation is the clearest instance. Union is completely absent. Even here, individuals typically imagine a union, sometimes encouraging their imagination by way of pornographic images. So ingrained is the need for bodily union that in the lonely and solitary action of masturbation, the image of union cannot be abandoned. People will go so far as to have life-sized dolls on which to masturbate.

Other actions, although less solitary than masturbation, amount to not much more than mutual or assisted masturbation. So-called oral and anal sex seek the stimulation of masturbation with the assistance of someone else's body. Consequently, something of union is present, but it is not the union of male and female in sexual intercourse. It is not the joint action aiming to achieve the male ejaculating into the vagina of the female.

These activities can provide, beyond mere physical pleasure, the sense that someone else is willing, in a manner, to give him or herself to me. A true mutual giving, however, is absent. No human shared good unites the couple. Underlying the desire is self-interest, the desire to be wanted. The union, which is a union of utility (as is the band of thieves), ultimately exacerbates the desire. Like tearing off a scab, it leaves an open wound of acute dissatisfaction.

The intense pleasure, when joined to the frustration of an inadequate union, results in profoundly addictive behavior. The desired goal appears always just beyond grasp. The consequent emptiness leads to a renewed yearning. On account of gnawing anxiety, the victims of these behaviors seek distraction in intense bodily pleasures. We do them no kindness by telling them that these desires are integral to their identities.

Unfortunately, a profound confusion grips our perception of these deviant behaviors. Recognizing the importance of union with others, we conclude that sex is one of the most essential elements of the human good. We fail to recognize, however, that sexual union is neither the most consummate nor the most essential element of the human good. We fail to recognize that these sexual behaviors are poor imitations of true sexual union. We fail to recognize that these distorted unions set aside our human good; they set aside the part that nature has given us to play.

Consequently, we conclude that individuals should be able to follow their desires wherever they lead. They should be able to define for themselves the kind of union they want, the kind of union where they can find "love." We suppose that if we do not allow people to define themselves, then we rob them of the greatest good, or at least of the good as perceived under the dim light of a world unmoored from nature. In short, we deprive them of "love." In the empty solitude created by our world of relativism, a world of products and results, a world with no truly transcendent good to share, no greater torment can be imagined than the loss of this sexual gratification. In our aversion to this torment, we elevate the right to "love" (in whatever manner the person defines) to the status of a fundamental human right.

The argument in favor of diverse sexual expressions may be advanced yet further. If love is really a good of sexual union, then it seems that a couple should be able to pursue this union as they see fit; they should not be constrained by the mechanisms of reproduction. True love—the argument proclaims—will be advanced by granting sexual liberty rather than by fettering human desire with the limitations of nature.

This argument distorts the true good of sexual union. It correctly observes that sexual union should indeed be a union of love. Even apart from any thought of having children, the couple can unite to express physically the deep spiritual bond between them. Not every physical union, however, is a true expression of a spiritual love. The physical expression of love within marriage is a particular kind of expression meant for a particular kind of union. We do not have sex with everyone to whom we are united by a bond of love. Sexual union, for instance, does not express the bond a father has for his children. Rather, sexual union is meant to express the giving of oneself to another in commitment for life. It expresses not just any commitment. It expresses the commitment to be united for the possibility of raising children.

Outside of marriage, then, the particular love of sexual union is absent. The sexual bond becomes a lie, expressing a love that is not there. Even within marriage, certain perversions express a lie because they remove an element of the commitment. They affirm the bodily union but deliberately remove the union as ordered to children.

What Good Is at Stake?

Our confusion may be aggravated by the manner of reasoning underlying these sexual norms. The reasoning seems divorced from the goals we pursue and the means we choose to attain them. In this regard, the reasoning used in the last chapter to explain monogamy is more palatable. We recognize the goal of raising children, and we recognize the means of parents uniting to achieve this goal. Some people might disagree with the ultimate conclusion, but they can at least recognize how the reasoning works.

This connection with recognizable moral reasoning is often absent for some other moral standards concerning sexual union, such as the norms against oral sex or anal intercourse. In these cases, we do not seem to begin with a goal and then search for possible means to achieve the goal. Rather, we begin with nature and the part that nature has given to us. We then reach the conclusion that these behaviors do not conform with the role given to us by nature. No goal appears in this reasoning, and without a goal, we have no means to the goal. The reasoning seems alien and unpersuasive. What does it have to do with the human good?

All too often, however, we have come to the table of discussion after having already excluded the only goal in which this reasoning makes sense. We have lost sight of the shared human good. We have lost sight of the human good that arises from nature and that is shared by way of our nature. We can see only desires and the satisfaction of these desires. We have forgotten that desires arise because we have first perceived a good, which is the completion of some function.

Let us not begin with a want or an urge that we happen to have. Rather, let us begin with the human good, which is the completion of our human nature. Let us begin with the good of reason, and let that good give rise to our wants and desires. This good is not found in a result or a product. Rather, it is found in activity. We are not completed by having things or feelings; rather, we are completed by doing.

Furthermore, we are not completed by solitary activity; rather, we are completed by acting in concord with others. Like the members of an orchestra, we want to play a kind of music together with others. The good of sexual intercourse must be placed within this human good of coordinated activity. Although sexual intercourse is useful for bringing about children, its good is not found only in results. Its good is realized in being part of a united activity, an activity in which we work together to achieve our human completion.

The members of the couple cooperate with one another in sexual union by working together to place the sperm within the woman. The man does not masturbate and then place the sperm in the woman. Rather, through a union of bodies, the two bring what is in the man into the woman. This cooperation is an intimate mystery, but at the moment we are not addressing this cooperation.

Instead, we are addressing a more profound cooperation for the human good. The couple themselves, in their joint activity, cooperate in something even greater than their own union of love. Their action, of bringing the sperm into the woman, is part of a greater action, an action that is not completed by the couple but by nature. The couple cooperates in the united activity of working together with nature for the human good of reproduction. Just as the pen, when moved by the author, contributes only a small part to the act of writing, so the couple, when moved by nature, contributes only a small part to the act of reproducing.

Together with nature, they achieve the human good of united activity. This good makes sense only in a world in which giving is more important than the gift. This good makes sense only in a world in which sexual intercourse is itself an act of giving. We might perceive it as an act of taking, of getting the satisfaction of physical pleasure and of getting the satisfaction of being close to someone else. But in fact, sexual intercourse is an act of giving. It is first of all an act of working together for the human good of future generations.

The couple provides their small part in the orchestrated movement of human beings working to achieve the human good. The natural law, arising from the design of our nature, defines the parameters by which their sexual activity fits within the shared good of the whole. By following this guidance, avoiding the pitfalls of distorted sexual activity, they avert a perilous entanglement in pleasure devoid of love. In addition, they themselves take part in the orchestra.

chapter 27

The Divine Plan

The world is charged with the grandeur of God.

—Gerard Manley Hopkins, *God's Grandeur*

Socialism is before all things the atheistic question, . . . the question of the tower of Babel built without God, not to mount to Heaven from earth but to set up Heaven on earth.

—Fyodor Dostoevsky, *The Brothers Karamazov*

In many of the preceding chapters, we have seen that modern human beings have viewed the good through inversion glasses, glasses that turn the world upside down. Having lived so long with this inversion, the truth—the right-side-up vision—appears alien and distorted. It may be hard for us to believe that we are seeing things inverted. Indeed, we may feel antipathy for the right-side-up world, the world in which we are parts of a greater whole. Being a part may seem too limiting; it cramps our style. We want, by ourselves, to define who we are; we do not want to accept a role that is given to us by our nature.

In the upside-down world in which we dwell, we are not parts. Rather, we are sovereign. We may be surrounded by a multitude of people, but we are not united with them. They may prove useful in achieving our separate goals, and we may feel the need to help them out in return. Nevertheless, we are isolated. We do not pursue a joint project, of which we contribute only a part.

Our imagined sovereignty extends to the definition of our own good. Our good is what we want it to be. It is ours and only ours. We even define who we are. We are not *given* an identity; we *choose* our identity. We are given only a variety of powers, such as the powers to move about, reproduce, remember, desire, reason, and so on. These powers just happen to reside in a single individual, perhaps because they have proven useful—over the eons—for leaving a greater number of offspring. Confronted with this haphazard collection, we choose to give it shape according to our own designs.

In this inverted world, we might choose to create an ethics of production, a consequentialist greatest good of the greatest number. We do not, thereby, make ourselves belong. The greatest good does not give us a role to play. Rather, it turns us into a mere number, a quantity of independent and isolated goodness. The only role available is to become a productive instrument, an instrument for a good alien to our own.

The Divine Artist

As we further examine the contours of the right-side-up world, the world that now appears foreign to us, it is best to approach the very beginning. This world does not stand on its own; it is not independent. Rather, from the beginning, God created this world, and he continues to hold it in existence.

Imagine that Anna, in her artistic creativity, paints a picture abundant with beauty. Perhaps she paints it in order to sell it and make money. Perhaps she paints it in order to secure a name for herself as a great artist. Perhaps, on the other hand, she paints it in order that others might share in the vision of beauty that she herself enjoys.

Only this last possibility is available to God (*SCG*, III, chap. 18, no. 5).

He enjoys complete goodness in himself. He can gain nothing from his creation. Only his creation stands to gain. And it, of course, can gain everything. From being nothing, it comes to be something. But if it *merely* existed and had no goodness, then it would not have gained anything worth having. The one and only good, however, is the divine good. What creation stands to gain, then, is a share in God's own goodness.

When God creates, he paints a picture. The created universe is a kind of work of art, a painting that reflects the beauty found in God. It radiates forth goodness, but not only its own goodness. Its action of radiating goodness is also the divine action. Between a pen and the author who writes with the pen, there is only one act of writing. The pen's act of writing is itself the act of the author, who gives movement to the pen. Similarly, when Anna creates artistically, the painting's act of radiating beauty is, in a way, the action of Anna, who gives the beauty to the painting. Likewise, all that creation has is from God. When it shines forth beauty, it shines forth the divine beauty (*ST*, I, 44, 3; *ST*, I, 65, 2).

The beauty within Anna's picture, we might say, is Anna's beauty. We do not mean her own physical beauty. We mean the beauty that she possesses in her mind and by which she creates. She gives this beauty to her painting. In a way, then, the painting shares in the goodness of beauty that Anna herself possesses. Similarly, any goodness found in creation is a sharing in the divine goodness. Creation is truly good, but it has no independent goodness, nothing it can claim as belonging to itself alone; any goodness it has is the divine goodness (*ST*, I, 6, 4; *DV*, 21, 5).

God creates, then, not to gain anything from his creation. He creates only to share his own goodness, to extend his goodness, so that it is now found in his created universe as well (*ST*, I, 47, 1).

A Design and a Purpose

The whole of creation is one vast design (*ST*, I, 47, 1–3). It is not a chance event. It is not a haphazard collection of particles that randomly bump into one another (Denton 1998). Like Anna's painting, it is carefully crafted. Anna orders the parts in proportion to one another to shine forth beauty. Similarly, God orders the parts of the universe to shine forth his own beauty. The universe is one, as God is one, but it is one only to the degree that its many parts are crafted to fit together (*ST*, I, 47, 3).

Each part is likewise carefully designed. Human beings are not chance events. They are not a haphazard collection of capacities that happen to have survived over the eons. Instead, they are like a car, which is designed to provide transportation. The many parts and the many subcapacities all fit together for this one purpose of transportation. Likewise, human beings are designed for a purpose. Their many parts and their many capacities all fit together for one purpose, which is to reason, to know the created world and to know the author of this world (*SCG*, III, chap. 37, no. 7).

God wants his creation to be truly good. As we have seen, however, the good is that which completes a movement to an end. When God creates, then, he gives his creatures a movement to an end; he gives them a purpose (*In Meta*, lib. 12, lect. 12). God's creation is not static, like the nature of a triangle or the nature of a circle. Rather, his creation is dynamic, stretching beyond itself. God creates trees that are inclined to grow and to reproduce. He creates bears that are inclined to grow, to reproduce, and to perceive the world around them. And he creates human beings, who dynamically move out, with their reason, to comprehend the world around them and the author of this world.

We do not have static minds. We have minds impelled by their very nature to grasp the truth (*ST*, I-II, 3, 8). Our minds are made complete—*we* are made complete—by this understanding of the truth. This good is truly our good, our completion. But it is not ours alone. We know the truth only as impelled by the divine movement acting in our nature. Our acts of knowing the truth are actions of sharing in the divine good because they are not only our own. They are divine acts carried out through us, carried out in our nature. We are made to be an echo of God.

The Purpose of Limited Parts

In the right-side-up world, then, we are not sovereign. We are parts. We do not define our nature; rather, we are *given* a nature. We are given a part to play within the story of creation. Within the orchestra, Clare must play her part not only as her own but also as part of a greater action, as part of the act of the whole orchestra. We also must play our part. Our actions must be parts of a greater action, parts of the divine action.

Our sharing is not only with the divine; we also share our good with other human beings. We have been created to know the world around us and to know its author, but each of us is only a tiny fragment. However learned we become, we remain—by ourselves—of little consequence. We know but a sliver of the divine truth. However accomplished Clare becomes as a cellist, she can never by herself play symphonic music. She must unite with others. Similarly, we must unite with other human beings, so that together we might know the truth of our creator.

Because of the inadequacy of our individual actions, we form a transcendent union with others, a union by which our actions are united with their actions, so that together we might play the music of the universe. This call to union is a call to friendship. Our actions must not remain only our limited actions; they must belong to others as well. They must belong to our friends. We must be made complete together with others. In friendship, we unite to transcend our limitations. Through a web of friendships, we reach toward a union that extends far beyond our limited selves.

Our inadequacies—our needs—are far more significant than this brief account so far suggests. We have not only an inadequacy of transcendence but also profound inadequacies of deprivation. Not only are our individual actions inadequate unless joined into a united action; in addition, we lack even the tools to perform our part. We are born into the world with a nature by which we can know, but we do not have much more. We cannot even feed ourselves. We must be assisted in every step forward.

We have noted four domains where we suffer deprivation. First, we have individual bodily needs for food and protection. Second, we have educational needs to learn about the world around us. Third, our desires lack proper formation; we must be trained to desire what is truly good. Finally, even if all these needs are met, we are still mortal; we will all die.

All these needs can be met only with the assistance of others. With others, we can get the food we need and the protection we need. With others, we can get beyond a superficial knowledge of the world. With others, we can overcome our many disordered desires. And only with others—with future generations—can we overcome our mortality.

These inadequacies of deprivation might tempt us into a union of utility, a union like a band of thieves. We must avoid this temptation. We must not forget the transcendence with which we began. When we unite with others to meet our bodily needs, our educational needs, our moral needs, and our needs of mortality, we still must form an orchestra of united activity.

Our acts of giving must always be greater than the gift. Our actions of assistance toward others must always be more than usefully productive. They must be part of a coordinated activity, by which together we achieve our many individual completions. Together we are seeking a united good, attained by a united activity. By helping others, we are not simply producing their good; we are acting with them to attain their good.

In human affairs, we form many groups or societies to coordinate our activities for the human good. We form families, charitable societies, educational societies, economic societies, and so on. None of these, by themselves or collectively, have the full force needed to reign in the many unbalanced human desires by which individuals are continually harming one another. Only the coercive force of law, found in political society, is sufficient to restrain destructive behavior, thereby preparing the way for the peaceful environment in which virtue and friendship can flourish (*ST*, I-II, 95, 1). All of us, then, are members of the human community, but we must also become members of some political society. Human beings are political by nature.

In the right-side-up world, then, we are parts of many wholes. We unite with our friends and other human beings to transcend our many limitations. We unite in various groups to overcome our deprivations. Ultimately, all this coordination with other human beings is one great coordination with the divine. All our actions—our individual actions and our united actions—reflect the divine action within us. All our actions are a sharing in the divine good. We are all parts, and only by being parts, by playing our roles within the whole, can we find fulfillment.

Human Free Will

Human beings differ dramatically from the rest of material creation. A tree follows its natural movements spontaneously, with no choice. The same can be said of a bear or a squirrel. These animals do exhibit a great variety of behaviors, and their activities follow upon an awareness of their environment; nevertheless, they are ultimately impelled by instinct. In contrast, human beings make deliberate choices. The fulfillment of some of their powers depends upon these choices. The fulfillment of the power of reproduction, for instance, depends upon a choice to engage in sexual intercourse. The impetus that God has given us to reproduce is not an impetus to grow buds out of our thighs. Rather, it is an impetus that includes a choice.

Within our overall design, the very ability to choose is itself a power given us by God. It is meant to fit within this design. This power, we have seen, is the human will, which has a natural impetus to pursue the true human good. The will is our power for the good, just as reason is our power for the truth (*ST*, I-II, 8, 1; *ST*, I-II, 9, 1, ad 3; *ST*, I, 82, 3, ad 1). We truly attain our human good, and thereby radiate the divine, only by way of loving the good with our wills. We do not reflect the divine automatically in the way that a tree automatically follows its impulse. We reflect the divine only by willing God's good.

No action is truly our own apart from our willing it. We do what we will to do. George, for example, reads a book because he wills to do so. An act of reading that happened apart from his choice would not be his action, at least not fully his action. Through this disembodied activity, separate from his deepest self, he himself would not possess the good found in the book. He himself would not become a subject of the divine good. He can become the subject of this good only through his choices, by which he most completely possesses the good. George is not just a collection of powers. He is a human being, meant to be a subject of the human good, which is a sharing in the divine good. God wants George to reflect his divine goodness by acting as a voluntary, rational subject. Consequently, God moves George to fulfill—with voluntary choice—the purpose embedded within his human nature. In the same way, God moves each one of us.

All our various powers move out to some endpoint and are fulfilled by attaining this goal (*ST*, I, 78, 1, ad 3). All our powers, then, move out to some good. Only the will, however, moves to attain the good precisely as good (*ST*, I, 82, 5). Reason, for instance, moves out to the truth precisely as the truth. With our wills, however, we move out to the truth as a certain good; we desire to attain the truth as good for us. As reason is the power for the truth, the will is the power for the good.

The Special Role of Human Beings

Consequently, only intellectual beings can truly be subjects of the divine good, for we alone can know the good truly as good and we alone can love the good truly as good (*SCG*, III, chap. 112, no. 3). While a tree and a bear reflect God's good in some manner, human beings not only reflect his good but attain it. Of all material creation, then, we alone share in the divine good. God created in order to share his good with others. He cannot really share his good with a tree or a bear; he can only give them some reflection of his goodness. In contrast, he can share the good with human beings, for we not only reflect his goodness but are also made in his image and likeness (*ST*, I, 93, 1–2).

Only creatures made in God's own image and likeness can truly possess the divine. Only spiritual creations, who have intellects by which they can know God and wills by which they can love God, can genuinely share in the divine good. Any created good, if it is to be divine, must return to its source in God. But a tree, once it has attained its completion or goodness, cannot love this goodness as coming from God, for the tree does not know God. Likewise, a dog or cat, however perfect it may be in its canine or feline nature, knows only sensible things in the world around it; it does not know, and cannot truly love, the God who gave it this nature. Only intellectual creatures can understand the source from which they spring (*QDV*, 22, 2). Within material creation, then, human beings alone are possessing parts of the shared good (*SCG*, III, chap. 112, no. 4).

But human beings are still parts. We must still play our roles within the whole. When we know the world around us, and when we know God himself, our acts of knowing must not be simply our own. We must know together with God; our actions must also be God's actions. We must be the pen in the hand of God. God has given us a nature stretching beyond itself, stretching outward to a united act of reflecting the divine good. We must not stay locked up in ourselves; we must return to God.

In the movie *Chariots of Fire*, the character Eric Liddel, who won the gold medal in the 1924 Olympics for the 400-meter race, says, "I believe God made me for a purpose, but he also made me fast. And when I run, I feel his pleasure." Running is no great accomplishment. In the great scheme of the universe, even winning the gold medal is no great accomplishment. It is simply a worldly glory that passes quickly. But running for God's pleasure is a great accomplishment. It is a sharing in the divine, if only a small sharing.

Liddel had a much greater purpose than running. He went on to live a humble and dedicated life as a missionary in China. Nevertheless, even in this small act of running, he shared in the divine good. When we do that at which we excel—and Liddel excelled at running—we live out the divine within us. We should not think our role is too small because we have not accomplished great deeds. Rather, we should rejoice in the activity that God has given us; we should rejoice in the activity that we enjoy, especially that which we enjoy together with others. These small acts are part of the role God has given us to play.

In the right-side-up world, then, human beings are not random events with no purpose or meaning (Meyer 2009; Johnson 2010). In the right-side-up world, human beings are designed to play a part: they are designed to take part in the very good of God. Human beings are possessing parts of the good of the universe.

In this universe, we are not sovereign. We are parts, but precisely because we are parts, we are not alone. We are united with others in sharing the good. We are united with God himself.

chapter 28

Natural Laws

To scorn the dictate of reason is to scorn the commandment of God.

—Thomas Aquinas, *Summa Theologiae*, I-II, 19, 5, ad 2

There exists a true law, a right reason, conformable to nature, universal, unchangeable, eternal, whose commands urge us to duty, and whose prohibitions restrain us from evil. This law cannot be contradicted by any other law and is not liable either to derogation or abrogation. It is not one thing at Rome and another at Athens; one thing today and another tomorrow; but in all times and nations this universal law must forever reign, eternal and imperishable. God himself is its author, its promulgator, its enforcer. He who obeys it not, flies from himself, and does violence to the very nature of man.

—Cicero, *On the Republic*

The whole of human life is a life of coordinated activity. We coordinate with our friends and other human beings to transcend our limited acts of knowing. We coordinate with others to work together in overcoming our deprivations. Ultimately, these multiple coordinations must form one great coordination with the divine.

We coordinate our activity by way of some authority. When the coordination is simple, no overt authority is needed. Two people singing together, for instance, might manage the coordination with no overt authority; together, they serve as the authority for themselves. Often, however, a visible authority is needed to provide the proper coordination, as when a conductor is needed for an orchestra.

Human laws provide coordination within groups or societies. Lesser societies coordinate their activities by way of rules, which do not have the full coercive power of the law. Political societies, however, coordinate activities by laws, which have the coercive sanction of punishment. In either case, these rules or laws set the parameters by which actions fit within the community; they set the standards by which the members can share the good by playing their part within the community.

A Dynamic Nature

By what rules are our human actions coordinated with the divine? Clare ensures that her actions are not simply her own but are part of the united action of the orchestra by submitting her actions to the guidance of the conductor. How do we ensure that our actions arise not simply from ourselves and our own impetus but from God, so that we can thereby follow the divine movement and radiate the divine power within us? Just as a pen writes well by following the movement imparted to it by the author, so must we allow God to act through us.

God acts within us, we have seen, by giving us an internal impetus (*ST*, I-II, 91, 2). He does not create us static but gives us a nature impelled beyond itself. We make pens and give them a purpose, but realistically they have no internal impetus by which they move out to write. When

God creates, he also gives a purpose, but he embeds the purpose within the nature. Unlike the pen, God's creation does have an inherent movement, stretching out to act. The movement of this nature is the divine movement in creation.

God has given us minds with a natural movement. Presented with the world, our minds move out to grasp it. Our minds do not have to be pushed by an external force in the way that the pen is pushed by the author. Of course, we direct our various mental capacities. We move our eyes to the right or to the left, for instance, to look at this or that object. When presented with objects, however, our minds quite spontaneously become aware of them.

Other powers as well, such as the power of reproduction, have a natural impetus to move toward their goal. We do indeed engage the power of reproduction with freely chosen actions. A couple, for instance, must choose to have sexual intercourse, but they do not create the subsequent movement that unfolds toward new life. Indeed, we create nothing just by choice. Rather, with our choices we use the powers that are given to us. These powers have their own capacities or their own movements to an endpoint, independent of the choices we make. The power of reproduction is no different. By its nature, this power moves out toward the union of sperm and ovum within the woman.

We act with God, then, by acting in accord with these natural movements, which he has given to us. Likewise, a tree acts with God by following its natural movements, its tendency to grow and to reproduce. A bear, as well, radiates the divine by acting according to the impetuses that God has placed within it: its tendencies to grow, to perceive the world around it, and to have emotional desires.

As we have seen, however, human beings differ from the tree and the bear, which follow their natural movements spontaneously, without choice. If the tree fails in its action, its failure depends on no choice. Instead, the failure arises on account of some defect, such as a genetic defect by which the tree might fail to reproduce (*ST*, I, 49, 1). The tree does not choose to reject the impulse of reproduction. Rather, the impulse is thwarted by some obstacle or defect.

In contrast, as human beings we can choose to follow the movement of nature, coordinating our actions with the divine, or we can choose to thwart the movement of nature, acting in opposition to the divine. A pen has no choice but to follow the movements of the author, but God has given us a choice. We can follow his movement, which he has embedded within our nature, or we can reject it.

Knowing the Good

A choice implies knowledge of the options. Suppose that Jane is presented with three boxes. The first contains a diamond ring, the second contains an orange, and the third contains a pebble. Unfortunately, Jane does not know what is in the boxes. Consequently, she cannot choose the diamond ring. She might choose the box that happens to contain it, but that would not be a choice for the diamond ring; rather, it would be blind luck. In order to choose the diamond ring, Jane must have knowledge of it.

Similarly, if God has given us a choice to follow his divine movements, then he must give us knowledge of them. Otherwise, acting in accord with his movements would be just blind luck.

God has indeed given us a mind by which we can know the world around us, by which we can know the natures of things. With our reason, we can understand our own nature; we can know the dynamic movement of our nature to various endpoints. Human beings, for instance, understand that they have the power of reproduction. With modern science, we have come to understand this power in minute detail, but even without science, human beings were aware of the power, and they were aware of the voluntary part that a couple must play. Similarly, with our reason we can understand our own minds. We can understand that we have a mind that can grasp the truth, a mind that spontaneously moves out to understand the world (*ST*, I, 16, 4, ad 2).

So it is with other powers. We understand that we have a power to grow, and we understand our voluntary contribution to this power (by way of eating food). We understand that we have various emotions and that we have some measure of voluntary control over them, at least by controlling what we think about. God has not left us in the dark, but he has provided us with the means to grasp the movements he has placed within us.

As we have seen, we also grasp the nature of the good. With our reason, we understand that the good is found in that which completes some movement to an endpoint. God, then, has given us the minds by which we can know our own good. We know our natural movements to an endpoint, and then we know that the fulfillment of these movements is good. We can even grasp how it all fits together, how these diverse capacities all harmonize for one chief purpose, which is to know the truth, to know the world around us and its author.

Our Knowledge of Policies Arising from Nature

Our minds not only grasp what is good but also how we ought to behave. We know that as a doctor, Teresa ought to heal her patients, even those she dislikes. We know that a lawnmower ought to cut the grass and that a tree ought to put out roots. In each case, our knowledge depends upon the awareness of a movement to an endpoint, most especially a function or purpose. The function of a doctor is to heal, so Teresa ought to heal. Trees are moving to the endpoint of growth and reproduction, so they ought to take in nutrients. The function of a lawnmower is to cut grass, so it ought to cut grass.

The same reasoning applies to our own functions (or movements to an endpoint). We readily grasp, for instance, that in order to attain the human good—the good of a rational animal—we ought to know the truth. Likewise, we grasp that in order to complete the movement found within the power of reproduction, a man and a woman ought to unite, bringing the sperm into the woman. In short, by noting the movements to an endpoint, we come to know certain rules of behavior.

These rules of behavior follow the pattern of traffic laws. When we say that we ought to drive on the right side of the road, we do not mean that everyone must always be driving; if Mary never drives in her life, then she does not break the law. Rather, we mean that at the time when we are driving, then we ought to drive on the right side of the road. The rule is not a command to go driving at this moment; it is a guideline about how to drive when we choose to do so. In short, it is what we earlier called a policy.

Similar conditions apply to our knowledge that a man and a woman ought to unite and bring the sperm into the woman. This rule is not a command to have intercourse. Rather, it is a guideline about how to have intercourse when we choose to engage our power of reproduction. Likewise, we grasp that we ought to consider the evidence before coming to a judgment concerning the truth; we are not, thereby, grasping a command to consider the evidence at this very moment. Perhaps at the moment it would be better to sleep. Rather than a command to act now, then, this ought-statement sets the parameters of how we ought to act when we engage our reason.

It follows that by knowing our various powers, we can know that we ought to pursue the truth, control our emotions, reproduce in the manner that nature provides, and help those in need. These ought-statements are not commands to act right now. They are guidelines about how to engage in certain behaviors. When we see someone in need, we ought to help (if we are able). When confronted with the emotion of anger, we ought to make sure that it is guided by truly rational considerations. And when a man and woman unite, engaging the power of reproduction, they ought to play the part that nature has given them.

Negative ought-statements are slightly different. The statement that we "ought to do harm to no one," for instance, can be fulfilled at all times. When we are sleeping, we do not fulfill the affirmative ought-statement to seek the truth, but we do fulfill the negative ought-statement to avoid harming others. Negative ought-statements, then, do not simply set a policy to be carried out when we are performing a certain kind of action; they set a standard to be fulfilled at all times.

Knowing the Divine Plan in Us

We have seen in previous chapters that we have minds by which we can know all these various ought-statements. With our one power of reason, we understand our human nature, its various powers, and how we ought to behave. We can now see that this awareness is an awareness of how to act in accord with the movements that God has placed within us. It is an awareness of how to unite our actions with the divine action, of how to play our part in the greater action of radiating God's goodness (*ST*, I-II, 91, 2).

By giving us the power of reason, then, God has provided us with the knowledge we need to make a choice. We are not like Jane, who cannot choose the diamond hidden in the box because she lacks the needed knowledge. We have been given the knowledge. Consequently, we can choose to follow the divine movement or to reject the divine. We are not blind. We do not act automatically, like a tree. Our actions are voluntary. We can choose to accept God's gift of sharing in his good, or we can choose to act on our own, not taking our part within the divine action of radiating his good. We can choose either to fulfill the role God has given us or to reject it. We can recoil from the part God has given us, thinking that we are more than parts; we can prefer to be sovereign instead.

In either event, whether we carry out our role or reject our role, we do not act blindly. We have the insight by which we know our nature and its completion. We know the way needed to achieve this good (*ST*, I, 79, 12).

Natural Policies Constitute a Natural Law

Aquinas thinks that the awareness of the human good and of how we ought to behave deserves the name of law; it deserves to be called the natural law (*ST*, I-II, 91, 2). Without doubt, this awareness can be called a rule or set of rules, but we have seen that not every rule is a law. Ariel might have rules about how to behave at work, but these rules are not laws. Bob might give himself rules about how to execute his exercise program, but these rules are not laws. Likewise, when we discover that we ought to pursue the truth, we have discovered a rule of behavior; does it follow that we have discovered a law?

Recall that Aquinas gives four characteristics of a law (*ST*, I-II, 90, 1–4):

(1) It is a rule of reason about how to behave.

(2) It concerns the common or shared good.

(3) It is made by the proper authority, having care over the common good.

(4) It is promulgated.

In some sense, these four characteristics apply to mere rules and not only to laws. Rules unquestionably meet the first condition. Likewise, they often meet the second condition, at least in some manner. The rules at Ariel's workplace, for instance, concern the shared good of her work.

In this regard, however, these rules are not quite like laws. The rules concern the very parochial or local shared good of Ariel's workplace. In contrast, says Aquinas, laws concern the shared good of human happiness (*ST*, I-II, 90, 2). In other words, laws are concerned with the ultimate shared good. The laws of a political society aim to instill virtue, by which the citizens can attain the shared good of human life. If laws were only concerned about increasing human wealth, then they would not deserve the name of law. They might indeed aim at a shared good but not at the overall shared good of human life.

Some rules can also meet the third condition. The rules at Ariel's workplace, for instance, are made by those in charge. Ariel herself is not imposing them upon her fellow workers.

This third condition, however, has an ambiguity that follows upon the ambiguity in the second condition. Ariel's supervisors might be the appropriate authority for the shared good of her workplace, but they are not the appropriate authorities for aiming at the overall good of human life. That authority is given (by election or by some other means) to certain representatives of the people, who must decide the best rules to coordinate human actions in order to restrain evil and encourage good.

The fourth condition, like the first, can apply straightforwardly to mere rules. The rules in Ariel's workplace, for instance, are likely promulgated (that is, made known) by her supervisors.

Only this fourth condition is problematic for the natural law. We might describe the natural law (in this context) as those rules that coordinate our activity with the divine movement embedded in our very nature (*ST*, I-II, 91, 2). The first three conditions of a law apply to these rules without difficulty. First, these ought-statements are reasoned rules of behavior. Second, they do concern the shared good. Indeed, they concern the ultimate shared good of human life, which is to share in the divine good. Third, they do arise from the proper authority, for God himself has instilled in us the movements to various endpoints and he has given us the mind by which we can know these movements.

But in what sense are these rules promulgated? They are not written down, nor are they proclaimed orally. Nevertheless, these rules are made known. They are made known by our natural capacity to grasp the truth. Since God has given us this capacity, these rules are made known by God himself (*ST*, I-II, 90, 4, ad 1). Aquinas thinks that our natural capacity allows us to grasp the most basic precepts of the natural law, such as the precept to love other human beings. The details of how to carry out these primary precepts are sometimes understood with confusion because of bad arguments, misguided societal customs, or bad desire (*ST*, I-II, 94, 4). Nevertheless, we have the tools to understand fundamentally how we should behave.

In some way, then, the natural law meets the four conditions of a law. We should recognize, however, that the primary meaning of law is found in human laws. The natural law can indeed be called a law, but the meaning of the word "law," and the meaning of some of the conditions, may have slightly shifted.

This shifting, however, is a common occurrence in human language, for which Aquinas uses the term "analogous names" (*ST*, I, 13, 5). We use the word "see" analogously, for instance, when we first say that we see with our eyes but then extend the word to say that we see with our minds, as Kenny might say that he sees the point Christine is trying to explain to him. Besides this example, Aquinas often gives the example of the word "healthy." Primarily, this word refers to the proper functioning of an animal, but it can be extended analogously, as when we say that medicine is healthy (because it causes health) or that a complexion is healthy (because it is a sign of health in a person). The extension of words by way of analogy is a natural use of language, so Aquinas does not abuse the language when he applies the word "law" analogously to natural laws.

Partaking in the Divine Plan

According to Aquinas, the natural law is our human and rational participation in God's governance of the created universe (*ST*, I-II, 91, 2). All of creation, he says, shares in this governance in a very limited sense, for all things have embedded within them at least some natural movements to an endpoint. Even a rock is inclined, through its weight, to move downward to the center of gravity. This gravitational movement is part of the order in the universe that God has instilled so that creation might reflect his goodness.

Like the rest of creation, human beings have this manner of participating in the divine governance. We have various powers with their various movements to endpoints. Like trees, we have the power to grow and the power to reproduce. These powers, which originate from God, are inherent movements to various endpoints. Like bears, we have the power to see and to hear, the power to get angry, and the power to desire. These powers, as well, are certain inherent movements. Finally, as human beings we have some distinctive powers not found in the rest of material creation, whether rocks, trees, or bears. We have reason, by which we stretch out to understand the truth, and we have a will, by which we stretch out to the good.

Since these last two movements to an endpoint are peculiar to human beings, we might suppose that they represent the peculiarly human participation in God's governance. Ultimately, however, they are not distinctive enough. They are not a new *way* of participating in the divine governance. They still follow the manner of being an embedded movement to an endpoint. Admittedly, the objects to which these movements are directed are peculiar to human beings. Nevertheless, reason and will remain embedded movements to an endpoint, just like those found in the bear.

On account of these two powers, however, human beings do have a novel participation in the divine governance. Not only are we moving to an endpoint; we are also aware of this movement. Not only are we stretching out toward the truth; we are also aware that we ought to stretch out toward the truth. We, and we alone, are aware of the part we must play in the symphony of creation. We know how we must move ourselves—by way of making choices—to accomplish our part. In this way, we have a far greater participation in the divine governance. Not only do we move to various endpoints; in addition, we move with understanding. With our minds, we understand where we must go in order to fulfill the purpose we have in the universe. This knowledge, this awareness, is the natural law. Through the natural law, then, we partake in the divine governance of the universe.

Natural law teaches us that we are parts, parts within a greater whole. Our nature gives us a role within a greater picture. The natural law sets the boundaries of where we belong within the whole. Just as an actor is given a role to play within a drama, so we are given a role to play within the story of the universe. Natural law teaches us that we are not alone. Together with others, we must strive to live out the story. We must freely radiate God's goodness.

chapter 29

Virtue

If we wish to put the nation in order, we must first put the family in order; to put the family in order, we must first foster our personal life; to foster our personal life, we must first set our hearts right. In order to set our hearts right, we must first be sincere in our thoughts.

—Confucius, *The Great Learning*

By doing just acts, we become just; by doing temperate acts, we become temperate; and by doing courageous acts, we become courageous. But most people fail to do these things. They are like patients who listen attentively to their doctors but fail to do what the doctor orders.

—Aristotle, *Nicomachean Ethics*

Speaking of a "natural law ethics" can be dangerously misleading. It might leave the impression that ethics is about following a set of rules. As we have already mentioned, Thomas Aquinas actually speaks very little about the natural law. He prefers to speak about virtue and vice. He discusses monogamy within the context of the virtue of chastity and the vice of lust (*ST*, II-II, 154); he discusses war within the context of the vices of discord, contention, and strife (*ST*, II-II, 40); he discusses authority within the context of the virtue of obedience (*ST*, II-II, 104–105); and he discusses private property within the context of the virtue of justice (*ST*, II-II, 66). Aquinas himself, it seems, does not think so much in terms of rules and laws; rather, he thinks in terms of virtues and vices. He steadfastly avoids the misperception that ethics is a matter of following a set of rules.

Action and Desire

In two important ways, ethics is not a matter of following rules. An explanation of the first way, which has not yet been discussed in this book, begins by noting that human beings do not act like a computer algorithm, inescapably following a set of commands. Rather, we act according to desires. Larry knows the rule that he should not steal from others, but he ignores the rule (robbing banks instead) because he has an excessive desire for wealth and a diminished concern for the welfare of others. We all experience moments, sometimes quite regularly, when we know what we should do—we know the rule we should follow—but on account of strong desires, we disregard the rule. Christine knows that she should leave the last piece of chocolate for Kenny, but her desire gets in the way, and she chooses to take it for herself.

As we have already observed, human beings are free. We are not determined to follow our desires, but then neither are we determined to follow rules. Whether we follow the rules or not, we do so to attain some good; we do so on account of some desire. If Christine forgoes the chocolate, she does so because she desires some good, perhaps Kenny's good or the good of friendship or some such thing. None of her desires—her desire for chocolate, her desire for friendship, or her desire to stay healthy—determine her action. Nevertheless, all these desires influence her action. She acts only because she desires.

Our strongest desires do not determine our actions, but they tend to exert a greater force upon our decisions. Christine struggles with her decision (whether to eat the chocolate or not) precisely because of her strong desire for chocolates. If her desire were less demanding—if she could take chocolates or leave them—then her decision would be easier. She might more readily side with the good of friendship. We are not determined by our desires, but we do tend to make certain choices precisely because some of our desires are stronger than others.

As we have noted, even when we follow the rules, we do so on account of some desire. Furthermore, it is not a desire simply to follow rules. Rather, it is a desire to attain some good. Rules simply tell us the best way to achieve the good. Bob follows the rule to exercise three times a week because of his desire to get in shape. The rule tells him how to achieve this goal. Ought-statements, we have seen, are always hypothetical or conditional; they express some necessity or fittingness for achieving an end. In no way, then, do we act based on rules apart from some desire for a good.

The rules of the natural law are no different. They tell us how to achieve the good. In this case, however, the good is the overarching human good; it is the true human fulfillment shared with others. The rules of sexual ethics, for instance, are not arbitrary dictates imposed by an overly controlling God. Rather, they are the guides by which we can attain the shared human good in the domain of sexuality. Bob is more likely to follow his rule to exercise three times a week if he has a strong desire to get in shape. Similarly, the greater our desire to attain the shared human good, the more apt we will be to follow the natural law.

Virtue and Habit

An important feature of human psychology is that our desires are not set in stone. They change over time. More importantly, we ourselves can modify them (*ST*, I-II, 49). As we have seen, Maria's anger at John does not determine her action. She does not need to yell at him. More importantly, she can actually modify her anger; she can calm herself down. She might choose to take some deep breaths in order to diminish her anger. She might reconsider the situation, perhaps recognizing that John meant her no harm or that the offense against her was insignificant in the big picture. These techniques may not eliminate her anger, but they might at least lessen it.

Maria, then, can control her anger in two ways (*ST*, I, 83, 3). First, she can simply choose not to act upon it; she can choose not to yell. Second, she can actually modify her anger, so that it becomes less demanding. Both these manners of control (and especially the second) lead to a third, to the most important control we can have over our desires: they allow us to reshape the overall pattern of our desires. Not only can Maria modify her anger right here and now; she can also modify her irritable disposition so that she is less likely to become angry in the future.

Human beings are habitual creatures. The manner in which we sit, stand, or walk, for instance, follows a habitual pattern, so much so that we might recognize someone in the distance based solely upon his stride. Of course, we can break our patterns, but it takes effort. If John has back pain on account of poor posture, he can choose to stand or sit erect, but he is apt to slip back into his old posture. Changing his posture long-term requires a concerted effort to change his habit. By repeatedly correcting his posture, he can form a new habit over time.

Not only do we have patterns of posture; we also have patterns of desiring in certain ways. Christine has a habit of desiring chocolates, and Maria has an irritable disposition, a habit of getting angry. These habits can also be modified with effort. Maria can change her disposition so that she becomes angry less readily. Just as John changes his posture only with concerted effort, so also Maria can change her disposition only by repeatedly taking the time to control her anger. Such changes do not occur overnight. Indeed, they take months and years. At times, it may seem to Maria that she is making no progress: she is just as irritable as before. When she reflects over the past several years, however, she begins to recognize that her disposition has indeed changed; she does have better control of her anger.

Our habits of desiring have a more profound influence over our well-being than do our habits of sitting or standing. The latter may lead to poor physical health, but the former can lead to poor spiritual health.

If Maria continues to get angry, then her anger will only grow over time as she develops a stronger and stronger disposition to get angry. She will become an unpleasant person, both to herself and to others. She will lose sight of the shared good, focusing only upon retribution to satisfy her own private welfare.

Few things are more important than making the effort to develop the right sorts of habits in our desires. We must form habits of desiring what is truly good. We must diminish those habits by which we desire false goods. In this manner, when presented with the true good, an appropriately strong desire will arise. We will then find it easy, almost second nature, to seek what is good and to reject what is bad. We will, in short, follow the natural law almost by instinct, with little reflection.

The moral virtues are precisely those habits by which we desire what is truly good (*ST*, I-II, 58; Jensen 2013). The virtue of chastity, for instance, is the habit by which we desire sexual pleasures in accord with the good of reason. Just as Maria has a habit of getting angry, so someone with the virtue of chastity has a habit of desiring sexual pleasure within the context of the shared human good. The virtue of generosity is the habit by which we desire our possessions as something to be shared with others. If Don has the virtue of generosity, then he has a giving heart; he quite spontaneously desires to share his possessions with others. Likewise, the virtue of courage is the habit by which we brave and fear appropriately. Braving danger for the shared good comes as second nature to the person with the virtue of courage.

A virtue occupies a middle ground between two extreme vices (*ST*, I-II, 64). At one extreme, for instance, stinginess is opposed to generosity (*ST*, II-II, 118). At the other extreme, a careless looseness with money is opposed to generosity (*ST*, II-II, 119). Likewise, cowardice is the extreme of fear opposed to the virtue of courage (*ST*, II-II, 125); at the other extreme (of daring or braving) is a foolhardy rashness (*ST*, II-II, 127). Chastity avoids the extreme of lust, which is an excessive desire for sexual pleasure, but it must also avoid the (comparatively rare) opposite extreme of a deficient desire (*ST*, II-II, 154). A husband, for instance, might desire his own wife insufficiently.

The moral life, then, is a matter of forming the proper virtues, of rooting out vices and of planting the appropriate desires in their place. Virtues, like any habit, are formed by repeated actions. By repeatedly controlling her anger, for instance, Maria develops the virtue of patience. The development of these virtues takes time and effort. Indeed, it is a lifelong project.

Viewing the ethical life as a matter of following a set of rules loses sight of this important aspect of ethics. Ethics is not a matter of following rules; rather, it is a matter of becoming a certain kind of person. It is not merely a matter of doing what is good; it is a matter of *becoming* good. For this reason, Aquinas focuses upon the virtues rather than upon the rules. Of course, when the virtues are discussed, the rules come into play. When discussing chastity, for instance, Aquinas argues that sexual relations should be kept within marriage. Nevertheless, he is not giving a rule book. Rather, he is giving a guide for self-improvement, a guide to transforming one's life.

Duty Calls

This self-transformation might be misunderstood in a way that will lead us to the second manner in which ethics is not merely a matter of following rules. Someone might misconceive the virtues as so-called "deontological virtues." In this understanding, virtues are good because they are the habits by which we can follow the rules well. Don, for instance, is supposed to follow the rules about sharing his wealth, but he can consistently follow these rules only if he has a habit of following rules. He should work to transform himself, then, to become the sort of person who follows moral rules.

This account profoundly misunderstands the role of rules within the ethical life. It supposes that our ultimate goal is to bring our actions in conformity with a set of rules. We often say that we should do the right thing just because it is the right thing to do. This common saying may express an important truth: when we do what is right and just, we should not be propelled by ulterior motives, such as personal profit. Don should not be generous, for instance, merely because the reputation of generosity will increase the profits from his business.

On the other hand, this common saying might be misleading. It might suggest that we should do the right thing simply because it conforms to a standard of being "right," because it conforms to a moral rule of behavior. Don should be generous, for instance, just because morality tells him that he should do acts of generosity. He should be generous just because it is his duty to be generous. This misconception of morality dislodges rules from their proper place as needed guides and elevates them to the role of the crowning jewel of ethics.

Virtuous Actions

We have discussed at length—as a major focus throughout this book—the ultimate goal of the ethical life. We can now view this previous discussion in the light of virtues. Most properly, the moral virtues are certain habits of desiring well. The term "virtue," however, is ambiguous. It can refer to the habit itself, but it can also refer to the desire to which the habit gives rise; in yet another way, it can refer to the actions that are desired. The virtue of generosity, for instance, refers to the habit of desiring well with regard to our possessions. But we also speak of virtuous desires. Don's generous desire to share his wealth with the poor is a virtuous desire. Furthermore, the actions that he desires—sharing his possessions with the poor—are virtuous actions.

Between these three (the habit, the desire, and the action), the last has a certain priority. The habit is itself defined in terms of the desire. The habit of generosity, for instance, is the disposition by which someone consistently has generous desires. And the desire is likewise identified by way of the action. Don's desire to be generous is a desire for the act of sharing his possessions. Similarly, the habit of courage is defined in terms of braving and fearing appropriately. Furthermore, braving is appropriate when it is directed to an action of facing danger for the true human good.

The priority of action over desire and of desire over habit runs deeper than definitions. More profoundly, the priority concerns the goal or purpose. It concerns the good at which we aim. Don does not want the habit of generosity simply for its own sake; rather, he wants the habit ultimately for the sake of the action. He wants to act generously, for he shares the good by way of generous actions. A generous action, however, is not mere physical activity; it is not simply handing over money to a beggar. Rather, a generous action includes the desire within it. Don acts generously only if he gives the money from a generous heart. But Don knows that he can consistently act generously only if he develops the appropriate habit. He wants the habit, then, for the sake of the desire, and he wants the desire lived out in action.

This priority of action over habit—a priority concerning the goal at which we aim—is no surprise. We have already seen that a thing is most complete by performing its distinctive activity well. A knife is made complete by being sharp, but it is most complete by cutting well. The value of being sharp is found precisely in its order toward the activity. Similarly, the habit of generous desires is a kind of completion of Don, but the ultimate completion is found in the activity toward which the habit is directed.

The parallel is expressed in the following table (which adds the examples of an eye and a doctor, to provide further aid in understanding).

The first column lists the thing with its movement to an endpoint. The second and third columns give us completions of this movement. The ultimate good of the thing is found in the third column. The second column identifies a completion (and not merely a useful good), but this good is ultimately directed beyond itself to the activity found in the third column.

The ultimate goal of the ethical life, then, is not conformity with a set of rules. Rather, the ultimate goal of ethics is virtuous activity. This activity, as we have seen, completes the individual. Since individuals are parts within a greater whole, their own completion is to be shared with others. Virtuous activity, then, completes not only the individual but also the whole community. The ultimate goal of ethics is to share the good through our activity, for which reason Aquinas says that all human law is directed toward friendship (*ST*, I-II, 99, 2). And friendship, we have seen,

Table 29-1. Different instances of virtue

Thing and its function	Virtue (that quality by which a thing performs its function well)	Activity of acting well (virtuous activity)
Knife	Quality of being sharp	Cutting well
Eye	Spherical eyeball, clear lens, and so on	Seeing well
Doctor	Knowledge of health, illness, and treatments	Healing well
Human being	Habit of desiring possessions as something freely given	Virtuous acts of appropriately sharing one's possessions with others

is realized in activity. Friends are most properly friends not while asleep but when they are actively sharing the good with one another.

The Role of Law

The schema seems to be missing an important element. Indeed, it is missing the focus of this book, for it does not explain the place for rules or laws. Where, in Table 29-1, should we place the natural law?

The natural law is not hiding far in the background. With the virtue of chastity, for instance, someone will desire sexual pleasure according to the order that is laid out by the natural law. He will desire sexual pleasure within marriage, but he will not desire it outside of marriage. A similar point can be made for generosity. We should share our possessions with others, but it is not always clear with whom we should share and how much we should share. If Don is overly generous, for instance, then he may bankrupt himself and be unable to care for his own children. He must discern when to give and how much to give. The natural law provides guidance for his discernment. Through the natural law, he becomes aware that his possessions are not simply for himself. At the same time, he becomes aware that he has a responsibility to care for his own children.

Every virtue is the mean between two extremes, but the boundary between the mean and the extremes is not always clear. Sometimes it is rather straightforward. Don, for instance, should not steal from the rich in order to give to the poor. Typically, however, no algorithm is available to determine a precise line separating virtue from its opposite vices. An individual must make the determination by applying general principles to the concrete situation. When Don determines whether to share his goods with someone in need, he considers the general principles mentioned here (among others): he has a responsibility to share his goods but also a responsibility to care for his children. Ultimately, Don must begin with some general rules of behavior, rules that can be described as laws, *natural* laws.

The natural law, then, is something like a map. It shows us the way. The natural law itself is not the goal; rather, virtuous activity is the goal. We aim to share the good, but we do not always know how to do so. We are like Aristotle's ignorant archers, who want to hit the target but do not know where it is. We need a map to show us the way. The natural law provides this map. It provides the light by which we can see where to go and illumines our path so that we can choose well. In addition, we can transform our very selves; we can, as Aristotle says, develop the divine element within us (*NE*, bk. 10, chap. 7). We can take our part within a world charged with the grandeur of God.

affirmative precept: a law that commands us to do some good action. An affirmative precept has force always but not in every situation. The law to love our neighbor as ourselves, for instance, is an affirmative precept.

agent: a thing or person that acts. A knife, for example, is the agent of cutting, and a doctor is the agent of healing.

categorical imperative: according to the philosopher Immanuel Kant, a categorical imperative is an imperative (or ought-statement) that derives its force not from any desire for an endpoint but simply from itself. For instance, the norm commanding us to treat others as an end, and not merely as a means, is a categorical imperative.

categorical ought-statement: see *categorical imperative*.

civil law: the human law that varies from country to country; it is opposed to the law of nations. Traffic laws are an instance of civil laws.

common by causality: a good that moves many individuals to act as a united agent. The good of playing symphonic music, for instance, is a good common by causality to the diverse members of the orchestra.

common by predication: many instances of something belonging to the same kind. A rose being red and a car being red, for instance, have the color red in common by predication.

community of utility: a union of individuals solely for the sake of a useful good. A band of thieves, for instance, is merely a community of utility.

completion: that which makes something whole or complete; the state of having all that is needed to make something whole. Those things moving to an endpoint are complete to the degree that they can realize their functions. A thing is complete (1) by having all its parts, (2) by having those qualities by which it performs its function well, and (3) by actually performing its function well. In these ways, (1) a knife with a handle and blade is complete, (2) a sharp knife is complete, and (3) a knife that is actually cutting well (at the moment) is complete.

conditional necessity: see *hypothetical necessity.*

conditional ought-statements: an imperative (or ought-statement) that derives its force from the movement to an endpoint arising from some function or role. A doctor, for instance, ought to heal her patients on account of her role as a doctor.

consequence: an effect that falls outside the action itself.

consequentialism: the ethical view that we should seek to produce the greatest number of goods for the greatest number of people.

deontological virtue: a habit of following moral rules.

desiring powers: capacities that move us out to the world. These powers include the emotions and the will.

dropping options: see *error of dropping options.*

emotions: conscious desires that involve bodily changes—for example, anger, envy, anxiety, and so on.

emotivism: the relativist view according to which evaluative terms (such as "good," "bad," "right," and "wrong") simply mean that we have a positive or negative attitude toward the object evaluated. Calling rape evil, for instance, simply means that I do not like rape.

error of lumping together: an error in identifying consequences (as opposed to actions) that fails to distinguish what a person plans to do and what he or she foresees, thereby lumping all consequences together as part of the action.

error of dropping options: an error in identifying consequences (as opposed to actions) that includes within the means only what is absolutely necessary within the means of an action, thereby classifying optional means as consequences. For the goal of building a shed, for instance, this error would not include the means of pounding nails, because the use of nails is optional (since the shed might be built with screws instead).

error of slicing thin: an error in identifying consequences (as opposed to actions) that separates a single action into multiple actions, as long as the action can be described in multiple ways, thereby making actions as thin as the multiple descriptions we can imagine. The action of killing a human being, for instance, might be described merely as killing a mammal.

error of turning a blind eye: an error in identifying consequences (as opposed to actions) that fails to take note of certain causes chosen as a means to achieve the goal, thereby placing some things essential to an action in the category of consequence. When Barb defends herself with a gun, for instance, this error might describe her action as "firing a gun," but it would not include the description "harming the assailant," even though this latter description is an essential means in her defense.

error theory: the relativist view according to which evaluative terms (such as "good," "bad," "right," and "wrong") refer to fictional things, even as the word "unicorn" refers to something fictional. According to this view, for example, calling rape evil is to attribute a made-up idea (evil) to the act of rape.

ethical realism: The view that ethical terms (such as "right," "wrong," "good," and "evil") express something real about the world. In addition, ethical realism claims that we are able to know the real moral aspects of the world. See also *objective ethics*.

ethical relativism: the view that ethical terms (such as "right," "wrong," "good," and "evil") do not identify anything real about objects or actions; they either assert something fictional or they assert something about our own subjective states. Moral relativist views include prescriptivism, emotivism, and error theory.

ethical skepticism: the view that we are unable to know moral aspects of reality. According to ethical skepticism, for example, we are unable to know that rape is wrong.

evil: a word to refer to what is bad; the opposite of good; that which undermines the completion of a movement to an endpoint.

function: the unique purpose of a thing; the action for which something is made; the characteristic action of a thing. Writing is the function of a pen, for instance, and reasoning is the function of a human being.

functional thing: a thing that has a function and is defined in terms of its function, as an eye is defined as an organ for seeing or a knife is defined as a tool for cutting.

good: an adjective or a noun that has three primary meanings: (1) it describes a functional thing that performs its function well, as a good knife cuts well; (2) it identifies that which completes something moving to an endpoint, as being sharp is the good of a knife insofar as it completes the knife; (3) it identifies that which produces the completion of something moving to an endpoint, as a knife sharpener is good for a knife.

greater good: according to consequentialism, the greater good is an accumulation of individual goods. According to natural law, the greater good is what belongs to many people together.

hypothetical necessity: the necessity of something in order to attain an end. Going on a diet, for example, may be hypothetically necessary in order to attain the end of losing weight.

hypothetical imperative (or hypothetical ought-statement): an imperative (or ought-statement) that derives its force from the desire for some endpoint. The command "go on a diet" is hypothetical, for instance, if it has force only on account of a person's desire to lose weight.

inadequacy of deprivation: an inadequacy by which an individual needs the help of others to attain his or her own private good. The need of a child (or of an adult) for assistance in attaining food, for instance, is an inadequacy of deprivation.

inadequacy of transcendence: an inadequacy by which an individual who has already attained his or her own private good still needs others to achieve a greater good in union with them. An orchestra of accomplished musicians, for example, must unite to transcend their limitations in order to play symphonic music.

instinct: an internal sensing power (a kind of knowing power) by which animals (including human beings) make evaluative judgments. A bird, for instance, might judge that twigs are good for making a nest.

interior senses: knowing powers that begin with the content provided by the external senses but then develop beyond the senses, knowing in ways not available to the external senses. The power of memory, for instance, recalls what has been sensed in the past, and the power of instinct knows that some things are fitting or worth pursuing.

intuitionism: the view that we come to know the human good by way of some immediate intuition, depending upon no prior knowledge.

is-statement: a statement concerning the way the world is. Is-statements are sometimes contrasted with ought-statements.

knowing powers: powers by which we are aware of the world; these powers take in the world around us rather than move out to the world. Examples of knowing powers include the external senses, the internal senses, and reason (or intellect).

law: a directive of reason for the common good, given by the proper authorities and made known (or promulgated) to those who must follow the directive.

law of nations: the human law derived from the natural law as conclusions or as necessary determinations; the human law that is common to all countries or nations; it is opposed to the civil law. The law against murder, for instance, belongs to the law of nations.

legal positivism: the view that all human laws are posited (or asserted) merely by human will, without deriving any force from the nature of things.

lumping together: see *error of lumping together*.

monogamy: the family structure in which one man and one woman unite until death to bear and raise children. One man cannot join himself to multiple women, nor one woman to multiple men.

moral realism: see *ethical realism*.

moral relativism: see *ethical relativism*.

moral virtues: habits of desiring and choosing what is truly good.

naïve realism: the view that maintains the existence of special kinds of attributes, such as rightness or wrongness, that can be found in actions, just as whiteness can be found in snow; these real attributes can be perceived with a special power of the mind.

negative precept: a law that commands us not to do some evil. It holds always and in every situation. The precept "do harm to no one," for example, is a negative precept.

new natural law: see *revisionism*.

objective ethics: the view according to which "right," "wrong," "good," and "evil" are real aspects of the world around us. See also *ethical realism*.

ought-statement: a statement expressing necessity concerning some endpoint. A doctor, for instance, ought to heal; in other words, given his or her endpoint, it is necessary for a doctor to heal. Ought-statements are sometimes contrasted with is-statements. Is-statements state the way the world is, but some modern thinkers suppose that ought-statements do not, even though they can be true or false. Ought-statements can express some of the same content as imperatives. The ought-statement "you ought to turn right," for instance, expresses some of the same content as the imperative "turn right!"

per se knowledge: knowledge that is achieved simply by understanding the ideas involved in the relationships between the ideas; it is achieved without deductive reasoning. That a whole is greater than its parts, for example, is a proposition that is known per se.

policies: general directives of behavior that cover a whole class of actions. A military major, for example, might have a policy according to which soldiers running across an open field must move in a zigzag fashion; traffic laws are examples of policies.

positive precept: see *affirmative precept.*

precept: a rule or command of the law.

prescriptivism: the ethical relativist view according to which evaluative terms (such as "good," "bad," "right," and "wrong") express a prescription or command. Calling rape evil, for instance, simply means "do not rape."

realism: see *ethical realism.*

reason: a knowing power by which we are aware of the natures of things, the relations between things, and the causes of things. It is found only in human beings.

relativism: see *ethical relativism.*

revisionism: a view that attempts to modify natural law theory to accommodate certain modern conceptions. It rejects, for instance, the importance of the endpoint, of human nature, and of the role God plays within morality.

Robinson Crusoe: a fictional character (based upon a real-life character) who was stranded on an island and survived on his own (making shelters and tools, planting crops, hunting animals, and so on) for many years before he was rescued.

shared good: a good that belongs to several people together; a good that is possessed in union. Playing symphonic music, for example, is a shared good for the members of the orchestra.

skepticism: see *ethical skepticism.*

slicing thin: see *error of slicing thin.*

subsidiarity: the idea that society should be structured around smaller communities uniting to form medium-sized communities, which form yet larger communities. What *can* be managed in a smaller community *should* be managed in a smaller community.

theorist: those who espouse some version of a theory.

turning a blind eye: see *error of turning a blind eye.*

union of deprivation: a union of individuals in which the members need the help of others to attain their own private goods.

union of transcendence: a union of individuals in which the members unite to transcend beyond their individual goods to attain a good together with others.

union of utility: see *union of deprivation.*

virtue: see *moral virtues.*

virtue ethics: an ethical view that emphasizes the role of virtue within ethics; some versions emphasize that virtues, such as courage, generosity, and justice, complete the individual human being.

will: a desiring power moved by reason that has the good in general as its object.

bibliography

Ackerman, Felicia. 2000. "'For Now Have I My Death': The 'Duty to Die' Versus the Duty to Help the Ill Stay Alive." *Midwest Studies in Philosophy* 24, no. 1: 172–85.

Anscombe, G. E. M. 1958. "Modern Moral Philosophy." *Philosophy* 33, no. 124: 1–19.

Ayer, A. J. 2014. *Language, Truth and Logic*. New York: Dover Publications.

Behr, Thomas C. 2019. *Social Justice and Subsidiarity: Luigi Taparelli and the Origins of Modern Catholic Social Thought*. Washington, DC: The Catholic University of America Press.

Bennett, Jonathan. 1995. *The Act Itself*. Oxford: Clarendon Press.

Boyle, Joseph M. 1977. "Double Effect and a Certain Type of Embryotomy." *Irish Theological Quarterly* 44, no. 4: 303–18.

Bratman, Michael E. 1987. *Intentions, Plans, and Practical Reason*. Cambridge, MA: Harvard University Press.

Cavanaugh, Thomas A. 2006. *Double-Effect Reasoning: Doing Good and Avoiding Evil*. Oxford: Oxford University Press.

De Koninck, Charles. 1997. "On the Primacy of the Common Good: Against the Personalists." *Aquinas Review* 4: 1–100.

Denton, Michael J. 1998. *Nature's Destiny: How the Laws of Biology Reveal Purpose in the Universe*. New York: Free Press.

Finnis, John. 1980. *Natural Law and Natural Rights*. Oxford: Clarendon Press.

———. 1983. *Fundamentals of Ethics*. Washington, DC: Georgetown University Press.

———. 1987. "Natural Inclinations and Natural Rights: Deriving 'Ought' from 'Is' According to Aquinas." In *Lex et Libertas: Freedom and Law According to St. Thomas Aquinas*, vol. 30, ed. Leo Elders and Klaus Hedwig, 43–55. Rome: Studi Tomistici.

Geach, P. T. 1956. "Good and Evil." *Analysis* 17, no. 2: 33–42.

Grisez, Germain. 1965. "The First Principle of Practical Reason: A Commentary on the *Summa Theologiae*, 1-2, Question 94, Article 2." *Natural Law Forum* 10, no. 1: 168–201.

———. 1983. *The Way of the Lord Jesus 1: Christian Moral Principles*. Chicago: Franciscan Herald Press.

Hardwig, John. 1997. "Is There a Duty to Die?" *The Hastings Center Report* 27, no. 2: 34–42.

Hare, R. M. 1981. *Moral Thinking*. Oxford: Oxford University Press.

———. 2013. *The Language of Morals*. New York: Oxford University Press.

Hart, H. L. A. 2012. *The Concept of Law*, 3rd ed. Oxford: Oxford University Press.

Hobbes, Thomas. 1994. *Leviathan*. Indianapolis, IN: Hackett Publishing.

Hume, David. 1983. *Enquiry Concerning the Principles of Morals*. Indianapolis, IN: Hackett Publishing.

Jensen, Steven J. 2013. *Living the Good Life: A Beginner's Thomistic Ethics*. Washington, DC: The Catholic University of America Press.

———. 2014. "The Roots of Transhumanism." *Nova et Vetera* (English edition) 12, no. 2: 515–41.

———. 2018. *The Human Person: A Beginner's Thomistic Psychology*. Washington, DC: The Catholic University of America Press.

Johnson, Phillip E. 2010. *Darwin on Trial*. Washington, DC: Regnery.

Kant, Immanuel, and James W. Ellington. 1983. *Grounding for the Metaphysics of Morals*. Indianapolis, IN: Hackett Publishing.

Lewis, C. S. 1947. *The Abolition of Man*. New York: MacMillan Publishing Co.

Mackie, J. L. 1990. *Ethics: Inventing Right and Wrong*. Harmondsworth: Penguin Books.

Meyer, Stephen C. 2009. *Signature in the Cell: DNA and the Evidence for Intelligent Design*. New York: HarperOne.

Mill, John Stuart, and George Sher. 2002. *Utilitarianism*, 2nd ed. Indianapolis, IN: Hackett Publishing.

Moore, G. E. 1903. *Principia Ethica*. Cambridge: Cambridge University Press.

Pigden, Charles R. 1990. "Geach on 'Good.'" *Philosophical Quarterly* 40, no. 159: 129–54.

Ross, David. 2003. *The Right and the Good*. Oxford: Oxford University Press.

Simon, Yves R. 1962. *A General Theory of Authority*. Notre Dame, IN: University of Notre Dame Press.

Skinner, B. F. 1971. *Beyond Freedom and Dignity*. New York: Vintage.

Tadros, Victor. 2011. *The Ends of Harm: The Moral Foundations of Criminal Law*. Oxford: Oxford University Press.

Thomson, Judith Jarvis. 1994. "Goodness and Utilitarianism." *Proceedings and Addresses of the American Philosophical Association* 67, no. 2: 145–59.

Tollefsen, Christopher. 2006. "Is a Purely First-Person Account of Human Action Defensible?" *Ethical Theory and Moral Practice* 9, no. 4: 441–60.

Wallerstein, Judith S., Julia Lewis, and Sandra Blakeslee. 2002. *The Unexpected Legacy of Divorce: A 25 Year Landmark Study*. London: Fusion.

Zimmerman, Michael J. 2001. *The Nature of Intrinsic Value*. Lanham, MD: Rowman & Littlefield.

index

The letter t following a page number denotes a table.